T0305154

Vietnam and the East Asian Crisis

Vietnam and the East Asian Crisis

Edited by

Suiwah Leung

Director and Fellow, National Centre for Development Studies

The Australian National University, Canberra, Australia

Edward Elgar

Cheltenham, UK • Northampton, MA, USA

Published by
Edward Elgar Publishing Limited
Glensanda House
Montpellier Parade
Cheltenham
Glos GL50 1UA
UK

Edward Elgar Publishing, Inc.
6 Market Street
Northampton
Massachusetts 01060
USA

A catalogue record for this book
is available from the British Library

Library of Congress Cataloguing in Publication Data

Vietnam and the East Asian crisis / edited by Suiwah Leung.
    Includes index.
  1. Financial crises—East Asia. 2. Business cycles—East Asia.
  3. East Asia—Economic conditions. 4. Financial crises—Vietnam.
  5. Business cycles—Vietnam. 6. Vietnam—Economic conditions.
  I. Leung, Suiwah, 1947–
  HB3816.5.V54   1999
  332.1'0959—dc21   99–21830
                                           CIP

ISBN 1 84064 089 8
Typeset by Japan Online, UK

Contents

List of Figures   *vii*
List of Tables   *ix*
List of Contributors   *xi*
Preface   *xiii*

PART ONE   VIETNAM AND THE REGION

1. Crisis in Asia and Vietnam's Economic Policy Response   3
    Suiwah Leung

2. Needed: A Strategic Vision for Setting Reform Priorities   9
    in Vietnam
    James Riedel

PART TWO   THE ASIAN FINANCIAL CRISIS AND VIETNAM

3. Asia's Financial Crisis: Lessons and Implications   31
    for Vietnam
    Ramon Moreno, Gloria Pasadilla and Eli Remolona

4. Current and Capital Account Liberalisation: 55
    Issues Facing Indonesia
    Hadi Soesastro

5. Paradise Lost: The Pernicious Impact of Exchange Rate   66
    Policy on Indonesia's Banking System
    Ross H. McLeod

6. Dollarisation and Financial Sector Developments in Vietnam   83
    Suiwah Leung and Ngo Huy Duc

7. Borrower Transaction Costs and Segmented Markets: 96
    A Study of the Rural Credit Market in Vietnam
    Tran Tho Dat

PART THREE   EAST ASIAN EXPORT-ORIENTED
             INDUSTRIALISATION AND VIETNAM'S
             STRATEGIC DIRECTIONS

8. Industrialisation in ASEAN: Some Analytical and   121
    Policy Lessons
    Hal Hill

9. Developing with Foreign Investment: What Can   146
    Vietnam Learn from Malaysia?
    Prema-chandra Athukorala

10. Experiences in the Region and Private Sector Incentives   165
    in Vietnam
    Raymond Mallon

11. Implications for Vietnam of Rural Industrialisation in China 193
    Yiping Huang

12. Market Reform and Vietnamese Agriculture   206
    Nhu Che, Tom Kompas and Neil Vousden

References   *219*
Index   *231*

Figures

2.1 Ratio of Value Added to Fixed Capital by Firm Type in   16
     Taiwan Manufacturing, 1986
2.2 Capital Inflows to the Crisis-stricken Five   21
2.3 Current Account Deficits and FDI Inflows   23
2.4 Index of Real Dong/Dollar Exchange Rate   25
3.1 Decline of East Asian Currencies against the US Dollar,   34
     5 January 1996 – 8 May 1998
12.1 Rice Output in Vietnam, 1976–94   209
12.2 Index of Average Rice Price, 1981–94   214
12.3 Average Variable Profit in Rice Production   214
12.4 Cumulative Growth of Rice Output, TFP and 'Incentive'   215
     Component of TFP (%)

Tables

2.1	Comparative Economic and Social Indicators	13
3.1	Change in Stock Price Index, Recent Peak – April 1998	33
3.2	Short-term Borrowing from Banks in BIS Member Countries, 1990–97	41
6.1	Monetary Survey, 1986–93	85
6.2	Ratio of Foreign Currency Deposits to M2 in Selected Asian and Transitional Economies	87
6.3	Estimation of Dollarisation Coefficient	90
6.4	Estimation of the Impact of Dollarisation on Inflation	93
7.1	Distribution of Loans by Transaction Cost of Borrowing from the Formal Sector	100
7.2	Components of Borrower Transaction Costs in Selected Countries	101
7.3	Average Borrower Transaction Costs from Formal Sector by Loan Size	102
7.4	Comparison of Borrower Transaction Costs for Selected Countries	103
7.5	Average Borrower Transaction Costs for Formal and Informal Sectors	104
7.6	Effective Interest Rates on Loans from Various Sources by Loan Size	106
7.7	Estimation of the Transaction Costs Function	110
7A.1	Statistical Summary of Variables Used in Equations (7.2) and (7.3)	116
7A.2	Correlation Matrix of Variables Used in Equation (7.2)	117
7A.3	Correlation Matrix of Variables Used in Equation (7.3)	117
9.1	Inward Flows of FDI, 1981–96	148
9.2	Malaysia: Composition of Value Added and Employment of MNE Affiliates in Manufacturing	150
9.3	Vietnam: Contribution of MNE Affiliates to Total Manufacturing Production and Employment	152
9.4	Vietnam: Industry Distribution of Licensed FDI, 1988–94	154
9.5	Vietnam: Structure of Exports, 1985–96	155
10.1	Key Economic Indicators, 1995–98	167

10.2   FDI (1988–97) and Exports (1996–97) to Vietnam from Asia   170
10.3   Share of Private and State Sectors in the National Economy,   172
       1986–96
10.4   Industrial Output by Ownership, 1994–97   173
10.5   Trends in Numbers of Business Enterprises, 1990–97   175
10.6   Laws Regulating Business Entities   178
10.7   Bank Lending to State and Non-state Enterprises, 1991–97   183
11.1   Employment and Output of TVEs in the Rural Economy   197
11.2   Rural Income in China, 1983–95   199
12.1   Rice Output in Vietnam, 1976–94   210
12.2   Annual Growth Rates   211
12.3   Implied Growth Rates of Rice Output during Stages of   217
       Liberalisation

Contributors

Suiwah Leung is Director and Fellow, Graduate Studies in the Economics of Development, at the National Centre for Development Studies, Australian National University. From 1995 to 1998, Dr Leung was the Coordinator of the AusAID/NCDS Vietnam Economic Research Project. She has published widely on international financial issues in relation to the Asia–Pacific region and on the Vietnamese economy.

Prema-chandra Athukorala is Senior Fellow, Division of Economics, Asia Pacific School of Economics and Management, Australian National University. Dr Athukorala is an expert on the Malaysian economy and has published widely on trade and development issues in the Asia–Pacific region.

Nhu Che was recently awarded her PhD at the Australian National University for her work on developments in the Vietnamese agricultural sector.

Hal Hill is Professor of Economics, Division of Economics, Research School of Pacific and Asian Studies, and Asia–Pacific School of Economics and Management, at the Australian National University. Professor Hill, who is also Head of the Southeast Asian Economy Project at the Australian National University, has published extensively on trade and foreign investment issues affecting the region.

Yiping Huang is Senior Lecturer at the National Centre for Development Studies at the Australian National University. He has published extensively on rural sector developments in China.

Tom Kompas is Senior Lecturer, Faculty of Economics and Commerce, at the Australian National University. Dr Kompas publishes in the field of micro-economic theory.

Raymond Mallon is currently a consultant to the Asian Development Bank and economic adviser to the Central Institute for Economic Management in Hanoi. He has been working in Southeast Asia since 1984 and has been based in Hanoi since 1991.

Ross H. McLeod is Fellow in the Indonesia Project, Asia Pacific School of Economics and Management, at the Australian National University. He is an acknowledged expert on the Indonesian economy and is Editor of the Australian National University's *Bulletin of Indonesian Economic Studies*.

Ramon Moreno is Senior Economist at the Federal Reserve Bank of San Francisco and Associate Director of its Center for Pacific Basin Monetary and Economic Studies. The Center has been responsible for generating an extensive range of high-quality research on financial and exchange rate issues in the Asia–Pacific region. Dr Moreno's own research focuses on open economy macroeconomics and economic growth.

Ngo Huy Duc is Lecturer at the Ho Chi Minh Political Academy in Hanoi. Dr Ngo recently completed his PhD at the Australian National University, where he carried out research on currency substitution with application to Vietnam.

Gloria Pasadilla is Assistant Professor and Research Director of the International Economics Group, School of Economics, at the University of Asia and the Pacific, Manila. She has served as program adviser for the ADB Institute in Tokyo.

Eli Remolona is a Research Officer in the Capital Markets Function of the Federal Reserve Bank of New York. His research interests are term structure models, market microstructure and emerging markets.

James Riedel is Professor of Economics at the Paul H. Nitze School of Advanced International Studies, Johns Hopkins University, Washington DC. He is currently on leave, teaching in the Fulbright Economics Teaching Program in Ho Chi Minh City. Professor Riedel has published extensively on trade and economic development issues in the Asian region.

Hadi Soesastro is Executive Director of the Centre for Strategic and International Studies in Jakarta. The Centre is well known for its high-quality independent research on economic policy and political economy issues in the Asia–Pacific region. Dr Soesastro is also Adjunct Professor, Asia Pacific School of Economics and Management, at the Australian National University.

Tran Tho Dat is Lecturer at the National Economics University in Hanoi. Dr Tran recently completed his PhD studies at the Australian National University, where he conducted research on the rural credit market in Vietnam.

Neil Vousden is Reader and Senior Fellow at the National Centre for Development Studies and Department of Economics, Faculty of Economics and Commerce, at the Australian National University. Dr Vousden has published widely on international trade theory and policy.

Preface

This book is the second in a series published under the auspices of the AusAID/NCDS Vietnam Economic Research Project, which ran from 1995 to 1998. The first book, entitled *Vietnam Assessment: Creating a Sound Investment Climate*, was published at a time when Vietnam was opening its economy to the global market place in an effort to join the ranks of the fast-growing Asian economies. The present volume, in contrast, is being published in the aftermath of the Asian financial crisis, when uncertainties about Vietnam's economic policy directions inevitably arise. It is hoped that this book will contribute to the speedy resolution of some of these uncertainties.

The Vietnam Economic Research Project was made possible through the financial support and foresight of the Australian Department of Foreign Affairs and Trade (DFAT) and the Australian Agency for International Development (AusAID). However, the project would not have been possible without the intellectual support of my colleagues at the Australian National University, some of whose work appears in the present volume. The project has also been strongly supported by economists and academics in Vietnam's institutions. Our special thanks go to Dr Le Dang Doanh of the Central Institute for Economic Management in Hanoi, whose personal contribution and advice made our collaboration both fruitful and enjoyable. We are also very appreciative of the cooperation of the National Economics University in Hanoi and the University of Economics in Ho Chi Minh City, which hosted two of our workshops. Our thanks go also to the various resident representatives in Vietnam of the International Monetary Fund, the World Bank and the Asian Development Bank, whose contributions added to the quality of our work.

Special thanks are due to Beth Thomson, the copy editor and typesetter of both books, and Billie Headon, the administrator of the Vietnam Economic Research Project. Without the skill and dedication of both these professionals, none of this would have been possible. Special thanks are also due to my husband, Ron Dean, whose intellectual and emotional support saw me through many difficulties in connection with the project. Last but not least, I would like to thank the many PhD scholars from Vietnam who presented their research at the five workshops and two conferences held during the course of the project. Their intellectual contributions, personal dedication and sheer sense of fun made all the hard work worthwhile.

Dr Suiwah Leung
Director and Fellow
Graduate Studies in the Economics of Development
The Australian National University
Canberra

PART ONE

Vietnam and the Region

1. Crisis in Asia and Vietnam's Economic Policy Response

Suiwah Leung

The banking and currency crisis that hit Thailand in July 1997 spread rapidly through countries in Southeast and East Asia, albeit with varying degrees of intensity. The crisis poses a number of important questions for Vietnam, three of which are addressed in this book. First, will the crisis spread to Vietnam, now tied more closely to the rest of Southeast Asia through its membership of the Association of South East Asian Nations (ASEAN)? Second, will it have a significant adverse impact on Vietnam's economy? And third and perhaps most important, is the export-oriented industrialisation model of East and Southeast Asia still valid as a long-term development strategy for Vietnam, and what are the lessons that can be learned from the experiences of countries in the region?

WILL THE CRISIS SPREAD TO VIETNAM?

Causes of the Crisis

In considering Vietnam's vulnerability to crisis, Ramon Moreno, Gloria Pasadilla and Eli Remolona suggest in Chapter 3 that the East Asian crisis was caused by a combination of a run on domestic financial institutions and a run on currencies. Directed credit on the part of governments to 'favoured' sectors, together with implicit and explicit government guarantees, had weakened the ability of financial institutions in the crisis-stricken countries to manage risks and to evaluate lending on its commercial merits. These policies also encouraged aggressive lending to expand market shares, which helped fuel real estate and share market booms. At the same time, weaknesses in the financial sectors of the affected countries were masked by very rapid growth. Furthermore, the pegged exchange rate regime in existence in all the countries up to the time of the crisis discouraged financial institutions and individuals from managing exchange rate risks, including through the

use of hedging facilities. Consequently, forward markets in many Asian currencies did not develop (Leung 1997).

The situation was exacerbated by very large inflows of short-term capital,
mostly from institutional investors in the US and Europe, to take advantage
of the high yields to be gained in the 'emerging markets'. These yields were
artificially inflated by the removal of exchange rate risks through the pegged
exchange rate regimes of the Asian countries. Capital inflows were predominantly intermediated through the local banking systems. Moreno, Pasadilla
and Remolona point out that by about mid-1997, short-term currency deposits
in financial institutions in Thailand, Indonesia and Korea exceeded 100 per
cent of the stock of these countries' international reserves. When investor
sentiment turned, the rush on currencies brought about a collapse of the
domestic corporate sector. This in turn exposed the weaknesses of the financial institutions and brought on a banking crisis.

Is Vietnam at Risk?

The structural weaknesses in Vietnam's financial sector are probably more
severe than those in the crisis-affected countries. As Raymond Mallon points
out in Chapter 10, however, the failure to apply internationally accepted
accounting and auditing practices makes it very difficult to assess the 'true'
financial status of Vietnamese financial institutions. The use of direct controls over these institutions, as well as subsidised credit given to major state-
owned enterprises, certainly gives very strong disincentives to proper risk
management. It is perhaps indicative that the survey referred to by Tran Tho
Dat in Chapter 7 found that, in the Binhluc district in the Red River Delta,
the Vietnam Bank for Agriculture did not seem to consider a borrower's past
record with the bank relevant to the assessment of a loan proposal. This
would seem to suggest, at best, that the bank does not make efficient use of
customer information in assessing credit risk, and at worst that it is not cus-
tomary for credit risk to be a factor in lending decisions.

In fact, as shown by Suiwah Leung and Ngo Huy Duc in Chapter 6, Vietnam still has a substantially underdeveloped financial sector, with one of the
lowest ratios of M2 to GDP in the Asian region. Added to this is a pegged
exchange rate, strict foreign exchange control and a currency that is not fully
convertible. Given that the 'contagion effect' of the Asian crisis stemmed
from a reassessment of risks on the part of international investors – induced
to a large extent by the existence of significant amounts of unhedged foreign
currency debts in the crisis-affected countries – the underdeveloped nature of
Vietnam's domestic financial sector, together with its relative isolation from
international financial markets, makes it unlikely that the banking and currency crisis will spread to Vietnam, at least in the short run (James Riedel,
Chapter 2; see also Leung and Doanh 1998).

However, while a financial crisis may not 'spread' to Vietnam in the sense that there may not be a significant reversal of short-term capital inflows, capital flight accompanied by hyperinflation could still occur. Leung and Ngo estimate in Chapter 6 that both the volume of US dollars circulating in Vietnam expressed as a ratio of GDP, and the propensity of the Vietnamese people to switch from the domestic currency into dollar holdings, are among the highest in the world. Given this very significant degree of dollarisation, Leung and Ngo show that there is a real risk of macroeconomic instability. Dollarisation means a decrease in domestic currency holdings and hence a dwindling of the inflation tax base. To generate a given amount of inflation tax revenue, higher inflation rates are needed. Indeed, Chapter 6 shows the existence of a mechanism in Vietnam whereby, once inflation is entrenched, dollarisation can lead to further inflation, leading to increased expected depreciation of the currency, more dollarisation and so on in a vicious circle. While Vietnam's record of sound macroeconomic management in the 1990s would seem to militate against a sudden and large increase in inflation that could trigger this instability, the economy is nevertheless vulnerable.

WILL THE CRISIS HAVE AN ADVERSE IMPACT ON THE ECONOMY?

James Riedel points out in Chapter 2 that many of the factors responsible for the current drop in exports and foreign direct investment (FDI) were in existence *before* the eruption of the Asian crisis. Vietnam's real exchange rate vis-à-vis the US dollar had been appreciating since 1992, resulting in a decrease in international competitiveness. In addition, statistics on foreign investment approvals would have begun falling in 1996 – before the onset of the crisis – if not for the last-minute inclusion of a couple of large real estate projects. It is certainly true that since the crisis the implementation rate of approved projects has fallen, as have exports to the region.[1] As a result, an incipient balance of payments crisis is looming in Vietnam. It is being contained, for the time being, by strict controls over imports.

LESSONS FROM THE EAST ASIAN CRISIS

The Implications for Export-oriented Industrialisation

In the longer term, the Asian crisis has raised the issue of whether the export-oriented industrialisation model followed by countries in East and South-east Asia is still a valid strategy for Vietnam to follow. The experiences of

Japan in the postwar period, of the Asian newly industrialising economies (NIEs) – Taiwan, Korea, Hong Kong and Singapore – in the 1970s and of the ASEAN-3 (Thailand, Malaysia and Indonesia) in the 1980s have clearly demonstrated that balance of payments constraints cannot be eased permanently through a policy of international isolation or of import substitution. Export-oriented industrialisation in these countries has not only provided a sustainable solution to their balance of payments constraints, but has also generated the employment needed for their large and growing populations. The banking and financial crisis in Asia has not undermined the validity of this strategy. It has, however, highlighted the danger of implementing export-oriented industrialisation through giving credit subsidies to selected sectors, and through the government's assuming exchange rate risks on behalf of the private sector (Ross H. McLeod, Chapter 5). Such subsidies and protection can cause grave damage to the country's financial institutions.

Added to this is the more general observation, made by Hal Hill in Chapter 8, that subsidies of all kinds to selected industries (including fiscal incentives, special credit allocation and import protection) have not been the major factor behind sustained growth in the ASEAN-3. Special incentives to attract FDI have been found to be less successful in Southeast Asian countries than good macroeconomic performance, consistent policies towards foreign investment and a liberalised trade regime. In particular, as Premachandra Athukorala points out in Chapter 9, Malaysia's success in export-oriented growth through FDI is based on an open trading regime where there is minimal import licensing so that foreign companies can import their inputs freely, subject only to broad-based tariffs. There is also little protection of the output of local industries owned by foreign companies, so that these companies make use of Malaysia's abundant labour supply to produce goods for export to the global market.

These considerations lead both James Riedel (Chapter 2) and Raymond Mallon (Chapter 10) to the conclusion that the export-oriented industrialisation model remains a valid strategy for a labour-abundant and relatively resource-poor country such as Vietnam, but that this strategy has to be implemented by unshackling the domestic private sector (particularly small to medium-sized firms) rather than by subsidising selected firms or industries. The resilience of the Taiwanese economy to the financial crisis in the region, and the vulnerability of the Korean economy, attests to the superiority of implementing an export-oriented industrial strategy that is free from special incentive schemes to promote selected industries. In other words, the Asian crisis has not diminished the validity of export-oriented industrialisation per se as a development strategy, but it has conclusively demonstrated the unworkability of 'picking winners' in the implementation of this strategy.

This is a valuable lesson for Vietnam, whose political thinking and recent history are inclined towards a much more interventionist role for the state. Instead of picking winners, governments in Asia are currently engaged in setting the framework in which markets can operate. For the financial markets, this includes prudential supervision and regulation of banks. In Vietnam's case, such a framework would include the establishment of basic legal/commercial infrastructure, clarification of property rights, and the provision of reliable market and firm-level information so that markets (including the financial markets) could function effectively. Prudential supervision of banks could then be given real meaning, as Mallon concludes in Chapter 10. The benefits of this approach have already been shown in the agricultural sector. In Chapter 12, Nhu Che, Tom Kompas and Neil Vousden point to the dramatic growth in rice productivity in Vietnam that resulted from the very large incentive effects of market opening and the establishment of land use rights in the period 1988–94. This is a clear example of the important role of the state in setting the framework for markets, and of the benefits that can accrue from the implementation by the government of market-friendly policies.

Political philosophy and the belief in the 'dominant role of the state' have induced Vietnam to look closely at China's experiences. The success of township and village enterprises (TVEs) in China in the 1980s, documented by Yiping Huang in Chapter 11, has suggested one possible alternative to export-oriented industrialisation as a development strategy for Vietnam. The TVEs were owned collectively under the auspices of the local government authorities. Supplying simple manufactured goods to the domestic market, they grew rapidly in the mid-1980s. The TVEs played a valuable role in providing employment for the growing rural labour force while keeping the rural population away from the cities. Huang suggests, however, that the TVEs were a suboptimal (albeit temporarily successful) response to the opportunities and constraints that existed in China at the time, and that the same opportunities and constraints are not currently present in Vietnam. For instance, China's TVEs took advantage of the gap left by its heavy industry-oriented state-owned enterprises in the supply of consumption goods to the domestic market. In Vietnam this gap in consumer goods is already being filled by urban enterprises as well as by imports. Furthermore, there does not appear to be quite the same degree of political constraints on private ownership in rural Vietnam today as there was in China in the early 1980s. As pointed out by Che, Kompas and Vousden in Chapter 12 (p. 208), 'Although the ultimate ownership of land still rests with the state, the system of land tenure has shifted considerably in the direction of private property rights, providing farmers with reasonable security of tenure'. Export-oriented industrialisation based on clearly defined property rights therefore remains the 'first best' solution for Vietnam as it industrialises.

What Can Vietnam Learn from Its Neighbours?

To reorient the Vietnamese economy towards exporting will require significant structural change. What are the political economy lessons from the rest of the region in undertaking such changes?

Indonesia embarked on labour-intensive export-oriented manufacturing from about 1982 and began deregulating its domestic financial sector in the mid-1980s. In both cases, significant structural reforms were undertaken in response to adverse external circumstances rather than in a well-planned 'sequenced' manner. The export-oriented industrialisation drive was undertaken in response to falling oil prices (Hadi Soesastro, Chapter 4); domestic financial deregulation began in response to the cessation of international bank lending and hence the need to mobilise domestic savings (McLeod, Chapter 5). Furthermore, deregulation of Indonesia's *domestic* financial sector brought significant benefits in terms of increased domestic savings and access to the formal financial sector for many Indonesians. However, Indonesia's failure to follow up with deregulation of its pegged exchange rate regime threatened to undermine the gains of the past one and a half decades.

Like Indonesia, Vietnam was responding to external events – the break-up of the former Soviet Union and the cessation of foreign aid and trade with the Soviet bloc – when it adopted its policy of *doi moi* [economic renovation] in 1989. Unlike Indonesia, however, deregulation of Vietnam's domestic financial sector has barely begun. The lesson of the interaction between domestic financial liberalisation and the exchange rate regime is therefore timely. The current crisis in the Asian region and the looming balance of payments crisis could well provide the impetus for a second *doi moi* – this time focused on structural reforms and their interrelations with macroeconomic stabilisation in Vietnam.

NOTE

1. The World Bank (1998) estimates the combined effect of falling FDI and exports resulting from the East Asian financial crisis to be about US$3 billion (or around 12 per cent of Vietnam's GDP).

2. Needed: A Strategic Vision for Setting Reform Priorities in Vietnam

James Riedel

Vietnam has made the transition from a centrally planned to a market economy, albeit one in which the government plays a heavy role. In this respect it is no different from many economies that are commonly regarded as market economies. The issue is no longer whether Vietnam will have a market economy, but rather what kind it will have – a dynamic, prosperous one, or a cumbersome, inefficient one like many in the developing world.

Looking back over the past six years of economic accomplishments – near double digit growth rates, inflation in the single digit range and foreign direct investment (FDI) flooding in – one might be persuaded that Vietnam has already laid the foundation for a dynamic, prosperous market economy. That of course would be a mistake, as it is well recognised, both inside and outside of the government, that without further reforms the strong performance of the past will not be sustained. Local and foreign experts clamour daily for one reform or another, the most common targets being state enterprises, trade policy, the financial sector, the tax system and the administrative apparatus.

In each of these areas of policy there are major problems that need to be tackled. However, even if the authorities were willing to tackle them all at once, they would lack the resources and administrative ability to do so. What is necessary therefore is to establish a set of reform priorities based on a strategic vision of long-term economic development in Vietnam. At present there is no consensus in the government about such a strategy, and so there is no agreement as to what the priorities of reform should be.

A long-term economic development strategy that is appropriate for Vietnam's circumstances cannot be invented de novo; it can only be found by studying the experiences of other countries in similar circumstances. Many, indeed most, developing countries have tried to chart a new course, a 'third way', a strategy custom-designed to fit what they have perceived to be their unique economic and political circumstances. But in every case they have been forced to abandon their 'third way' and look to the experiences of other countries for guidance. Since 1985 nothing short of a revolution in policy making has swept the developing world, as one country after another has undertaken to liberalise its trade and industrial policy in an effort to emulate the success of the East Asian 'Tigers' (Dean, Desai and Riedel 1994).

It is ironic that Vietnam, which lies in the very midst of these economic Tigers, has been one of the last countries to embrace the strategy that propelled their success. For as we shall argue below, there is no other proven path to rapid, long-term growth for a country in Vietnam's circumstances than the export-oriented industrialisation strategy that each and every one of the successful East Asian countries followed. Vietnam is poised to replicate their success: it satisfies the preconditions in terms of resource endowment; and it has to a large extent established the policy framework needed to make the strategy work (although there are many areas in which the policy framework could be improved). However, one critical ingredient of the strategy is missing – the network of private small and medium-sized companies that was the backbone of export-oriented industrialisation everywhere that it succeeded.

Correcting this deficiency by creating an environment conducive to private corporate development should, we argue, be the highest policy priority. In setting the agenda for reform of trade policy, the financial system, the tax regime and so forth, the authorities should pay utmost attention to the consequences of their actions for the private corporate sector. Even in dealing with immediate economic problems, consideration should be given to the implications for longer-term strategic objectives (Riedel and Turley 1998).

The case for an export-oriented industrialisation strategy in Vietnam has recently been clouded by the financial crisis that has swept East Asia since mid-1997. In the popular press the 'Asian miracle' is now the 'Asian myth', and the 'Asian Tigers' are dismissed as 'paper tigers'. It is therefore necessary to consider whether the export-oriented industrialisation strategy followed by the Asian Tigers remains a reliable strategy for Vietnam in light of the regional financial crisis, and at the same time to address the widespread concern that the crisis will spread to Vietnam – or at least severely diminish its economic prospects in the near to medium term.

Knowing the priorities of reform is not enough; there must also be willingness on the part of leaders to undertake the reforms needed. Since every change, even from worse to better, involves costs to some and benefits to other vested interests in the economy, the willingness to make changes inevitably revolves on the interplay of economics and politics. Therefore, in the final section of this chapter, we address the question of whether the leadership will meet the political challenge of keeping reform on track.

THE IMPORTANCE OF PRIVATE SECTOR DEVELOPMENT

The argument that private small and medium-sized companies are critically important to Vietnam's economic development is based on three fundamental propositions that are solidly supported by empirical evidence. These are: (1) that export-oriented industrialisation is the only viable strategy for rapid economic growth in Vietnam; (2) that Vietnam satisfies the prerequisites of the strategy in terms of the resource endowment and policy framework needed to make the strategy work; and (3) that critical to the success of the export-oriented industrialisation strategy is the emergence of private small and medium-sized companies as the dominant (but not exclusive) form of industrial organisation in the manufacturing sector.

The Imperative of Export-oriented Industrialisation

In the vast literature on economic development over the past 100 years, there is no empirical regularity that is more robust across time and countries than the positive relation between openness to trade and economic growth. This fact was not always known or appreciated, and indeed most developing countries commenced their industrialisation by closing their economies to international trade. The import substitution strategy of industrialisation, which virtually every developing country (except Hong Kong) adopted at the outset of industrialisation, was based on two false premises. One was that export-oriented industrialisation was bound to fail because developing countries would find no market for their products in the developed countries. The other was that developing countries, by closing their economies and protecting domestic industry, would be able to capture economies of scale and time (learning by doing), which would eventually make them competitive in industries in which they initially lacked comparative advantage.

Both of these premises have been proved false by the cumulative experience of developing countries over the past four decades. The experiences of Hong Kong, Singapore, Taiwan and South Korea – the first countries to abandon the conventional wisdom of the day and adopt the export-oriented industrialisation strategy – were a powerful demonstration of the fallacy of the premise of export pessimism. In spite of the evidence, however, export pessimism persisted in the form of the 'fallacy of composition' argument, which held that the success of the first-comers to export-oriented industrialisation (the 'Four Tigers') could not be replicated by latecomers because the former had saturated the market for labour-intensive manufactures in developed countries. This last stand of export pessimism was thoroughly demolished when, following the success of the Asian Tigers, a succession of other

developing countries, including China and most of the Southeast Asian countries, adopted and succeeded with the export-oriented industrialisation strategy in the 1980s.

The second premise – that scale economies and learning by doing would
allow developing countries to revoke the law of comparative advantage and
instead put their scarce investable resources into capital-intensive, high-
technology industry – proved equally false, and was disastrously costly for
developing countries. Certainly the import substitution strategy did create
large industrial bases in the larger continental developing countries (China,
India, Brazil, Turkey), but in every case it carried an enormous cost in
terms of economic inefficiency, and often brought with it macroeconomic
instability.

The positive experiences of countries following adoption of an export-
oriented industrialisation strategy, combined with the overwhelmingly negative experiences of countries following adoption of an inward-oriented
import substitution strategy, have impelled many countries to undertake
broad-based programs of economic reform since 1985. Indeed, outside of
Sub-Saharan Africa, there is nothing short of a revolution in policy reform
under way in developing countries, as one country after another has undertaken unilaterally to lower its barriers to trade and institute market-oriented
reforms.

An Export-oriented Industrialisation Strategy for Vietnam?

The export-oriented industrialisation strategy is appropriate for Vietnam for
two reasons: (1) there is no alternative strategy that will work as well; and
(2) economic conditions in Vietnam are similar to those that existed in other
countries that have succeeded with an export-oriented strategy.

The only countries that have achieved a high level of per capita income
without industrialising are those with an extraordinary abundance of natural
resources, mainly oil. Unfortunately Vietnam is not such a country. It has
substantial mineral resources (mainly oil and gas), which in recent years
have contributed significantly to exports and to government revenues, but on
a per capita basis Vietnam's oil reserves are only a fraction of those of, say,
Indonesia or Malaysia.

Vietnam is also blessed with about 70,000 square kilometres of fertile
agricultural land, which at present provide employment for about 80 per cent
of the population and in good monsoon years generate a food surplus (mainly
of rice) for export. Relative to the population of about 75 million, however,
Vietnam's agriculture is already close to the limit of its capacity to feed the
country, and agricultural productivity will therefore need to rise. An export-
oriented industrialisation strategy will not relieve Vietnam of the necessity of

having to invest heavily in the agricultural sector to raise productivity. Even with substantial investment in agriculture, the sector will not be able to provide productive employment for the millions of people who reside in the countryside and the millions more who will be born into the rural sector in the years to come. Indeed, the only way to raise agricultural labour productivity is to transfer a large proportion of the agricultural labour force to the industrial sector.

Industrialisation is therefore the key to raising per capita income in Vietnam over the long term. Moreover, industrialisation must follow Vietnam's comparative advantage and be, for the most part, labour intensive and export oriented. As shown in Table 2.1, Vietnam's comparative advantage lies first and foremost in the abundance of its human resources. Like all other East Asian countries that have succeeded with export-oriented industrialisation, Vietnam is a densely populated country with meagre natural resources and with the majority of its population in the rural sector. Furthermore, as the

Table 2.1 Comparative Economic and Social Indicators

	Taiwan (35–40 years ago)	Thailand (20–25 years ago)	China (10–15 years ago)	Vietnam (most recent)
Population density (population/sq km)	300	108	96	195
Agricultural population density (population/sq km)	629	240	219	934
Agricultural land/total land (%)	24	45	44	21
Life expectancy (years)	63	60	65	67
Secondary school enrolments (% school age children)	30	26	47	42
Illiteracy rate (% population aged over 15 years)	30	7	27	16

Source: Riedel (1993).

table shows, Vietnam has achieved levels of human resource development comparable to those that existed in other East Asian countries when they launched their export-oriented industrialisation strategies.

One area in which Vietnam is relatively deficient is industrial development; current levels are far below those achieved by other countries when they shifted from an inward-looking import substitution strategy to an outward-looking export-oriented strategy. Per capita output of Vietnam's principal industrial products is only about one-tenth to one-twentieth that of, for example, Taiwan or China when they launched their industrialisation strategies.

Because Vietnam's industrial base is relatively small, some might be led to suggest that, like most other countries, Vietnam should follow an inward-looking policy to build up its industrial base before undertaking an export-oriented industrialisation strategy. This would be a major mistake, for the export-oriented strategy succeeded elsewhere by being 'footloose' and hence able to circumvent the inefficient industrial base built up during the earlier import substitution phase. The essence of the strategy is, for the most part, to combine low-cost labour, drawn chiefly from the rural sector, with mainly imported raw materials and capital goods. Seen in this light, the relatively small size of Vietnam's industrial base is an advantage rather than a disadvantage, because it largely obviates the necessity (though not the desirability) of attempting to privatise or close down state-owned industries that are unable to compete internationally.

Vietnam meets the prerequisites for a successful export-oriented industrialisation strategy not only in terms of resource endowment, but also in terms of the macroeconomic framework that is required. At least three macroeconomic conditions are common to all the successful applications of such a strategy: (1) macroeconomic stability; (2) relatively high and rising domestic saving and investment rates; and (3) if not free trade, as in Hong Kong and Singapore, then free access for exporters to imported inputs and capital goods.

One of Vietnam's most remarkable achievements has been its ability to reduce inflation and keep it down, a tribute to the government's commitment to a prudent fiscal policy. Moreover, in the past six years Vietnam has achieved a doubling of the share of gross domestic investment in GDP and a tripling of the private saving rate. Finally, it must be acknowledged that Vietnam has gone a long way towards lowering trade barriers, especially for exporters, although much remains to be done to put them on an equal footing with their competitors in world markets. Of the three key ingredients of the policy framework for export-oriented industrialisation, this final one has suffered the most in recent years as the government has tried to manage an incipient foreign exchange crisis by compressing imports.

The Role of Private Small and Medium-sized Enterprises[1]

There is a body of opinion in development economics and in some international development institutions that 'small is beautiful', and therefore that small and medium-sized companies should be promoted because they are small. That opinion is not shared by the present author, who advocates efficiency rather than any particular form of industrial organisation. If efficiency is served by large state-owned enterprises (SOEs), then so be it. Indeed, there are some industrial branches, such as steel and chemicals, in which large enterprises are no doubt more efficient than small ones. There are even some industries in which state ownership might be preferable to private ownership, as for example in the case of natural monopolies, which must be closely regulated if privately owned.

The importance of private companies in export-oriented industrialisation is grounded not in theory or ideology, but in the fact that this form of industrial organisation is the most successful in low-wage, labour-abundant, open economies. By 'most successful' what is meant is that, if treated fairly, private companies earn higher returns on investment than larger SOEs or smaller private household businesses. As a result they are better able to compete for scarce investable resources and emerge as the predominant form of business enterprise in relatively labour-intensive, export-oriented branches of manufacturing.

Evidence of the superior performance of private companies in labour-abundant countries can be found in any of the successful East Asian countries. Here we draw evidence from Taiwan, which is the most successful of all the East Asian countries and the one most appropriate for purposes of comparison with Vietnam since, as shown in Table 2.1, Vietnam bears a striking resemblance to Taiwan as it was 35–40 years ago.

One similarity that would come as a surprise to many is that SOEs dominated the manufacturing sector in Taiwan in the late 1950s, just as they do in Vietnam today. Indeed, the real (US dollar) value added of state-owned manufacturing firms in Taiwan in the late 1950s was greater than that of such firms in Vietnam currently. However, the contribution of state-owned manufacturing firms was entirely eclipsed by the growth of private manufacturing after the export-oriented industrialisation strategy was launched in the 1960s.

The private companies that grew to overwhelm SOEs in Taiwan were for the most part small and medium-sized companies with an average of about 40 employees per firm. Their share of manufacturing value added rose from about 35 per cent in 1960 to about 85 per cent in 1995. It is apparent why such companies emerged as the dominant form of enterprise in Taiwan. As shown in Figure 2.1, the average return on capital in Taiwan's private small and medium-sized companies is almost three times higher than in the much

Figure 2.1 Ratio of Value Added to Fixed Capital by Firm Type in Taiwan
Manufacturing, 1986

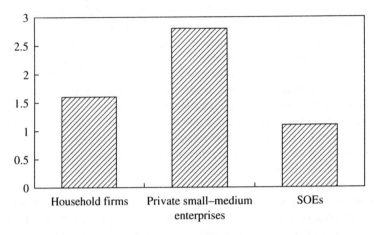

Source: Riedel and Tran (1997).

larger and more capital-intensive SOEs, and about two times higher than in
the smaller and slightly more labour-intensive family firms. In a labour-
abundant, low-wage, open economy, the private companies predominate
because they are small enough to be flexible and large enough to be efficient.
Their beauty is not in their size but in their profitability.

PROBLEMS FACING PRIVATE COMPANIES AND
THE PRIORITIES FOR REFORM

'Credit, Credit and Credit'

The former Communist Party Secretary-General, Do Muoi, has described the
problems of economic development in Vietnam as being three-fold: 'capital,
capital and capital'. Private small and medium-sized companies in Vietnam
share this view, identifying the main obstacles to their growth as 'credit,
credit and credit'. Private companies acknowledge that ambiguities about
property rights, restrictions on international trade, irrationality in the tax system, and excessive bureaucracy and red tape complicate business and carry
costs, but these problems are viewed as secondary to credit – or more precisely, the lack of it.

The inefficiency of the financial system is a burden to all forms of business, public and private, large and small. It is, however, especially critical for

the emerging private companies, which unlike state-owned firms cannot rely on the government to guarantee their bank loans, and unlike household firms have to face relatively large capital investment requirements and long gestation periods. Without access to formal financial markets, the emerging private companies are forced either to borrow at exorbitant rates in the informal market or to amass personal savings to meet the capital requirements for investment. As a result, many potentially able entrepreneurs with profitable projects are no doubt discouraged from investing, which means that fewer jobs are created in the manufacturing sector, that less foreign exchange is earned from exporting manufactures and that less revenue is collected from taxing Vietnam's most profitable companies.

Finding solutions to the problem of financing private corporate investment should be the main priority of policy reform. The establishment of the long-awaited stock market is a step in the right direction, but it will not go far towards solving the financing problems of new private companies. Much more important are measures that would deal directly with the problem of securing bank loans and guaranteeing foreign currency credits on imports of machinery and equipment for private companies. To assist them to overcome the problems they face in formal financial markets, the government should consider establishing a fund to provide credit guarantees to private companies, as many other governments in East Asia have done. In Taiwan, for example, the fund established by the government in 1974 with an initial endowment of only US$400 million has guaranteed in excess of US$58 billion in credit to small and medium-sized businesses and generated a surplus to the fund of more than US$200 million.

In addition to taking steps to remove existing obstacles to financing private investment, the government must also make every effort to avoid creating new obstacles. Caution is especially warranted at the present time, when some in the government are recommending restrictions on imports and on the use of deferred letters of credit to finance imports as a means of dealing with the country's large trade deficit. If the trade deficit is a problem, it is one that was created by the SOEs, not by the emerging private companies. Indeed, Vietnam's private small and medium-sized companies, as the essential ingredient of a successful export-oriented industrialisation strategy, are the long-term solution to the balance of payments constraint the country faces. It would therefore behove the government to consider establishing special programs in the State Bank to give Vietnam's new export-oriented private companies priority in accessing foreign exchange.

Property and Land Use Rights

The fledgling status of the private corporate sector in Vietnam is hardly surprising, given that the legal protection of private property was first established with the adoption of the 1992 Constitution. Furthermore, it was not until 1994 that a basis for resolving disputes over property rights, through civil and economic courts and non-governmental arbitration centres, was established. As matters stand, the legal framework for a free enterprise market economy is still incomplete and in need of reform. In particular, the legal requirements for government intervention in private economic decision making, especially with respect to investment, and the differentiated rules and incentives applying to different forms of business ownership, constitute serious obstacles to the establishment and growth of private small and medium-sized companies.

Property rights with respect to land are far and away the most problematic. Vietnamese law establishes the right only to use – not to own – land, and imposes severe limitations on the transfer of land. As a result, land use rights are often not transacted openly, leading to extreme price volatility, speculation and inefficient use of land. Of course, in such an environment the most disadvantaged firms are those that are just starting to get established: in short, Vietnam's private manufacturing companies.

The Tax System

The problem with the tax system in Vietnam and its implications for small and medium-sized companies is not the level of taxation per se, which by international standards is quite low, but the irrationality of the system and the way in which it is administered. What is irrational about the tax system is its multiplicity of taxes and taxation rates. Private companies, for example, are subject to three major taxes: a turnover tax, a special sales tax and a profit tax. Furthermore, the rates applicable for each kind of tax vary across types of business and commodity category, with turnover tax ranging from zero to 40 per cent and profit tax from 25 to 45 per cent. With the proliferation of taxes and tax rates, a great deal of discretion is introduced into the administration of the system. This in turn encourages businesses to keep multiple sets of books and in general to avoid transparency in their financial records. The consequence of such a system is not only inefficient and inequitable tax collection, but also the undermining of accurate accounting and financial record keeping, which are critical ingredients of a sound financial system.

The Trade Regime

Like the tax system, the trade regime is not regarded by small and medium-sized companies as a major obstacle to business. The past growth rate of trade at about 30 per cent per annum, or three times the rate of growth of

GDP, testifies to the overall openness of the economy. Nevertheless a number of trade-inhibiting measures remain, and for the most part these bear disproportionately on private small and medium-sized companies.

Although import duties on raw materials and capital goods are relatively low (under 20 per cent), the administration of trade policy in Vietnam demonstrates a strong inclination on the part of officials to protect domestic industry from international competition. However, by applying for membership of ASEAN, the ASEAN Free Trade Area (AFTA) and the World Trade Organisation (WTO), the government is committing itself to the kind of liberal trade regime that is critical for the success of the export-oriented industrialisation strategy.

Bureaucracy and Red Tape

The logic of a market economy is that a person investing his or her own money is the best judge of whether that investment will succeed, since the investor profits if it does and loses if it does not. The Vietnamese authorities have accepted the necessity of a market economy but still do not completely trust its underlying logic. Individuals are not free to invest their own money in legal business ventures, but must first get the permission of the state to establish, dissolve or change a business. In the case of private small and medium-sized companies this process is especially burdensome.

IMPLICATIONS OF THE ASIAN FINANCIAL CRISIS

The financial crisis that erupted in a number of Asian countries in 1997 has raised serious concerns in Vietnam, the most immediate being that it will spread there (Hai 1998). Even if Vietnam can avoid a similar financial crisis, there is concern that the regional crises will have negative spillover effects on its economic prospects, at least in the near to medium term. Finally, there is concern that the much vaunted 'Asian model' of economic development, advocated here as Vietnam's best hope for long-term economic growth, is no longer reliable in light of the Asian financial crisis. Each of these is a legitimate concern that deserves consideration, but first it will be useful to examine briefly the nature of the financial crisis in the region.

The Nature of the Crisis

The crisis began, according to most reports, when the Bank of Thailand announced on 2 July 1997 that it was abandoning the peg of the baht to the US dollar, sparking a sell-off of the currency. The weakness of the baht encouraged speculative attacks on other Asian currencies, some of which held their value while others collapsed. Six months after the onset of the crisis, the currencies of Thailand, Malaysia, the Philippines and South Korea had each fallen about 50 per cent in value. The Indonesian rupiah suffered the most, losing about 75 per cent of its value. The currencies of Singapore and Taiwan were each devalued about 20 per cent, mainly as a competitive response to the wholesale devaluations in the region, while the Hong Kong dollar and Chinese renminbi have remained unchanged against the US dollar. The Vietnamese dong has been devalued less than 10 per cent in the past six months, an issue taken up later.

The massive devaluations in the crisis-stricken countries (Thailand, Malaysia, Indonesia, the Philippines and South Korea) were the product of a classic financial panic. Foreign investors and creditors woke up suddenly in mid-1997 to the realisation that the assumptions they had made in the early 1990s were no longer valid. Back then it all seemed so easy. Stock prices and property values were soaring, interest rates were high, and the risks were assumed to be low because the currencies of these countries were pegged to the US dollar. In the rush to cash in, European and American fund managers pumped enormous sums of short-term credit into these newly discovered 'emerging markets' (Figure 2.2). Short-term foreign credit to Thailand amounted to 7–10 per cent of GDP in each year from 1994 to 1996. By the end of 1996, foreign bank short-term loans to Thailand stood at about US$70 billion. In Malaysia the amount was US$22 billion, in Indonesia US$55 billion and in Korea a staggering US$100 billion (Chanda 1998, p. 46).

What went wrong, and could it have been anticipated? Of course, both borrowers and lenders in international financial markets should have remembered lesson one of international finance, that a relatively high interest rate is associated with an expectation of currency depreciation. Even more basic, they should have kept in mind that every party comes to end, and the more raucous ones end most abruptly. It was not a secret that real estate markets were overvalued, that many banks were overextended and that foreign currency debt was accumulating rapidly, but nobody wanted to leave before the party was over. However, the collapse of the Bangkok Bank of Commerce in 1996, the default on a Euro-bond by a major Thai real estate company in February 1997, and then revelations of trouble in Thailand's largest finance company in March were enough to make investors run for cover (Chanda 1998, p. 46).

The crises were not only the result of panic by greedy investors, they were also caused by fundamental weaknesses in the economic and political systems of the affected countries. Corruption, crony capitalism and weak financial systems have been identified as the key culprits. These problems are, of course, not unknown in the Asian countries that have been spared a financial

Figure 2.2 Capital Inflows to the Crisis-stricken Five (US$ billion)

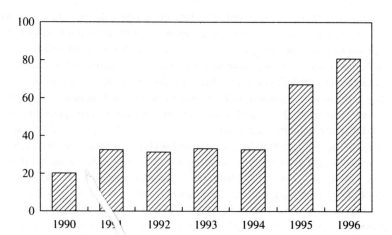

Sources: IMF (selected issues), *International Financial Statistics*; World Bank, Vietnam database.

crisis, in particular China and Vietnam – the latter two having so far avoided trouble mainly by steering clear of international financial markets and relying chiefly on FDI for foreign capital. Opening up to international financial flows exposed the political and economic weaknesses of the crisis-stricken Asian countries, it did not create them. In doing so the international financial markets rendered an invaluable service, and the crises may turn out to be a blessing in disguise, provided that the affected countries are willing and able to learn from their mistakes and change their ways.

The ability of the crisis-affected countries to make the necessary changes hinges mainly on the strength of their political systems, which is no doubt why Indonesia, which has perhaps the weakest political system of all, has fared the worst. Malaysia's fundamentals may well have been the most favourable, but the reluctance of Prime Minister Mahathir to acknowledge that anything was fundamentally wrong and instead to blame what was happening on 'immoral' currency traders certainly made matters worse. The market's cautiously optimistic reassessment of Korea's prospects is due in large part to the surprising resilience the country's political system demonstrated during the recent presidential election. No doubt the massive financial assistance offered by the multilateral financial institutions and the US government also helped, but this assistance was only made possible by Korea's show of political will to deal with its fundamental problems.

Will the Crisis Spread to Vietnam?

The concern that the crisis in neighbouring countries will spread to Vietnam arises not just because of geographic proximity to the regional troubles, but from the fact that many of the weaknesses in the economic and political systems of the crisis-stricken countries are shared by Vietnam. One in particular is the weakness of the banking system, which was at the root of the crisis in each of the affected countries. In Thailand, banks and finance companies affiliated with banks borrowed short term in international financial markets to fund a speculative bubble in real estate. In Korea, banks were directed by bureaucrats to lend money to projects and sectors favoured by government policy, which in all too many cases proved insufficiently profitable to be able to repay the banks' loans. In Indonesia, political connections dictated a large amount of bank lending, funded from abroad, which not surprisingly ended up as a mountain of bad debt. In each of these cases the root problem was improper banking practices made possible by inadequate regulation and lax supervision.

Bank supervision is still at a rudimentary stage of development in Vietnam, and many of the regulations that have been enacted recently have not yet been tested. In the past, bank regulation and supervision was less important than it is now because the banking industry was entirely state owned and under the direct control of the government. The credibility of the banks rested on that of the government. The banking sector is still dominated by the state-owned banks, but private banks are gaining ground and beginning to force competition on their large state-owned counterparts. Furthermore, with the opening of the economy, domestic banks – both state owned and private – have been required to establish credibility not only with domestic depositors, but also with their foreign counterparts on whom they rely to finance trade. With the loosening of government control over banking and the opening up of the economy, the need for transparency in the financial system has become all the more important. However, as noted recently, 'transparency has never been a strong point of Vietnam, which regards even its level of foreign reserves as a state secret' (Golin 1998, p. 38).

This lesson was vividly underscored in early 1997, when Vietnam experienced a so-called mini-banking crisis as a result of several defaults by both state-owned and private joint stock banks on deferred letters of credit owed to foreign banks. The difficulty of assessing the liquidity and solvency of domestic banks, and even of ascertaining what the government's policy was towards defaults on foreign letters of credit, rapidly undermined the international financial community's trust in Vietnamese banking institutions. It was only after the government was forced by events to disclose that the defaults occurred because of a mishandling of several financial scandals, and not because of bank illiquidity or government policy, that the matter was laid to rest.

In summary, Vietnam's banking system has the same weaknesses as the crisis-stricken countries in Asia, if not more. In these circumstances it would be a major mistake for Vietnam to open itself to free international capital mobility. Fortunately it has not done so, having maintained strict controls on foreign exchange transactions and restricted private capital inflows mainly to FDI. Indeed, as Figure 2.3 shows, since 1991 FDI flows have more than matched Vietnam's current account deficit in each year except 1996. However, while Vietnam has avoided the peril of a hot money attack on its currency, it has also forgone the advantages of integration into international financial markets, including the access to investment finance it sorely needs. It is therefore imperative that measures be taken to prepare the domestic banking system to become integrated into international financial markets. What needs to be done, and the consequences of not doing it, can readily be learned from the experience of neighbouring countries.

Negative Spillover Effects on Vietnam?

The spillover effect that has raised the most concern in Vietnam is the

Figure 2.3 Current Account Deficits and FDI Inflows (US$ million)

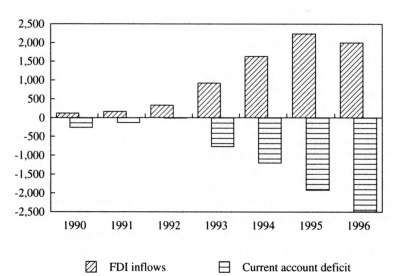

Source: World Bank statistics.

increase in competitive pressure brought about by the large devaluations in the crisis-affected countries. The degree to which Vietnam would suffer a loss of competitiveness through these devaluations depends on the extent to which it competes with such countries in world markets. A popular view is that the loss has been great, with the poor performance of exports at the end of 1997 being attributed to the regional crisis (Tran 1998, p. 2). However, an examination of the trade structures and world market shares of the affected economies suggests that the popular view may not be correct. The fact is that the world market shares of these countries are small in most of the commodity categories important to Vietnam, and therefore their devaluations are unlikely to affect significantly the US dollar prices of Vietnam's main exports (namely petroleum, rice, coffee and light manufactured goods). Where competitive pressure is likely to be most acute is in the domestic market, in which local goods compete with imports (legal and smuggled) from the crisis-stricken countries in the region. In this area, however, there is a compensation in that the losses suffered by the import competing firms are offset by the terms of trade gain that accrues to domestic consumers.

What this suggests is that the Asian financial crisis does not in and of itself provide a very strong case for a devaluation of the dong, contrary to popular opinion. A much stronger argument for devaluation rests on the real appreciation of the dong against the US dollar, which has been under way for a long time. As Figure 2.4 shows, the relative dollar price of Vietnamese goods has risen 60 per cent since 1992. This, far more than the devaluation of regional currencies, is the main source of declining competitiveness.

Vietnamese authorities have so far resisted devaluation, fearing that it could ignite inflation. Their fears may well be justified, especially if they are unwilling to accompany devaluation of the currency with appropriate macroeconomic and structural policy changes, including scaling back planned public expenditures and taking steps to encourage export-oriented industrial development. Without such measures, it is likely that a devaluation would result mainly in a higher domestic price level. The status quo is, however, equally unappealing, since the pressure on foreign exchange supplies will only increase, forcing the authorities to continue to restrict and compress imports, with deleterious effects on short and long-term growth prospects. Indeed, it is very likely that the fall-off in export growth in late 1997 was more a consequence of import compression than of competitive devaluations in the region. Furthermore, as expectations of a devaluation intensify, the black market rate will rise and a more internal substitution of dollars for dong will take place, putting upward pressure on interest rates in order to avoid official devaluation.

The impact of the Asian financial crisis on FDI in Vietnam is perhaps more serious. There is great concern that FDI is drying up, in part because of

Figure 2.4 Index of Real Dong/Dollar Exchange Rate*

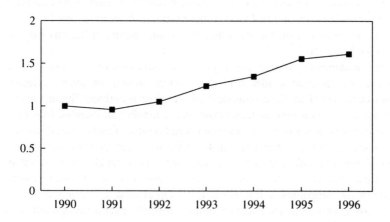

Note: *A rise in the index indicates real appreciation.*

Sources: IMF, *International Financial Statistics*; General Statistics Office, Hanoi.

the regional crisis and in part because of the growing hostility of foreign investors to the inhospitable business environment they face in Vietnam. Total new foreign investment of US$4.5 billion in 1997 was about half the record US$8.6 billion licensed the year before. In response to these pressures, Prime Minister Khai called a meeting with foreign investors in February 1998 to reassure them that the government was taking steps to address their complaints.

The actual impact of the crisis on foreign investment is hard to gauge, however. The available statistics on approved FDI have limited usefulness as they vastly overstate the amount of foreign investment that is actually implemented. Nevertheless, even if one takes reports of declining FDI at face value, the implications are far from clear. The fact is that Vietnam cannot and should not expect to rely on FDI to finance investment and balance payments to the extent that it has in the past. Therefore, even without the event of a financial crisis in the region, a slowdown of FDI may have resulted, and without necessarily implying a deterioration of economic prospects.

Should Vietnam Rethink Its Development Strategy?

The export-oriented industrialisation strategy has been the route to rapid growth both in the crisis-affected Asian countries and in those that have so far escaped a financial crisis. The strategy itself is therefore not called into question by the crisis. The tactics followed by the different countries pursuing export-oriented industrialisation have, however, varied significantly in some important respects, and it is in these tactical differences and how they influenced outcomes during the crisis that some important lessons may be found for Vietnam.

The fundamental issues are crystallised most vividly in the contest between the 'Korean model' and the 'Taiwan model' of export-oriented industrialisation. The Korean model, whose most prominent features are a high degree of economic concentration in the family-run *chaebol* [business conglomerates] and a heavy-handed industrial policy of picking and promoting 'winners', was a natural favourite of many in the Vietnamese government. Certainly it offers an approach with more of a socialist orientation than the Taiwan model, which features intricate networks of small and medium-sized private companies, and thus a low level of economic concentration and much less government guidance or support for industrial development. The Korean model was therefore seen as a way to have it both ways: a capitalist system, but with government in command.

The inherent contradiction of the Korean model – a capitalist system run by the visible hand of government rather than the invisible hand of the market – was revealed before the current crisis, most clearly in the late 1970s when government-led investment in heavy industry brought Korea to the brink of a debt crisis. However, with rapid GDP growth and booming exports, the lessons of the past were forgotten until 1997, when history replayed itself with a vengeance. Once again massive investments in heavy industry financed by short-term foreign borrowing with little regard for the bottom line, brought the country, this time past the brink, with a short-term debt amounting to a staggering US$100 billion and eight of Korea's 50 largest *chaebol* facing bankruptcy (Chanda 1998, p. 48). Meanwhile, Taiwan came through those turbulent months largely unscathed, and so now finds itself in a very good position to capture market opportunities from which Korean competitors are being forced to withdraw. The contest between the two models should therefore be considered over, although it would be naive to think that it will be.

WILL POLICY BE GUIDED BY A STRATEGIC VISION OR JUST CONTINUE TO MUDDLE ALONG?

At its fourth plenum in December 1997, the Central Committee passed a resolution approving direct export by private companies, more emphasis on labour-intensive industries, and trade in agricultural land use rights. These and other progressive measures were much welcomed, but fell far short of the strategic vision that recognises the central role of private small and medium-sized companies. It is an open question as to whether the leadership will continue with piecemeal reforms or take the bold steps necessary to sustain growth and equity in the long run.

Most observers doubt that the leadership will have the political courage to take the steps that are necessary to implement a viable long-term growth strategy. Certainly the leadership demonstrated boldness in 1986 when it adopted *doi moi* – its policy of economic renovation – and in 1989 when it launched comprehensive stabilisation and structural adjustment policies, but those were times of severe economic crisis and in the circumstances there was no alternative. In today's environment, with growth at a respectable 7–9 per cent and inflation in single digits, there is much less pressure for political boldness. No vital interests are currently threatened, and no emerging interest group is yet powerful enough to exert effective pressure for change. Therefore, in the absence of any sharp turn for the worse in the economy (so the argument goes), no decisive switch from muddling along to bold strategic reform should be expected.

It is hard to counter the pessimists' argument. It has on its side the weight of evidence from the past six years of incremental, unguided policy making. But there are some mitigating considerations to counter the pessimists' logic. The prospect of losing the momentum gained from past reforms poses a political threat not unlike the one the leadership faced in the late 1980s. If the hard-earned gains of the past ten years are allowed to slip away, a political price will be paid. In a sense, the pressure on the leadership is even greater today than it was in the 1980s: then they had nothing to lose; now they have one of the most remarkable economic turnarounds in history to squander.

Another factor favouring the kind of politically bold moves needed today is that they carry a much lower economic price than those taken in the 1980s. Stabilising the economy, dismantling the state procurement system and eliminating some 5,000 SOEs required enormous economic sacrifices on the part of every segment of the society, no less the government itself, which was forced to cut expenditures by a full six percentage points of GDP from 1989 to 1991. By contrast, adopting an export-oriented industrialisation strategy and creating an environment conducive to private small and medium-sized companies requires few public resources. What the private companies need is not so much to be promoted as to be unshackled, to be given the freedom and encouragement to exploit the enormously profitable market opportunities that await them. Indeed, if a conducive environment is created for the private companies, the government and other parts of the economy will profit along with the small and medium-sized companies. For it is a fact that only the small and medium-sized companies have the capability to generate employment for the millions who will migrate from the rural to the urban sector, to earn the foreign exchange that will be required to keep the engine of growth running in Vietnam, and to pay the taxes necessary to finance government expenditures and subsidise the SOEs. What is needed to implement the strategic vision set out here is, therefore, not economic sacrifice but political boldness. Will it be found again in Vietnam? Only time will tell.

NOTE

1. This section draws on Riedel and Tran (1997), which contains a full report of the results of interviews with some 50 private small and medium-sized companies.

PART TWO

The Asian Financial Crisis
and Vietnam

3. Asia's Financial Crisis: Lessons and Implications for Vietnam

Ramon Moreno, Gloria Pasadilla and Eli Remolona*

In recent years, Vietnam has had remarkable success in achieving rapid growth and stable inflation comparable to that observed in other East Asian economies. Annual real GDP growth accelerated from about 5 per cent in 1990 to close to 9 per cent or higher between 1994 and 1996. At the same time, consumer price index (CPI) inflation fell to single digit rates in the 1990s, well below the triple digit inflation experienced in the 1980s.

Apart from fiscal and monetary policy restraint, the key to these remarkable economic achievements was the adoption in the 1980s of *doi moi* – a 'new road' of economic liberalisation – which reduced the extent of central planning and led to an extensive set of reforms. Prices were liberalised in many sectors. Agriculture was decollectivised and farmers were granted land use rights. State enterprises were given greater autonomy in decision making and exposed to domestic and foreign competition. A legal framework was established to allow the operation of private businesses.

The challenge for Vietnam now is to maintain the momentum generated by these reforms and to sustain continued rapid growth in a stable macroeconomic environment. In particular, there is scope for further reforms and significant liberalisation, notably in the financial sector.

This chapter discusses lessons from the recent financial crisis in East Asia that may help guide policy makers in emerging markets such as Vietnam to identify sources of vulnerability to shocks. The most important of these is that the right set of institutional incentives and tools needs to be developed to ensure that East Asian financial institutions manage risks and operate effectively in a global market economy. Rapid growth and prudent macroeconomic policies do not guarantee a sound economic performance if an efficient and robust financial system is not in place.

To highlight this lesson, the chapter examines the sources of East Asia's financial crisis and policy responses. Fundamental weaknesses in financial systems, which had been masked by rapid growth, were at the root of East Asia's financial crisis. Government involvement in credit allocation, and implicit or explicit government guarantees against failure, meant that there was a lack of incentives for effective risk management. The weakness of the financial sector was accentuated by large capital inflows, which were partly encouraged by pegged exchange rates.

The short-run response of governments to the crisis must be to restore growth quickly while maintaining macroeconomic stability. The chapter discusses issues associated with the resumption of voluntary capital inflows (debt rescheduling and trade finance) and the repair of the balance sheets of financial institutions, both of which are crucial to restoring growth. The role of foreign investors, and obstacles to their participation in this process, is also discussed.

The chapter then touches briefly on macroeconomic policy, and the heated debate among economists on the appropriate degree of ease or tightness in monetary and fiscal policies to deal with the crisis. To facilitate analysis of the policy choices, we frame the issues in terms of a policy assignment problem. It is suggested that fiscal policy should be assigned to support growth and the financial sector, while monetary policy should be assigned to curbing inflation and stabilising exchange rate expectations. This implies some flexibility in fiscal policy and a relatively firm monetary stance. The appropriate degree of overall ease or tightness needs to be determined on a case-by-case basis, with the reaction of the market to policy initiatives providing some guide.

Long-run policies should aim to prevent a recurrence of the crisis by reducing the vulnerability of the financial sector. The chapter briefly discusses the implications for financial reform, supervision and regulation; exchange rate policies; and policies on capital flows. It emphasises the importance of effective banking supervision to reduce incentives for risky lending. It also points out that floating exchange rates are more likely to encourage better risk management and the hedging of foreign currency exposure. The lack of such hedging was a major contributor to the crisis. It is also noted that capital controls, which are currently in vogue in some quarters, are likely to discourage better risk management by insulating the domestic financial sector from the effects of poor decisions and inappropriate financial sector policies.

The final section of the chapter examines some of the implications for Vietnam of East Asia's experience, given conditions in Vietnam's financial sector and its desire to match the remarkable growth performance of the East Asian economies.

BOOM AND BUST IN ASIA

The outstanding economic performance of East Asian economies is familiar to observers. Operating in an environment of fiscal and monetary restraint, much of the region enjoyed high savings and investment rates, robust growth and moderate inflation for several decades. Starting some time in the second half of the 1980s, this rapid expansion was accompanied by sharp increases in asset values, notably stock and land prices. As shown in Table 3.1, stock price indices increased rapidly in East Asia from 1987, with the highest cumulative price increases being in Indonesia (934 per cent), Thailand (702 per cent) and the Philippines (556 per cent). Price indices for property markets are not readily available, but financial press reports suggest that increases in this sector were also significant.

Growth began to slow in a number of economies in the 1990s in reaction to shocks such as the devaluation of the Chinese currency in 1994, the depreciation of the Japanese yen against the dollar in 1995 and plunging semiconductor prices. However, the perception remained that East Asia was fundamentally healthy and that a 'soft landing' could be implemented successfully.

The collapse of the Thai baht in July 1997 rudely interrupted this scenario, triggering a wave of depreciation and stock market declines. As illustrated in Figure 3.1, from the second half of 1997 the values of the most affected East

Table 3.1   Change in Stock Price Index, Recent Peak – April 1998 (%)

	Date of Recent Peak	Jan 1987 to Recent Peak	Recent Peak to Apr 1998	Jun 1997 to Apr 1998
Indonesia	Jun 1997	934	−36	−36
Malaysia	Feb 1997	356	−51	−42
Korea	Oct 1994	256	−62	−43
Philippines	Jan 1997	556	−36	−22
Singapore	Dec 1993	120	−39	−21
Thailand	Dec 1993	702	−76	−22

Source: FAME database.

*Figure 3.1   Decline of East Asian Currencies against the US Dollar,
              5 January 1996 – 8 May 1998 (index, 27 June 1997 = 100)*

The NIEs and Japan

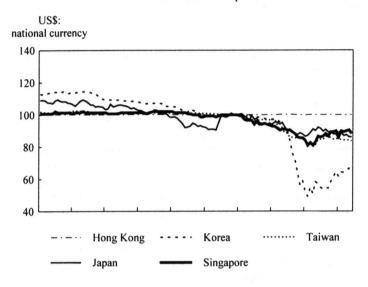

The NIEs and Japan legend:
Hong Kong   Korea   Taiwan
Japan   Singapore

Southeast Asia and China

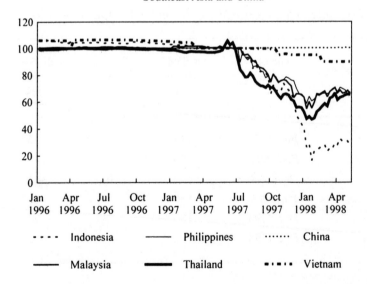

Southeast Asia and China legend:
Indonesia   Philippines   China
Malaysia   Thailand   Vietnam

Source: FAME database.

Asian currencies fell 33–75 per cent against the US dollar. Table 3.1 reveals that stock indices also declined sharply after June 1997, falling 36 per cent in Indonesia, 43 per cent in Korea and 22 per cent in Thailand. Measured against their peaks earlier in the 1990s, the stock price declines in Korea and Thailand have in fact been far sharper.

Disruptions in bank and borrower balance sheets associated with the collapse in currencies and asset prices have led to the closure of financial institutions and to numerous bankruptcies. They have also interrupted credit flows in the most affected economies.[1] Thus, although collapsing exchange rate pegs are expected to boost output in the medium term, short-term economic activity has slowed or contracted severely in the most affected economies, and interest rates have soared due to investor uncertainty. The anticipated severity of these effects is apparent in the sharp downward revision in forecasts of East Asian economic growth for 1998 compared to those made when the crisis began in July 1997. For example, the consensus (average) forecast of Indonesian GDP for 1998 fell from *growth* of 7.6 per cent (in July 1997) to a *contraction* of 6.3 per cent (in May 1998).

In spite of contractionary influences, the threat of inflation is significant due to unprecedented currency depreciation, pressure for monetary stimulus and the fiscal burden of repairing the financial sector. These inflationary pressures are also apparent in changes in forecasts of East Asian inflation for 1998 between July 1997 and April 1998, which in Indonesia's case rose from less than 7 per cent to 46 per cent.

FLAWED FINANCIAL FUNDAMENTALS

Observers have puzzled over the timing, severity and spread of Asia's financial crisis. Traditional macroeconomic explanations are unsatisfactory given the high rates of domestic savings in the region and its generally prudent fiscal and monetary policies. Even the conventional view that economies were 'overheating' may be questioned. Thailand's growth, for example, had slowed significantly after 1995. Recent research also finds that current account deficits – often used as an indicator of overheating – are not good predictors of balance of payments crises (Kaminsky, Lizondo and Reinhart 1997).

One interpretation of what happened that is broadly consistent with the facts and recent research is that the crisis in each of the Asian economies reflected closely related runs on financial institutions and currencies.[2] A generalised run on financial institutions can disrupt economic activity severely, weaken the balance sheets of borrowers and creditors, and threaten the flow of credit and the viability of the payments system. In an open economy, a simultaneous run on the currency worsens the situation by interrupting the flow of external funding, thus weakening the balance sheets of borrowers whose trade credits or investment funding is suddenly interrupted. Borrowers who have not hedged their foreign currency exposure are even more severely affected. Since a run on one currency causes uncertainty and creates the potential for runs on other currencies with financial systems viewed as vulnerable, this interpretation explains why the crisis spread throughout the region. It also suggests why the severity of the crisis – dependent on the complex interaction between conditions in the financial sector, the sentiments of market participants and the responses of governments and the international community – was largely unanticipated.

If there were indeed runs on East Asian financial systems and currencies, what caused them? One view is that the region's economies were inherently sound and could have continued functioning well indefinitely, but that an arbitrary shift in market expectations which interrupted fund flows to Asia induced the crisis. From this perspective, Asia's crisis mainly involved a sudden interruption in liquidity.[3] An alternative explanation, favoured here, is that recent events are attributable to fundamental weaknesses in the financial sector. It can be argued that the crisis in the region stemmed directly from policies that encouraged excessive risk taking, making East Asian financial sectors susceptible to shocks.

Two features of Asian financial systems encouraged risky lending. First, financial intermediaries were not always free to use business criteria in allocating credit. In some cases well-connected borrowers could not be refused credit; in others poorly managed firms were able to obtain loans to meet a specified government policy objective. For example, a former executive of a South Korean bank justified the extension of credit to a steel company by arguing that steel is an important national strategic industry. The steel firm subsequently went bankrupt. Hindsight reveals that the cumulative effect of such decisions can be to produce massive losses.

Second, financial intermediaries and their owners were not expected to bear the full costs of failure. Intermediaries are shielded from losses to the extent that they put 'other people's money' at risk. In part this is because they are highly leveraged.[4] But more importantly, they are typically protected by implicit or explicit government guarantees against losses. These guarantees may have arisen because the government's involvement in credit allocation decisions made it responsible for the outcomes of these decisions, because it was unable to bear the costs of large shocks to the payments system (McKinnon and Pill 1997), or because the owner of the financial intermediary was politically well connected (Krugman 1998a). Krugman points out that such guarantees can trigger asset price inflation, reduce economic welfare, and ultimately make the financial system vulnerable to collapse.[5]

The potential for loss is increased by the fact that the very nature of the banking business – to convey information about the quality of borrowers and their projects – implies a lack of transparency in loan decisions. This is particularly true in Asia, where accounting and disclosure practices are deficient. As a result, depositors and regulators may have difficulty telling if loans are sound, except when a bank faces serious difficulties. This condition hinders the governance of financial institutions, increases the incentives for risk taking, and may lead to fraud and undetected conflicts of interest.

WHY A CRISIS NOW?

Since the weaknesses in East Asian financial systems had existed for decades and were not unique to the region, why did Asia not experience crises of this magnitude before? Two tentative answers may be suggested pending further research.

First, the extent of risky lending in the region was disguised by rapid growth, which for many years allowed governments to pursue financial policies that shielded loss-making firms from the adverse effects of their decisions. This is apparent from the fact that, despite their outstanding economic performance, East Asian countries have had their share of financial sector problems (see Box overleaf).

In the 1990s, some of the affected economies tended to respond with forbearance; that is, they did not deal promptly with problem institutions. There was also a pattern of support for failing financial institutions. This suggests the existence of a very generous safety net that would tend to encourage risky lending. However, over time the safety net would also increase the financial sector's vulnerability to a sufficiently large shock.

Second, these countries were much more closely integrated with world financial markets in the 1990s than they had been in the past, increasing their susceptibility to changes in market sentiment. While financial market liberalisation is often cited as the main reason for rising vulnerability, the prime culprits may in fact be heightened awareness of profit opportunities in emerging markets and enhancements in information and transaction technologies. Although Indonesia's capital account has been open since the early 1970s, for instance, capital inflow surges did not occur until much later. What has changed is that international funds can now flow much more easily into emerging markets because of developments in the financial infrastructure.[6]

Closer integration with world financial markets adds an additional dimension of vulnerability that is not present in a closed economy. In a closed economy, bad loans caused by risky lending may not lead to a run because

SELECTED EPISODES OF BANKING DISTRESS IN ASIA

1980s

A study by Caprio and Klingebiel (1997) found that the Philippines (in 1981–87) and Thailand (in 1983–87) experienced major bank insolvencies in which most or all of the banks' capital was exhausted. Malaysia (1985–87) and Indonesia (1994) experienced insolvencies of a smaller magnitude. Restructuring yielded satisfactory results in Malaysia and mixed results in the Philippines and Thailand; the study found that it was too early to tell in the case of Indonesia. Sheng (1995) estimates Malaysian financial sector losses for the period at about 4.7 per cent of 1986 GDP. In North Asia, South Korean banks had for years borne a heavy burden of non-performing loans associated with policy lending, forcing large write-offs and the closure or restructuring of a number of industrial conglomerates in 1987. Policy loans continued to be an important feature of lending in South Korea in the 1990s.

1990s

Indonesia

A series of banking difficulties in the 1990s (prior to July 1997) were not large enough to be captured in Caprio and Klingebiel's index but suggest persistent financial sector vulnerability. These include a government-supported recapitalisation of Bank Duta in 1990, which reportedly lost about US$400 million speculating in foreign currency markets in 1989; the failure of Bank Umum Majapajit Jaya in 1990 to meet obligations to other banks in the central clearing system; a small run on Bank Danamon in 1991 necessitating government support following rumours of operating difficulties; and the liquidation of Bank Summa in late 1992–93 following losses of over US$1 billion. In early 1994 Bank Pembangunan Indonesia (Bapindo), the state development bank, incurred a potential loss of US$430 million – greater than its capital – from an unsecured letter of credit. The Ministry of Finance then indicated that all of Bapindo's obligations would be backed by the government. The bank was recapitalised in 1995, and the bank and its ownership were restructured by the Ministry of Finance and Bank Indonesia. In spite of this, Moody's described Bapindo's financial fundamentals as 'extremely weak' and assigned it a financial strength rating of E in February 1996. In early 1995 Lippo Bank failed to meet a US$4.5 million temporary clearing obligation due to underestimation of withdrawals caused by a large Telkom public offering. Bank Indonesia averted a crisis by issuing new guidelines permitting banks to use central bank certificates to meet clearing obligations. Since the financial crisis broke in 1997, the government has suspended the operations of, or placed under its supervision, a total of 30 banks. Another 40 are under the surveillance of the Indonesian Bank Restructuring Agency.

Korea
There were no reported signs of major difficulties in the financial sector during most of the 1990s. However, the very high debt ratios of corporations (of 400 per cent or higher) suggest that borrowers were counting on government support in case of adversity. This was confirmed by the government's response to the collapse of the Kia Group in July 1997, which was interpreted by private analysts as supporting insolvent banks and increasing the incentive for risk taking. In October 1997, before the currency crisis struck the won, Moody's and Standard and Poor's started to downgrade the Korean banks, specifically Hanil Bank, Korea Exchange Bank, Shinhan Bank, Korea First Bank, Korea Long Term Credit Bank and the Industrial Bank of Korea. Since the crisis, 16 financial institutions have reportedly been closed or suspended and another two taken over by the government.

Thailand
The banking sector was showing signs of stress well before the baht peg crumbled in July 1997. One of the largest bank failures was that of the Bangkok Bank of Commerce, which ran into trouble in 1994 but was allowed to continue operating through the forbearance of the Bank of Thailand. When a parliamentary debate made Bangkok Bank's problems public in May 1996, a run ensued, forcing the Bank of Thailand to inject US$7 billion in liquidity support and to take over the bank. In March 1997 the loan problems of finance companies came to light, but the Bank of Thailand provided the liquidity to let them stay open. In June 1997, 16 finance companies were suspended and told to find additional capital or merge. The biggest of these was Bank One. Further closures followed the devaluation of 2 July 1997: another 42 financial houses suspended operations, bringing the total to 58. In late January 1998 the government took over Bangkok Metropolitan Bank. Two weeks later it seized control of First Bangkok City Bank and Siam City Bank, Thailand's seventh and eighth largest banks.

depositors know that the government can supply enough liquidity to financial institutions to prevent any losses to depositors. In an open economy, that same injection of liquidity can destabilise the exchange rate. As a result, during periods of uncertainty, runs or speculative attacks on a currency can only be avoided if the holders of domestic assets are sure that the government can meet the demand for foreign currency.

To illustrate the ability of economies in the region to meet such a requirement in the 1990s, Table 3.2 reports short-term foreign borrowing in six East Asian economies; the ratio of such borrowing to foreign exchange reserves held by the central bank (illustrating the ability of central banks to make good on short-term claims in foreign currency); and the ratio to nominal GDP (illustrating the vulnerability of the economy to a change in sentiment that could prompt lenders to stop rolling over their short-term loans). The list excludes Hong Kong and Singapore because their role as international financial centres complicates the interpretation of the data, but includes Taiwan because, as a less affected economy, it can serve as a point of reference.

In the 1990s, short-term foreign borrowing in five of the affected East Asian economies expanded rapidly. The largest proportionate increases were in Thailand and Malaysia (600–800 per cent), with somewhat less rapid increases in South Korea (about 325 per cent) and moderate rises in Taiwan and the Philippines (140–170 per cent).

The ratio of short-term foreign borrowing to foreign exchange reserves gives a clearer picture of the external exposure of these economies. The ratio was well above 100 per cent for South Korea, Indonesia and Thailand – the three most affected economies – and below 100 per cent for the Philippines, Malaysia and Taiwan. The ratio surged in most East Asian economies in the 1990s, except in the Philippines where it declined.

In normal times a high ratio may be sustainable (in the same way that banks do not normally maintain 100 per cent reserves against their deposits). However, in the more vulnerable economies these ratios were clearly unsustainable when uncertainty spread throughout the region. As discussed below, in the current environment perceptions about the ability to meet short-term foreign claims, as indicated at least in part by the ratio, may affect the restoration of voluntary external financing.

The last column of Table 3.2 shows that short-term foreign borrowing increased relative to GDP in all economies in the 1990s, indicating that they had become more vulnerable to shocks that could deter foreign lenders from rolling over short-term bank loans. Such loans were equivalent to about 30 per cent of GDP in Thailand's case.[7]

The problem was compounded by a tendency not to hedge foreign currency borrowing in countries with pegged exchange rates. Market participants may have interpreted currency pegs as an implicit government

Table 3.2 Short-term Borrowing from Banks in BIS Member Countries, 1990–97*

	Amount of Borrowing (US$ billion)	Borrowing as % of Total Borrowing	Borrowing as % of Foreign Reserves	Borrowing as % of GDP
Korea				
1990	16.5	68	115	7
1994	34.9	73	165	9
1997	70.2	68	211	16
Thailand				
1990	6.4	58	54	7
1994	27.1	74	101	19
1997	45.6	66	148	29
Indonesia				
1990	n.a.	n.a.	n.a.	n.a.
1994	18.8	61	177	11
1997	34.6	59	174	17
Malaysia				
1990	1.8	26	23	4
1994	8.2	59	26	11
1997	16.2	56	63	17
Philippines				
1990	3.1	34	342	7
1994	2.6	43	41	4
1997	8.3	59	86	10
Taiwan				
1990	9.0	91	14	6
1994	17.1	93	19	7
1997	22.0	87	24	8

Note: *The loans are consolidated cross-border claims in all currencies and local claims in non-local currencies, expressed in US dollars. All data are for the position at the middle of each year.

Sources: Bank for International Settlements, *The Maturity, Sectoral and Nationality Distribution of International Bank Lending*, Basle; IMF (various issues), *International Financial Statistics.*

guarantee against the risk of currency volatility.[8] At the same time, banks and other borrowers viewed rising foreign reserves as an implicit bail-out fund that would be made available through currency intervention by the central bank. While the absence of hedging significantly lowered the cost of funds (in the short run) for those firms with access to foreign credit, the consequent mispricing of foreign credit contributed to excessive capital inflows and the vulnerability of borrowers with heavy exposure to foreign currency loans.

The lack of hedging added to the instability of Asian financial markets. First, since abandoning currency pegs was very costly, policy makers had to adopt harsh contractionary measures (involving skyrocketing interest rates in some cases) to defend the exchange rate in the face of adverse market senti-ment.[9] Second, borrowers who did not hedge their foreign currency borrow-ing have had difficulty servicing their debts and in some cases have gone bankrupt, thus worsening the crisis. Third, the efforts of market participants to cover previously unhedged foreign currency exposure after the onset of the crisis further weakened the domestic currency.

CRISIS TRIGGERS

While the growing vulnerability of the financial sector in East Asia was hid-den by rapid economic growth, historical experience suggests that such vul-nerability could lead to financial crisis following a sufficiently large shock.[10] Important international shocks in the 1990s have included the devaluation of the Chinese renminbi in 1994 (which ratified earlier depreciation) and of the Japanese yen after 1995. These events lowered the competitiveness of ASEAN and North Asian economies and became a disincentive for Japanese producers to relocate elsewhere in the region. In the mid-1990s semiconduc-tor prices plummeted, adversely affecting South Korea in particular.[11]

These shocks brought on the economic slowdown and decline in asset prices that ultimately caused the currency and financial crisis in Thailand. The events in Thailand were themselves a major shock to the financial sys-tems of the region. Under the interpretation offered in this study, the attack on the Thai baht prompted investors to reassess and test the robustness of the region's currency pegs and financial systems. Over time, the countries with less robust financial systems experienced collapsing pegs and financial crises.[12]

SHORT-RUN POLICY RESPONSES

The Asian crisis poses two main challenges for policy makers. One is to identify short-run economic policies that can restore growth quickly while maintaining macroeconomic stability. The other is to implement policies which, in the long run, will prevent the recurrence of, and reduce vulnerability to, future crises.

To meet these short-run goals, external and domestic voluntary financial flows must resume in order to restore growth, and macroeconomic policies consistent with stabilising inflation must be adopted. Significant effort has been invested in reviving external financial flows. In Indonesia, South Korea and Thailand, large programs of multilateral and bilateral assistance have been put together to reassure investors and meet short-term financing needs.

External Financing

The voluntary restoration of short-term external financing is hampered by uncertainty about debt service capacity associated with high ratios of short-term debt to foreign exchange reserves (Table 3.2). In South Korea, a recent external debt rescheduling agreement has produced some improvement on this score, although there are still loans coming due in the near term. In Thailand and Indonesia as well, the servicing of short-term debt has presented difficulties. In Thailand, short-term debt has not been rescheduled but is continually being rolled over. This has posed significant cash management challenges which, however, appear to have been met successfully. In Indonesia, many borrowers were technically insolvent at the exchange rates that prevailed after the crisis broke out, leading to problems in the servicing of short-term corporate debt. The issues that remain to be resolved are reminiscent of those that surfaced during the debt crisis of the 1980s. Two such issues are whether the government should assume or guarantee the debt, and to what extent creditors must absorb some losses.

Another key to recovery is ensuring financing for sound investment projects. For example, some firms in Indonesia and Thailand have had difficulty getting their bank letters of credit honoured, interrupting the normal flow of trade credit. A number of initiatives have been drafted to address this problem.[13]

Domestic Financing

To restore voluntary domestic financial flows, the balance sheets of banks and borrowers must be repaired. Assets will have to be disposed of, and financial institutions and borrowers must be recapitalised so that normal operations can resume. The costs of repairing the financial sector following a crisis are typically very high. Recent reports indicate that support for Mexican financial intermediaries and borrowers following the Mexican peso's collapse in 1994 represents nearly 15 per cent of GDP. Caprio and Klinge-biel (1997) reveal that, in some cases, costs have exceeded 25 per cent of GDP in the wake of banking crises.

Both South Korea and Thailand have expressed their intention of relying heavily on the private sector – including foreign investors – to support the process of recovery through the acquisition of weak domestic financial institutions and businesses, and the purchase of bankrupt lenders' and borrowers' assets. Allowing foreign investor participation could reduce the amount of government spending needed to support financial sector recovery and lead to efficiency gains. To the extent that such acquisitions would be subject to more stringent supervision from the foreign institution's home country, the incentives for risky lending cited earlier would also be mitigated.

However, there are significant obstacles to a market-based adjustment process of this kind. In a number of countries the absence of effective bankruptcy provisions makes it difficult to dispose of property. The true value of the assets being offered for sale is hard to determine due to a lack of transparency and deficient accounting and reporting procedures. At times the financial structure of corporations makes them unattractive buys (such as debt ratios of 400 per cent for Korean *chaebol*). Finally, there are disincentives – such as restrictions on ownership of real property – that specifically affect foreign investors.

To some extent, obstacles to foreign investment stem from concerns about transferring control to foreigners and selling assets at 'fire sale' prices. However, as noted by Krugman (1998b), if the initial inflation of the asset price reflected risky lending triggered by government guarantees, the subsequent deflation may be entirely reasonable. Selling to foreigners then becomes efficient, as assets fall under the control of those who can potentially use them best.[14]

As the costs of repairing the financial sector are so high, government funds will be needed to finance the repair. In some economies, government support for the financial sector has initially involved assuming bad loans and paying off depositors of failing institutions using central bank funds. (In certain instances these transactions have been offset by other transactions in order to limit the expansionary effect on money.) Policy makers also intend to have the government assume the costs directly, through deficit financing or tax revenues, to restore the central bank balance sheet and limit the creation of money.

Macroeconomic Policy

The repair of the financial sector thus raises questions about the extent to which policy makers should resort to money creation, raising taxes or deficit financing. This issue is closely related to the hotly debated question of the degree of monetary and fiscal restraint needed to stabilise expectations and restore growth. Observers disagree on whether tight monetary policies will attract financing and stabilise the exchange rate, or cause so much damage to the financial sector that they become counterproductive. As for fiscal policy, the main concern is how investors will react if they observe that a sudden gap in the financial sector, which may amount to a substantial fraction of GDP, is financed by budget deficits. (Usually, financing the gap will involve deficits spread out over many years, covering payments of principal and interest.)

In attempting to sort through these conflicting viewpoints, it may be noted that policy has two objectives: restoring growth, which requires supporting the financial sector; and stabilising exchange rate expectations, which can be accomplished by curbing inflation. At the same time there are two policy instruments, fiscal and monetary policy. The problem may then be seen as one of assigning monetary and fiscal policies to these two objectives in the most effective way.

While more research is needed to explore this new version of the 'assignment problem' – the effective pairing of instruments with policy objectives during a financial crisis – a good short-run rule of thumb is to assign the more flexible instrument to the more volatile market. From this perspective, it is immediately apparent that monetary policy should be assigned to stabilising exchange rate expectations by curbing inflation, and fiscal policy to supporting growth and the financial sector. If monetary policy were assigned to growth and the financial sector, this would most likely destabilise exchange rate expectations, as it would be expansionary, and raise inflation.[15]

However, solving the assignment problem does not entirely clarify the degree of ease or tightness needed (although it does make it clear that unrestricted monetary expansion is undesirable). For example, should support for the financial sector come from higher taxes or deficit financing? The bottom line is whether it is more appropriate to worry about growth or inflation in Asia at this time. Due to the severity of both economic contraction and depreciation, and the need to stabilise exchange rate expectations, the answer is not easily discerned and may vary from country to country. One useful guide is the response of markets, which immediately make it clear whether the policies that have been adopted are considered unsustainable or excessively expansionary.

Perhaps the most important point to bear in mind is that voluntary financial flows and exchange rates will remain volatile unless countries make a firm policy commitment and stick to it. The importance of making a clear commitment is best seen in South Korea and Thailand. After these countries opted for clearly defined macroeconomic programs involving some degree of restraint, there were signs of recovery in financing, as well as greater exchange rate stability.[16] Indonesia also decided to adopt a tighter monetary policy in response to double digit monthly inflation reports in the first two months of 1998.

LONG-RUN POLICY RESPONSES

Financial Reform, Supervision and Regulation

While financial reform is considered a long-run problem, in the present con-text it has short-run implications. The effectiveness of even relatively large assistance packages in restoring credibility and voluntary financing may be significantly impaired by the absence of meaningful financial sector reforms. The reason is that investors now know that, despite its outstanding growth performance, Asia is vulnerable to financial market shocks which can cause massive reductions in wealth.

Investors who have had their fingers burned by the financial crisis are now looking for reassurance that conditions have changed substantially, making a future crisis less likely. They also want to be in a better position to assess and manage risks that they may have glossed over in the past. Thus financial reform and transparency – issues which were previously ignored – have come to the forefront.

If the roots of Asia's financial crisis lie in excessive risk taking by banks, then financial sector reform should stress that credit be allocated strictly according to business criteria. Reform must likewise curb conflicts of inter-est and incentives for excessive risk taking arising from implicit or explicit government guarantees and lack of transparency.

The single most important financial sector reform to achieve these goals is the strengthening of the supervision of banks and other financial interme-diaries in a way that reduces unsound lending practices. There is no mystery to the principles of good bank supervision and regulation, most of which are well known to the supervisory authorities in East Asia and have in fact been incorporated in standard banking rules and procedures. The most important principle is that of arm's-length lending, and indeed all the countries have rules that limit lending to related companies and individuals.

Two other important principles are the allocation of adequate capital to absorb the risks being borne, and the management of market risk to consoli-date the various exposures in a bank's entire balance sheet. Prior to the cri-sis, the countries in the region had not consistently implemented the G-10 risk-based capital standards in the manner specified in the 1988 Basle Accord. And even if banks in Asia had adhered strictly to those standards, the capital required would not have been nearly adequate to absorb the risks they actually took. There is no substitute for intensive on-site examination to identify problems in individual banks, and for extensive and timely off-site examination to identify risk concentrations building up in the banking system as a whole.

The most serious problems faced by distressed banks in East Asia did not spring from highly technical transactions, but from asset quality problems and market risk exposures of the most ordinary sort. In Southeast Asia the asset quality problems stemmed from overlending to the real estate sector, often indirectly through finance companies in the case of Thailand, or through lending investors in the case of the Philippines. In many instances the rules for arm's-length lending were flagrantly violated. Market risk exposures have consisted largely of rather ordinary exposures to currency risks, with many banks having borrowed in US dollars and lent in the local currency. These are problems bank supervisors should have uncovered at an early stage by means of existing procedures. Only in South Korea have there been problems with financial derivatives, for which the regulatory authorities may not have fully understood the risks entailed. The failure of bank supervision in Asia was by and large that of implementation.

Why did supervision fail? In some cases supervisors were subjected to pressures that prevented them from doing their jobs effectively. There was also a lack of technical and other supervisory resources, making it easy for banks and other financial intermediaries to circumvent prudential rules. The high cost of Asia's financial crisis underscores the need to give supervisors the authority, incentives and resources to do their job effectively. Giving supervisors sufficient authority may require the abandonment of certain government practices that can lead to unsound credit, such as government-directed lending.

What bank regulators do after a bank has run into problems is as important as what they do to prevent them. In recent years, the workout process itself has come to be viewed as another way of mitigating moral hazard. The modern practice of bank workouts emphasises three elements: (1) prompt corrective action; (2) imposing costs on bank managers for their actions; and (3) calling supervisory authorities to account.

Prompt corrective action means closing banks down as soon as they are found to be insolvent. Any delay gives the bank an opportunity to 'bet the bank' in an effort to recoup. This has clearly been an issue in Asia. The Bangkok Bank of Commerce, for instance, compounded its failure massively following delays in resolving its problems (see Box, pp. 38–9).

Imposing costs on bank managers is a break from the traditional way of protecting depositors, which was to bail out the whole bank. Recent experience shows that it is possible to rescue depositors while letting the bank fail. When Barings Bank failed, for example, the Bank of England made sure the bank's depositors were protected while allowing the owners, even of such a major bank, to lose their capital.[17]

Finally, it is important to call the responsible supervisory authorities to account, particularly if their forbearance has imposed additional costs on the system. In the United States, for instance, the law requires banking authorities to explain their actions if a bank failure results in having to draw from the deposit insurance fund.

Exchange Rate Policies

The macroeconomic considerations involved in the choice of an exchange rate regime are well known, and are discussed by Wolf (1998). His analysis of various alternatives leads him to advocate a managed float with wide fluctuation bands. In this section we briefly explore the issue of exchange rate pegging by focusing on its implications for risk-taking behaviour and the robustness of the financial sector.

As discussed, a peg may be interpreted as an implicit guarantee against exchange rate risk. McKinnon and Pill (1997) show that government guarantees encourage capital inflow surges or 'overborrowing', as well as risk taking in the form of a lack of hedging for currency risk.[18] From this perspective, allowing the exchange rate to float would remove the implicit government guarantee associated with a pegged rate. Exposing domestic firms to currency risks would encourage hedging. Floating also helps to regulate capital flows. For example, capital inflow surges will be dampened if the currency appreciates.

Managed floats or basket pegs have practical advantages such as anchoring inflation (Wolf 1998), but judging by the behaviour of some Southeast Asian currencies, they tend to degenerate into single currency pegs. Alternative pegging arrangements may therefore not always succeed in encouraging hedging.[19]

Floating exchange rates are potentially a problem if policy makers have no alternative nominal target to anchor inflation. However, Glick and Moreno (1999) observe that in East Asia, countries whose currencies adjust more freely have had lower inflation rates. Furthermore, a number of nominal targets are available and have been used successfully, including the monetary base (Mexico after 1994), inflation (New Zealand since the mid-1980s) and nominal GDP.

Policies on Capital Flows

The Asian financial crisis seems to be generating a backlash against open capital accounts. While the appeal of capital controls is understandable, particularly as a way of insulating weak financial systems, they do not provide a long-term solution.

The root of the crisis was not capital flows per se, but distorted incentives which led to excessive risk taking and financing of asset price bubbles. Besides, there is ample evidence that small open economies can manage well even with open capital accounts. Singapore, for instance, has a largely open capital account but is the least affected among the ASEAN countries. Despite its restrictions on Singapore dollar loans to non-residents and offshore transactions in Singapore dollars, its domestic financial markets are highly integrated with world markets (Moreno and Spiegel 1997). New Zealand has both liberalised capital accounts and floating exchange rates, yet has posted one of the most remarkable economic turnarounds since the 1980s. The common feature between these economies is that institutional arrangements exist to limit the incentives for excessive risk taking. In Singapore this is done through supervision and regulation, in New Zealand through an emphasis on transparency and managerial accountability to stockholders and the public at large.[20]

The availability of foreign financing did accentuate the vulnerability of the financial sector in a number of Asian economies. However, the solution is not to limit these flows administratively, but to correct the incentives for risky lending through better banking supervision and more flexible exchange rates. From this perspective, capital controls are undesirable because they insulate weak financial sectors, thus creating incentives to defer the hard choices needed to improve bank supervision and enhance the robustness of the financial system. For this reason capital controls may increase, rather than reduce, the vulnerability of the financial sector to future shocks. The adverse effects of controls are often accentuated by the existence of a bureaucracy that has an interest in perpetuating controls well after the problems they were set up to address have disappeared.

Research and historical experience show that capital controls are effective only in the short run.[21] Sooner or later the private sector finds ways to dodge them – by adjusting import and export invoices to minimise taxes on short-term foreign borrowing, for example, or by increasing reliance on parallel financial and foreign exchange markets. The eventual ineffectiveness of capital controls was illustrated most dramatically in the early 1970s, when their erosion led to the collapse of the Bretton Woods system of fixed exchange rates.

While some studies find that portfolio and direct investments react in the same way to shocks, direct investments are generally considered less volatile. However, capital controls are a less efficient way of increasing long-term capital inflows than are credibility and clear, simple and market-oriented policies (Calvo, Leiderman and Reinhart 1996) – including price stabilisation programs, greater macroeconomic stability and institutional reforms. Indeed, controls that are not deemed complementary to more fundamental reforms can actually encourage outflows.

An alternative way of lowering capital market volatility is to encourage a switch from short to long-term maturity instruments. Since emerging economies typically lack well-developed capital markets in which long-term instruments can be traded, the shift from short to long-term debt can be achieved by promoting the issuance of long-term maturity instruments – without having to rely on capital controls. The government can act as a catalyst by issuing long-term debt instruments, which the private sector can use as the benchmark for its own long-term debt issues.

IMPLICATIONS FOR VIETNAM

What specific lessons does East Asia's recent financial crisis hold for Vietnam? Before addressing this question, it is useful to survey briefly developments in Vietnam's financial sector in the 1990s, when a series of reforms expanded the scope of banking services.

In 1990 the State Bank of Vietnam relinquished its commercial banking activities to newly created state-owned commercial banks, to focus on central banking functions. Since then a variety of financial institutions have proliferated, including joint stock banks, foreign joint venture banks, branches and offices of foreign banks and credit cooperatives, and savings and loans institutions (known as people's credit funds). As a result, although the Vietnamese financial system is still dominated by the four commercial banks, there is a greater diversity in the types of financial institutions than there was in the past.

However, like other countries at similar levels of financial development, Vietnam still focuses on direct controls rather than market-based mechanisms to regulate the flow of money and credit. The various control devices used by the government, such as the setting of bank interest rates and credit targets, restrict the banking sector's ability to allocate credit according to business criteria or to manage risk. The use of such criteria is further hampered by weaknesses in accounting practices that complicate the assessment of bank performance, and a lack of independent audited financial data for Vietnamese companies. For example, measuring non-performing assets is difficult, in part because of the reported lack of loan loss provisioning (Keenan 1997). Finally, the legal framework is insufficiently developed to permit the use of certain fundamental risk management tools such as collateral. For example, regulations make it difficult to mortgage or transfer assets, especially property.

The literature on banking crises (Goldstein and Turner 1996), as well as the recent experience of the region, suggests that these features of credit allocation can increase the vulnerability of the financial sector. Indeed, financial press reports suggest that a significant proportion of credit in Vietnam has been directed to unprofitable state-owned enterprises, and that non-performing bank loans are large (Keenan 1997). To what extent does this imply that Vietnam is immediately vulnerable to runs on its financial sector and currency of the type recently experienced by Asia?

In principle, in a state-controlled financial system like Vietnam's, the government can prevent a run on the domestic financial system by providing enough financing to cover losses. Thus dealing with losses in the banking sector can be seen primarily as a fiscal issue.[22]

This is not to say, however, that financial sector losses have no adverse effects. Aside from the impact on growth caused by the financing of unproductive investments, depositors may still withdraw from the domestic financial sector if they anticipate that the government will seek to cover losses through higher inflation (which is a tax on depositors earning a fixed nominal interest rate), or that it will not fully protect depositors in the case of financial sector losses. Indeed, it is apparent that in Vietnam the public is very cautious in dealing with the domestic financial sector. This caution is reflected in the extent of disintermediation, revealed by the low ratio of M2 to GDP in Vietnam of 25 per cent, half of that in Indonesia or the Philippines. It is also reflected in the phenomenon of dollarisation, in which Vietnamese residents use the US dollar as a store of value and medium of exchange. In 1993 the ratio of foreign currency deposits to M2 was 24 per cent, higher than Indonesia's 17 per cent (even if Indonesia had an open capital account, and Vietnam does not), and much higher than Korea's 0.6 per cent (see Chapter 6, this volume). At least two factors may contribute to the public's reluctance to rely on the domestic financial sector to store its wealth: the triple digit inflation experienced in the 1980s; and the bankruptcy of hundreds of credit cooperatives between 1989 and 1991. The resultant lack of depth in the financial sector poses a significant obstacle to development and may partly explain why Vietnam's national saving rate has remained in the neighbourhood of 15 per cent of GDP, less than half the rate observed in the high-growth East Asian economies.

Vietnam's extensive capital controls and reliance on foreign direct investment (FDI) also tend to insulate the domestic economy from the sudden interruption of external financing that has disrupted economic activity in East Asia. But neither is Vietnam invulnerable to the effects of changes in foreign investor sentiment. External financing accounts for close to 10 per cent of GDP, so any reductions in the flow of FDI would have a significant impact. In addition, the country's financial institutions have relied heavily on

short-term trade financing, increasing the vulnerability of producers to interruptions in such financing.

To sum up, recent reports suggest that Vietnam, like some of its neighbours in the region, has experienced difficulties in using business criteria or
managing risk effectively. While it can be argued that the socialisation of risk
in the domestic financial system, and the insulation of the system from the
external sector, makes Vietnam less vulnerable to runs than some other East
Asian economies, the weaknesses in the financial sector may still impose significant costs. In particular, lack of depth in the domestic financial system –
apparently because of past macroeconomic instability and financial crisis –
is an important obstacle to development. Furthermore, Vietnam has relied
heavily on external financing, making it vulnerable to interruptions in capital inflows, notwithstanding the large share of FDI in external financing.
These considerations are important in the short run as Vietnam seeks to
maintain the momentum of growth; they are even more important in the long
run as it tries to achieve higher levels of development. For these reasons,
applying the lessons of the recent experience of East Asia would most likely
benefit Vietnam. That is, for Vietnam, as well as for its neighbours in the
region, the development of a robust financial system that allocates credit on
the basis of business criteria and has the right incentives to manage risk, and
that can interact effectively with global capital markets, will be important in
ensuring sustained growth and macroeconomic stability.

NOTES

*   This chapter draws on an earlier study issued by the Asian Development Bank Institute,
    Tokyo. The authors thank Jesus Estanislao for encouraging this study, George Fane and
    Teresa Curran for helpful comments, Tania Luhde for information on episodes of stress to
    the banking system and Guillermo Pinczuk for research assistance. The opinions expressed
    are those of the authors and do not necessarily reflect the views of the Federal Reserve Bank
    of San Francisco, the Federal Reserve Bank of New York or the Federal Reserve System.
1. The reasons for credit flow interruptions when balance sheets are disrupted are discussed in
    the literature on debt deflation (Bernanke and Gertler 1995).
2. Strictly speaking, the literature distinguishes between domestic bank runs and balance of
    payments or currency crises. The term 'runs' is used for both, to emphasise the key similar-
    ity in the two processes – investors trying to unload their holdings of an asset before others
    manage to do so.
3. This is a possible interpretation of views expressed at the Asian Development Bank Insti-
    tute Workshops on Recent Financial Developments in Asia (see www.adbi.org), which
    brought together economists from Japan, Southeast Asia and the Asia–Pacific Economic
    Cooperation (APEC) economies to discuss the crisis. For recent models of bank runs and
    currency crises that do not always assume distorted incentives from government guarantees,
    see Chang and Velasco (1997), Calvo and Mendoza (1996) and Goldfajn and Valdes (1997).
4. Some observers argue that risk-adjusted capital ratios of 8 per cent are too low for emerg-
    ing markets. These ratios are below those maintained in industrial economies since the Great
    Depression of the 1930s by financial institutions not covered by deposit insurance, and do

not seem to take into account the fact that emerging market economies tend to be more vulnerable to shocks (Goldstein and Turner 1996).

5. The following provides an example of how guarantees work in practice. Because of the banks' special role in the payments system, a well-established principle dictates that depositors be reimbursed when a bank fails. Although this is an effective way of preventing bank runs, it also means that depositors have little incentive to monitor the safety and soundness of banks. This lack of monitoring creates a 'moral hazard' for bank managers – in the form of an undue incentive to take excessive risks. Risk taking is easy because banks operate on leverage, with relatively little capital supporting their lending and borrowing operations.

6. To give another example, in Thailand a noteworthy development was the establishment of the Bangkok International Banking Facility in 1993. While Thai residents could have borrowed abroad even without this facility, it lowered transaction costs between foreign and domestic residents.

7. While these data pinpoint a key area of external vulnerability, they understate its potential magnitude: net foreign portfolio inflows (which had also been on an upward trend throughout the 1990s) were reversed, and residents attempted to convert short-term assets or money into foreign currencies. However, data on stocks of portfolio investment relative to GDP are not readily available. Ratios of broad money (M2) to foreign reserves for these countries did not rise consistently over this period, though they were much higher than the ratios of foreign lending. For example, in South Korea the ratio fell from a peak of over 8 in 1991 to a still high 6.5 in 1996. In Indonesia, it reached a recent peak of 7 in 1995 but fell to 6.5 in 1996. In Thailand, the ratio was in the neighbourhood of 4 in every year between 1990 and 1996.

8. Dooley (1994) appears to have been the first to draw attention to the fact that pegged Asian currencies were a form of implicit guarantee that reduced the incentive to hedge. Lack of hedging when the exchange rate is pegged has been observed in other emerging markets. McKinnon and Pill (1997) show that the decision not to hedge is the rational (but undesirable) response to an implicit government guarantee caused by the large costs of financial system failure.

9. For a discussion of the costs that adjustable pegs may impose on the financial system, see Mishkin (1997).

10. For a survey of the literature on banking crises in emerging markets and an overview of historical experience, see Goldstein and Turner (1996). Latin American banking crises are analysed in Hausmann and Rojas-Suarez (1996), which contains selected case studies. Further case studies are provided by Sheng (1995).

11. Yen–dollar or renminbi–dollar shocks affect the real exchange rate (given sticky prices), while semiconductor price changes affect the terms of trade (the relative price of exports to imports). Recent research has shown that such shocks have been associated with banking and currency crises in emerging markets. For example, Caprio and Klingebiel (1997) found that 75 per cent of a sample of developing countries experiencing banking crises suffered a terms of trade decline of at least 10 per cent prior to the crisis; Kaminsky and Reinhart (1996) found that real exchange rate appreciation is a predictor of banking crises; and Kaminsky, Lizondo and Reinhart (1997) found that such appreciation predicts currency crises. The latter authors also discovered that 56 per cent of the banking crises in their sample were followed by a currency crisis within three years.

12. Similarly, it can be said that the pressure on a number of East Asian currencies following the collapse of the Mexican fixed peso–dollar rate in December 1994 led to a reassessment that involved the testing of the stability of pegs. This development, which was in some ways a prelude to the crises of 1997, set in motion a process of consultation and cooperation among East Asian policy makers, with a focus on short-term responses to deter or manage speculation in currency markets (see discussion in Manzano and Moreno 1998).

13. In February 1998, G-7 governments announced short-term insurance guarantees and re-insurance to creditworthy borrowers in Asia. In March, Singapore announced that it would launch a US$2 billion bilateral trade finance scheme for Indonesia. The funds would be drawn from the US$5 billion pledged by Singapore as part of the International Monetary Fund's (IMF's) US$43 billion package for Indonesia. At the time of writing, Bank Indone-

sia had placed US$100 million in each of five foreign banks to guarantee Indonesian letters of credit, and had plans to place funds in five more banks. The Asian Development Bank (ADB) has also stepped in. On 1 April it signed an agreement to guarantee US$950 million of credit facilities (pooled from 64 international financial institutions) for Thai exporters. A US$50 million ADB loan was also to be disbursed to help Thai exporters finance imports.

14. Krugman also points out that the transfer may not be efficient in this sense if the financial system was actually sound to begin with, but was disrupted by the run. However, even in this case he observes that the presence of foreign investors will limit the actual fall in asset prices. If there is a sufficiently large number of foreign investors, a run on domestic assets may actually be prevented by reassuring residents that there are buyers for their assets.

15. It is also possible to justify the proposed assignment on more fundamental grounds, but this would require research to specify government policy objectives and formulate assumptions about the characteristics of the economy. For a recent discussion of the assignment problem, see McCallum (1992).

16. Some of the most affected Asian economies have favoured easing fiscal policies over monetary restraint as economic conditions have deteriorated. For example, Indonesia and Thailand, by agreement with the IMF, have recently relaxed their fiscal conditions.

17. Not long before that, however, the Bank of England bailed out Johnson Matthey, a smaller bank than Barings and one that would otherwise have failed because of bad loans to Nigerian borrowers (Remolona 1990).

18. However, McKinnon and Pill do not necessarily advocate floating.

19. In spite of these arguments, other considerations may prompt certain economies to peg anyway. Close attention must therefore be paid to the incentives for risk taking created by such a decision.

20. For a description of New Zealand's system, see Brash (1997).

21. The literature on speculative attacks shows that although a government may use capital controls to buy time while it resolves policy conflicts, they do not prevent successful speculative attacks on inconsistent exchange rate policy regimes. Chile imposes non-interest-bearing reserves on short-term capital inflows and is considered by some as a model. However, the effect of restrictions on the total magnitude of inflows over the medium term is unclear. It is also hard to attribute Chile's successful growth performance to the brakes placed on short-term capital flows because the country has carried out many other macroeconomic reforms.

22. See the discussion of China's financial system by Fernald, Edison and Loungani (1998).

4. Current and Capital Account Liberalisation: Issues Facing Indonesia

Hadi Soesastro

Before the Asian financial crisis, Indonesia had been hailed by some as a model for Vietnam's economic development. As Indonesia has arguably been the hardest hit by the crisis of all the Asian economies, this and the next chapter explore Indonesia's economic policies and financial sector developments in some detail.

INTRODUCTION

Indonesia began liberalising its economy about 30 years ago, following a change of government in 1966. The program was not called 'liberalisation' at the time as this would have sounded too much like 'liberalism', until not long ago a dirty word in the Indonesian political lexicon. Rather, it was presented as a 'total correction' of the economic policies of the previous government. This reorientation of economic policies was intended to move the country away from *dirigisme* (central control and excessive government intervention in the economy), thought to be one of the main causes of the economic disaster that had befallen the country.

The process of liberalisation did not proceed on a linear track: there were times when it slowed down, came to a halt, or even experienced a reversal. Yet on the whole the Indonesian economy did become far more open and efficient, and the reforms helped to sustain growth for three decades. What is remarkable is that throughout the entire period the country was led by the same person, former President Soeharto, assisted by a team of technocrats. In times of crisis the technocrats' position was strengthened; in good times less attention was paid to proactive policy making. Macroeconomic policies, which were under the control of the technocrats for most of the period, remained sound, but microeconomic policies were less coherent.

Throughout the 30 years there were three distinct periods of liberalisation, each motivated by different events. The first, from 1966 to 1973, began with major liberalisation measures to rehabilitate an economy on the brink of collapse. Macroeconomic stabilisation was the immediate objective, and once this had been achieved measures were taken to restructure the economy. These major 'corrective' measures, accompanied by a total overhaul of the political system, gave the new government legitimacy. The second period, from 1982 to about 1990, was also driven by necessity. A fall in oil prices forced the government to restructure the economy further, moving it away from a dependence on oil revenues to become internationally competitive in a broad range of non-oil manufacturing products. The third period, from 1994 onwards, has been driven primarily by the emergence of a dynamic regional environment characterised by competitive liberalisation. This has been reinforced by Indonesia's involvement in such regional and global liberalisation initiatives as the ASEAN Free Trade Area (AFTA), the Asia–Pacific Economic Cooperation (APEC) process and the World Trade Organisation (WTO).

The intervening periods, during which the liberalisation process slowed, came to a halt or experienced a reversal, are no less interesting to analyse. Both the identifiable periods of liberalisation and the intervening years of increased protectionism were closely linked to major economic and political change (Pangestu 1991).

The reform agenda is far from exhausted. A number of important areas, including agriculture and some upstream industries, have not yet been sufficiently touched by the liberalisation drive. Moreover, in the current regional environment of competitive liberalisation, the goalposts for reform are continually shifting. The economic and financial crisis that has hit Indonesia so severely since the latter half of 1997 can also be expected to have a significant effect on the way the liberalisation process unfolds in the years to come.

Although much attention is currently focused on resolving the crisis, a number of questions about the wisdom and sequence of liberalisation have been raised by the wider public. Some argue that liberalisation of the current and capital accounts – the latter in particular – has largely been responsible for the crisis, with the associated reforms being carried out in the wrong sequence. Others regard liberalisation as a manifestation of the larger process of globalisation and feel that Indonesia may already have gone too far down this path. Still others view the liberalisation issue mainly in terms of the increased (and unchecked) role of the private sector in the economy. Finally, there are those who link the issues of economic and political liberalisation.

These concerns are not new but they are becoming more explicit. It is in this context that the issues surrounding current and capital account liberalisation in Indonesia can best be addressed. Two such issues stand out. First, how far, how fast and in what manner should liberalisation proceed? Second, who gains and who loses from liberalisation?

HOW FAR, HOW FAST?

The First Period of Liberalisation (1966–73)

Indonesia's process of economic liberalisation has been driven by pragmatism and necessity rather than theory or ideology. As there has never been a 'grand design' for reform, the question of how far liberalisation should go has not been addressed explicitly. The government has understandably been reluctant to embark on a debate about what policy measures and reforms are in accordance with, or in violation of, Article 33 of the 1945 Constitution, which would seem to stipulate a state-controlled economic system. An open debate on this matter could have necessitated an amendment to the Constitution, which would in turn have created a precedent for amending other articles. Because this would have had serious ramifications for national cohesion and political stability, the liberalisation policy has been kept at the level of 'low politics' (Soesastro 1989). Since the mid-1980s the preferred label for the liberalisation agenda has been 'deregulation'.

Packaged as a 'total correction' of the policies of the previous administration, the new government had no difficulty justifying the policies and programs adopted during the first period of liberalisation. To rehabilitate the economy, it moved decisively to restore macroeconomic stability and introduce market-oriented reforms. It eliminated the fiscal deficit, implemented the balanced budget principle as a cornerstone of macroeconomic management and adopted a stringent monetary program to deal with hyperinflation. Another major policy measure was to abandon the multiple exchange rate system in 1970, followed by a large devaluation in 1971 to bring the exchange rate to a realistic level. However, the most significant of the government's policies was the liberalisation of the capital account in 1971 to make movements of capital totally free. Despite being contrary to conventional wisdom on the sequencing of economic reform – according to which opening of the current account should precede opening of the capital account – this policy was instituted mainly to give credibility to the government's commitment to its open door foreign investment policy. Experience does indeed show that once the capital account is fully open, such a policy cannot be reversed, even slightly, without the risk of serious misinterpretation on the part of foreign as well as domestic investors.

Market-oriented reforms were introduced in the early years of the new government, to change the trade and incentive regime. A significant step on this path was the dismantling of the import licensing system. Although in 1968 tariffs on some products (such as textiles) were increased to encourage domestic production, levels of import protection were considerably less than they had been. The government also removed most domestic price controls.

Indonesia's open door investment policy was strengthened by the adoption of
the Foreign Investment Law of 1967, which removed all restrictions on foreign equity and the employment of expatriates and allowed 100 per cent foreign ownership. The public initially supported these policies and programs
with enthusiasm because they produced immediate results. Growth was
restored and inflation lowered; private enterprise was encouraged; and foreign capital and aid began once again to flow in.

However, a number of these policies and programs were subsequently
reversed. The sudden upsurge of foreign direct investment (FDI), made so
visible by the mushrooming of billboards and neon signs advertising Japanese consumer products, aroused a nationalist reaction that culminated in riots
during the visit of Japan's Prime Minister, Tanaka, to Indonesia in January
1974. Investment regulations were subsequently made more restrictive. All
new FDI had to be in the form of joint ventures, with Indonesian equity to be
increased to 51 per cent within a specified period. The list of sectors closed
to FDI was extended and tax incentives reduced. There was also a shift back
towards an increased role for the public sector in the economy, stimulated in
particular by the oil booms of 1973–74 and 1979–80. Public enterprises
began to take a dominant role in a number of sectors, and public investment
was increasingly directed towards heavy industries, petrochemicals and mining. The civil service also expanded rapidly, and bureaucratic intervention
became rampant.

Meanwhile, the incentive regime became progressively more inward-
oriented. Distortions in the trade regime were reinforced by investment
licensing and by credit allocation at subsidised interest rates (Bhattacharya
and Pangestu 1996). With the oil booms, the economy became heavily
dependent on oil revenue and the government was faced with the 'Dutch disease' problem – that is, the erosion of the competitiveness of the non-oil
economy due to a rise in the real exchange rate. The Dutch disease, the drop
in oil prices and world recession in the early 1980s eventually led to a recognition of the need for a total overhaul of the economy. This opened the way
for the second period of liberalisation (1982–90).

What lessons can be drawn thus far? On the positive side, compared
to other large oil-exporting countries, Indonesia did not squander its new
wealth. The oil windfall was used to reduce poverty, expand public education
and health facilities, and promote rural development by allocating substantial resources to agriculture and rural infrastructure. Macroeconomic policies
remained essentially sound; one could hypothesise that the very open capital
account had imposed discipline on macroeconomic management. The less
positive side was that liberalisation was not pursued consistently and tended
to be implemented in an ad hoc manner in response to external events. In
view of the lack of a blueprint for reform, this may have been inevitable. But

even if there had been the will to devise such a blueprint, it is questionable whether one could have been drawn up. In the final analysis the process of economic liberalisation is, after all, political in nature.

In the 1980s, to be politically feasible liberalisation had to be instituted in a gradual and pragmatic fashion. Ali Wardhana, one of the main forces behind the liberalisation drive, argued that gradualism offered the advantage of progressively winning over a new constituency for further reform (Wardhana 1989). He pointed out that the extended period of weak oil prices during the 1980s made the gradual approach a viable option and enabled policy makers and implementers to work within their capacities to plan and execute reforms. Proponents of rapid reform argued that fast and thoroughgoing liberalisation would be more effective in preventing vested interests from rallying their forces to oppose further reforms, while sending a strong signal on the government's commitment to liberalisation. In Indonesia, however, where a great deal of doubt existed about the benefits of liberalisation, gradualism was the only viable option. The credibility of the gradual approach would have been enhanced if the government had followed the release of major reforms with the announcement of a clear agenda for action and a timetable for further liberalisation. These were the elements missing from the liberalisation process of the 1980s.

As stated earlier, in Indonesia liberalisation has been driven by necessity and pragmatism rather than theory or ideology, although the universal trend in the 1980s towards economic liberalisation, deregulation and privatisation may have provided an additional source of inspiration. Theories about the proper sequencing of reform programs have been widely espoused, but their adoption is a matter of political feasibility. The sequencing issue has itself been put forward because it would not be feasible, or even desirable, to undertake all reforms simultaneously.

Conventional wisdom suggests that current account liberalisation be undertaken only after policies to ensure macroeconomic stability and exchange rate adjustment have been put in place, or in conjunction with such policies. Thus macroeconomic stability is a prerequisite of current account liberalisation and must be maintained throughout the process. The main objective of current account liberalisation is to improve resource allocation and economic efficiency by removing distortions, as well as to earn foreign exchange and improve the balance of payments by increasing exports and fostering efficient import substitution (Pangestu 1990). Trade (import and export) liberalisation would be followed by industrial sector reforms – including regulation of foreign investment, transportation and the domestic sector. Administrative reform would be crucial to the success of such a program. Liberalisation of the financial sector could then be tackled, with sequencing theory suggesting that the strengthening of institutional, legal and supervision capabilities be carried out first. Banking sector reform would precede capital market reform, with the domestic investor base being strengthened before full foreign participation was invited in capital markets. Only then should the capital account be liberalised. Supporters of sequencing argue that capital flight during the reform process could impede or even halt the liberalisation process. Another concern is that if a liberalised capital account and financial sector reforms were to precede reform of the real sector, there would be an increased flow of capital to sectors that had become attractive only because of prevailing policy distortions.

Indonesia is the only country in East Asia to begin by liberalising its capital account. As described earlier, this policy was adopted in the early 1970s to attract foreign investment. Indonesia's experience has often been cited as a 'successful' case of reversal of the usual order of economic liberalisation, although this seems less certain in light of recent events. Yet the open capital account did serve the country well by helping to impose discipline on macroeconomic management in difficult economic and domestic political circumstances.

Indonesia has much in common with other East Asian countries in the way in which current account liberalisation has been carried out. It launched a series of export policy reforms before undertaking import reforms; in other words, it maintained import protection while promoting exports. Facilities such as duty drawbacks and export subsidies were introduced to offset the high-cost economy created by import protection. This policy was successful in stimulating exports but did not increase overall economic efficiency. In the present international trading environment such a 'double distortion' policy cannot be sustained.

Import reform ideally begins with the removal of non-tariff barriers and their replacement with equivalent tariffs providing the same level of protection, to increase transparency, curb rent-seeking activities and improve the allocation of resources. The tariff system would then be rationalised to reduce the level and variance of tariffs to a progressively lower and relatively uniform nominal and effective rate of protection. On the whole, Indonesia's path of trade liberalisation has followed this pattern.

The Second Period of Liberalisation (1982–90)

Indonesia's second period of liberalisation, undertaken in response to a significant drop in oil revenues, was based on the following 'simple chain of economic reasoning' (Wardhana 1989). Economic growth and development depend on export growth to pay for imports and service debt. Reliable export growth requires non-oil exports based on agriculture and manufacturing. Non-oil exports flourish in an efficient, productive economy with a competitive domestic market. Protectionist policies and government controls are inimical to a competitive domestic market because they create a high-cost economy, and therefore need to be dismantled; that is, the economy must be liberalised and deregulated. As a corollary, the government must develop non-oil revenues if it is to play a constructive role in development. The benefits of liberalisation and resulting economic growth must be widely and evenly distributed, with the development of rural areas continuing to receive emphasis.

The reform process thus conceived did not proceed smoothly; indeed, it struck some initial difficulties (Syahrir and Brown 1992; Bhattacharya and Pangestu 1996). The first half of the period, from 1982 to 1985, was characterised by ambivalence (Pangestu 1991) and partial reform (Hill 1997c); substantial reforms were undertaken only in the second half (1986–90). In all, some 20 policy packages were introduced during the decade. The most significant of these were the trade liberalisation package of October 1986 and the financial liberalisation package of October 1988.

The steep drop in oil prices in 1986, together with the currency realignment that followed the Plaza Accord in 1985 – raising Indonesia's external debt payments – provided the immediate impetus for the more drastic measures. The deregulation measures carried out before these events had failed to address the issue of non-tariff barriers, which were adversely affecting a large proportion of imports. Import licensing, reintroduced at the start of the 1980s, had created opportunities for rent-seeking activities and become a major source of the high-cost economy.

Current account liberalisation was undertaken in 1982 in response to a deterioration in the country's balance of payments. Regulations affecting trade, such as export taxes and restrictions on trade with the Socialist bloc, were relaxed and a scheme for counter trade introduced. Later in the same year, however, the government introduced a licensing scheme in an attempt to curb imports. The use of import licensing measures proliferated rapidly. By October 1986 close to 1,500 items – or about 35 per cent of total imports by value – were affected by some form of non-tariff barrier, usually a licensing restriction. The system became a vehicle for rent-seeking activities and led to the emergence of what Mancur Olson has called 'distributional coalitions'. It was also used to promote the development of industries of questionable economic viability. The October 1986 package constituted the first serious attack on the licensing system. It ordered the dismantling of the plastic and steel import monopolies, regarded as symbols of the then newly emerging cronyism.

Financial sector reform was similarly slow to come to terms with the need for overall reform of the financial market, with early deregulation measures tackling only the problems of the state banks. The October 1988 package of financial reforms, widely regarded as being the most sweeping of this period, was aimed at increasing competition within the sector by removing some of the barriers to entry. State enterprises, which hitherto had been forced to use state banks, were now permitted to deposit up to 50 per cent of their funds in private banks. New foreign (joint venture) and domestic banks were allowed to enter the market, and foreign banks were permitted to open branches outside Jakarta. These measures brought about dramatic growth in the financial sector and significantly altered the market structure and competitive environment for banking. The number of banks increased from 61 in 1988 to nearly 120 in 1991, then to 230 in the mid-1990s. The private banks' assets and credit expanded rapidly, greatly enhancing the role of domestic private banks in particular at the expense of the state banks.

This rapid growth in credit may have been responsible for the overheating of the economy in the late 1980s and subsequent tightening of liquidity. This led to an increase in foreign borrowing, facilitated by an open capital account. Leakage from abroad meant that, despite the tight monetary policy, money supply growth remained high and inflationary pressures continued to increase. In 1991 the government took steps to manage offshore borrowing, placing a ceiling on borrowing for government-related projects and bank borrowing of about US$5–6 billion in total for the next five years. It was unable to control private sector borrowing directly, but indicated that total loans to the sector of up to US$2 billion annually would be acceptable. The limit on offshore borrowing by banks forced private corporations to seek funds directly from abroad. Because of the predictability of exchange rate depreciation and the implicit government guarantee against currency depreciation, firms began to borrow excessively. By mid-1997 accumulated debt in the private sector had reached over US$70 billion.

Against a background of increased problem loans and bank failures, concerns were expressed that the rapid expansion of bank credit would lead to financial instability and distress (Pangestu 1996). The open capital account was not at issue as it had been in place for some time, but the ability of the authorities to supervise a rapidly expanding banking sector was. Efforts to strengthen bank prudential regulations in 1992 and subsequent years appear to have been inadequate. The prevailing attitude seems to have been that both the new private banks and the central bank needed time to adjust to the sweeping financial reforms of the late 1980s.

A number of policy measures were subsequently taken to deal with the increase in capital flows, including a gradual widening of the exchange rate band, limits on offshore borrowing by non-bank financial institutions, and restrictions on new licences to operate non-bank financial institutions. In addition, reserve requirements were increased from 2 to 3 per cent and attempts made to control lending to the property sector. This was initially through moral suasion, complemented by the setting of ceilings, and then through a moratorium on lending instituted in 1997. The government simultaneously adopted a contractionary fiscal policy.

Although the process of liberalisation in the 1980s was widely supported in its broad outline, economists from the University of Indonesia expressed some concern over the widely held but simplistic notion that the reforms could provide a panacea to overcome the ills and inefficiencies of a high-cost economy. They argued that if liberalisation of the current account were pursued singlemindedly to promote non-oil exports, new distortions would be introduced, and that a heavy focus on reform of the manufacturing sector could result in a bias against the agricultural sector. They felt that the overall impact of liberalisation had been positive primarily in psychological terms, and that its impact at the sectoral or industry level needed closer examination (Anwar and Aziz 1987) to determine with accuracy who was benefiting – and who losing – from the process.

From 1991 to mid-1994, the country experienced a period of policy inertia (Hill 1997c) or 'reform fatigue' (Iqbal 1995). Efforts to liberalise the current account further came to a halt, and the average rate of nominal tariffs remained at the same level during much of the period. Things began to change in mid-1994 with the introduction of liberalisation measures in the investment field. This marked the start of a process driven by the need to compete in a region increasingly characterised by competitive liberalisation.

The Third Period of Liberalisation (1994–Present)

The investment liberalisation measures of June 1994 permitting 100 per cent foreign ownership were designed to increase Indonesia's attractiveness as an investment location in the face of increased competition from China, Vietnam and other East Asian countries. (The government had taken note of the fall in investment approvals in 1993 and the slowing of growth in non-oil exports.) In addition, nine sectors previously closed to FDI, including ports, power generation, shipping, air transport, railways, telecommunications and even, initially, mass media, were opened up.

In the trade field, the liberalisation package of May 1995 contained, for the first time, a timetable for the reduction of tariffs on most items up to the years 2003 and 2010. This unilateral liberalisation measure was issued in response to the competitive liberalisation environment in the region and signalled the government's determination to implement its commitments under AFTA, APEC and the WTO. The trade package was further refined in June 1996. While significant progress has been achieved in reducing tariffs, a few sectors remain highly protected. The dismantling of protection to these sectors has become a thorny political issue involving, not differences of opinion

among ministries about industrialisation and development, but the dismantling of rampant and entrenched cronyism.

Some saw the crisis that hit Indonesia in the second half of 1997 as an
opportunity to attempt to dismantle monopolies and cronyism, viewed as a
source of the high-cost economy and a major obstacle to the liberalisation
process. Having brought in the International Monetary Fund (IMF) to help
resolve the crisis, the government negotiated a program that included structural reforms to tackle the problem of cronyism. Although including these
reforms in the IMF package carried the risk that they might not be implemented in good faith, excluding them would have eroded the credibility of
the package (Soesastro and Basri 1998). It remains to be seen whether the
reforms will help sustain the liberalisation process, at least over the three
years of the IMF package.

WHO WINS, WHO LOSES?

The future of liberalisation will depend on a critical assessment by the body
politic and the public of its merits. The government urgently needs to study
the issue in some depth and respond to growing public concerns about the
negative impact of liberalisation and globalisation.

According to Hill (1997c), it is popularly believed that the liberalisation
(and deregulation) process has led to the creation of conglomerates and
monopolies, to increased inequality and poverty, to a widening of regional
disparities and to the demise of small firms. Hill assessed each of these
propositions based on available empirical evidence and concluded that the
reality was far more complex. A survey reported in Soesastro (1998) showed
that many Indonesians fear that liberalisation and globalisation will lead to
increased domination by foreign enterprises in the economy and a weakening of small and medium-sized enterprises. To test the common perception
that deregulation benefits larger companies disproportionately, Iqbal (1995)
examined the effects of reform on firms categorised according to their size.
His study of the probability of firm expansion, contraction or exit during two
periods, 1980–85 and 1986–91, concluded that both large and small companies benefited from liberalisation throughout the decade.

Perceptions are powerful and do need to be taken into account. The impact
of liberalisation and globalisation on different sectors of society is bound to
differ, with winners and losers emerging in the process. The challenge for
Indonesia and other developing countries is to move swiftly to identify these
groups and develop institutions and policy instruments to counter the adverse
effects of liberalisation.

CONCLUSION

Developing countries like Indonesia face two distinct orders of adjustment to the challenges of liberalisation and globalisation. The first is the task of restructuring and liberalising the economy so as to be able to take part in and benefit from the world economy more fully (Soesastro 1998), as discussed in the first half of this chapter. The second order of adjustment involves efforts to deal with the economic, social and political consequences of liberalisation. Without new initiatives to counter its negative impacts, it may be difficult to sustain the liberalisation process. It is in this regard that economic liberalisation may need to be supported as well by gradual political liberalisation.

The main issue now facing Indonesia in its liberalisation drive is to develop institutions and policy instruments to deal effectively with the current complex policy environment resulting from economic liberalisation. There is no alternative to sustaining the liberalisation process. The agenda has, in a sense, shifted from the first to the second order of adjustment.

5. Paradise Lost: The Pernicious Impact of Exchange Rate Policy on Indonesia's Banking System

Ross H. McLeod

Throughout the 1970s, Indonesia's banking sector was dominated by five state commercial banks, most of which were former Dutch banks that had been nationalised under former President Sukarno.[1] Regulations effectively prohibited the establishment of new private sector banks (whether domestic or foreign owned), and heavily constrained the expansion of existing branch networks. Only ten of about 70 private domestic banks were licensed to deal in foreign exchange, and it was practically impossible for others to obtain such licences. State-owned banks accounted for roughly 80 per cent of total commercial bank assets throughout this period.

The state banks were nominally restricted to operating in particular sectors of the economy (Panglaykim and Penny 1968, p. 76) and, although the boundaries were loosely drawn, did not compete strongly with each other. They had a huge captive market for both loans and deposits among the state enterprises, which were obliged to rely on them for their banking needs. They were not profit-driven institutions, but were seen more as an instrument for dispensing state patronage.

Two major deregulatory packages, in June 1983 and October 1988, took Indonesia's banking system in just five years from state bank dominance and bureaucratic suffocation to being an effervescent, private sector-driven collection of institutions, remarkably free of government intervention – a transformation so dramatic as to have been virtually unthinkable in the early 1980s (McLeod 1984, pp. 107–8). Unfortunately, however, the golden era of banking from 1983 through 1991 has not been able to be sustained.

This chapter discusses the interaction between certain aspects of macroeconomic policy and the evolution of microeconomic policies for the banking sector.[2] The broad argument advanced here is that there have been inherent weaknesses in macroeconomic policy which, rather than being corrected in the light of experience, have instead led to very damaging policy modifications in relation to the banking sector. As a result the immense achievements of the 1980s deregulation are now in grave danger of being overturned.

THE FUNDAMENTAL SHORTCOMING OF MACROECONOMIC POLICY

The present crisis aside, Indonesia's macroeconomic performance in general has been more than satisfactory. High growth rates have been maintained over a long period, inflation has been held to moderate levels, and poverty has been substantially reduced. But there has been a fundamental shortcoming that has caused problems from time to time and which, I argue, has been principally responsible for setting off Indonesia's current economic crisis. That weakness is the failure to accept the empirical reality, supported by theory, that governments cannot simultaneously control more than one of the nominal macroeconomic variables (the price level, the money supply, the nominal exchange rate and the nominal interest rate) – at least, not in the long run.

Indonesia has nearly always tried to control at least two, and sometimes three or all four of these variables. First and foremost, it has tried to control the nominal exchange rate. Second, it has tried to control the price level (usually indirectly, by controlling the money supply). Third, to a lesser extent, it has also tried to control interest rates. At times, of course, it is possible to 'control' all four, if the targeted values happen to be consistent with those that would emerge from the relevant markets. But in this case, 'control' is illusory. For brevity, I shall concentrate mainly on the conflict between trying to control both the nominal exchange rate and the money supply.

The problem is illustrated by the experience of the mid-1970s.[3] The government fixed the exchange rate against the dollar from 1971. In 1973–74 the Organisation of Petroleum Exporting Countries (OPEC) cartel began to flex its muscles, and the oil price jumped by a factor of four. As a significant oil exporter, Indonesia immediately began to experience a balance of payments surplus. Maintenance of the fixed exchange rate meant that the central bank had to buy dollars to prevent their rupiah price from falling (that is, to prevent a nominal appreciation). By doing so, however, the supply of base money was significantly increased, and inflation rebounded from close to zero early in the 1970s to an average 21 per cent per annum for the rest of the decade. In short, in order to control the nominal exchange rate during this period, the government had to sacrifice its control of money (and therefore prices). We shall return to this subject later to see how this impacted on the microeconomic policy settings.

By the late 1970s there was concern that Indonesian non-oil exports were losing competitiveness by virtue of high inflation, and the government decided to reverse its policy stance, temporarily sacrificing exchange rate control in order to regain lost competitiveness.[4] The rupiah was suddenly devalued by some 33 per cent. The new policy introduced thereafter was said to be a managed float against a basket of currencies. In choosing the weights for each currency in the basket, however, it appears that the government somewhat inexplicably used trade shares by currency in the invoicing of trade transactions, rather than shares by destination or source.[5] Since most trade is invoiced in US dollars, this meant that the US dollar had an extremely heavy weighting in the basket – in practice, very close to 100 per cent. Thus the new policy involved controlling the dollar exchange rate, much as before.

At first it seemed that Indonesia had reverted to having a fixed rate, but soon the view emerged that because its inflation rate was higher than that of its trading partners, it would be appropriate for the exchange rate to depreciate slowly to offset this inflation differential. As I have explained elsewhere (McLeod 1997a, pp. 33–6), this policy confused cause and effect, and resulted in Indonesian inflation continuing at a relatively high level for the same reason that it did in the 1970s: the quasi-fixed exchange rate generated balance of payments surpluses, causing money to increase too rapidly. This in turn generated inflation – albeit at a lower average rate in the 1980s than in the 1970s.

On occasion external events moved against Indonesia. Thus when the oil price fell in 1982–83 and in 1986, Indonesia was again forced temporarily to abandon its fixed exchange rate rather than face the monetary consequences of maintaining it – that is, falling money supply and deflation brought on by balance of payments deficits. The currency was devalued by about 30 per cent in March 1983 and again in September 1986. Never once, however, did the government question its basic policy of trying to control both the nominal exchange rate and the price level simultaneously. Instead it seemed prepared to live with the occasional need for greatly unsettling one-off adjustments to the exchange rate that this policy implied.

The consequences of this policy seemed of minor significance until 1997. Since the last major devaluation in 1986 Indonesia had substantially reduced its dependence on oil exports and oil taxes, so that fluctuations in world oil prices now had a far smaller impact than previously.

Because of the policy of steady depreciation of the rupiah against the dollar, the balance of payments has nearly always been in surplus during the last decade, and money has grown too rapidly to be compatible with the government's inflation targets. Indeed, inflation would have been much higher still except for the fact that the government was able to offset much of the monetary impact of its exchange rate policy by sterilisation. This took two main forms. First, the government built up large deposits with the central bank. Despite its nominal adherence to the balanced budget policy,[6] in fact it often ran a cash flow surplus, with inflows from taxes and foreign borrowing exceeding outflows from spending and debt amortisation. Second, the central bank engaged in open market operations, issuing its own certificates of deposit (SBIs) in order to soak up liquidity.

I argued previously that this policy was unsustainable (McLeod 1997a, p. 37; 1997b, p. 401) because the large negative interest spread between the central bank's rupiah liabilities and its rapidly increasing foreign assets would eventually cause it to modify its macroeconomic policies. As it turned out these policies were indeed unsustainable in the long term, but the manner of their demise was quite different from what I envisaged at the time.

A consequence of the twin policies of controlling the nominal exchange rate and controlling money growth through open market operations and budget surpluses was that the private sector was crowded out of the domestic financial market. Bank Indonesia borrowing (the issue of SBIs) and government cash flow surpluses caused larger private sector borrowers to go offshore for funds, and to build up a large stock of foreign debt in the period 1989–97. Moreover, because the government was promising to control the exchange rate (specifically, the rate of depreciation), and because it had done so successfully for the previous decade, they did not bother to hedge the foreign exchange risk. The same was true of foreign investors in rupiah-denominated bonds and shares.

When the Thai baht was unexpectedly floated and quickly devalued in July 1997, it became clear to borrowers and to offshore investors in Indonesia that there was a substantial exchange rate risk that could not safely be ignored. They responded by buying foreign currency in order to protect themselves against a possible exchange rate devaluation, as had occurred in Thailand. Their fears quickly became a self-fulfilling prophecy, and the rupiah plunged dramatically (McLeod 1998).

The government seemed to have been moving in the direction of floating the currency prior to the crisis, steadily widening its exchange rate intervention band to this end. This may have reflected recognition of the theoretical proposition mentioned earlier – that it is not possible in the long run to control both the nominal exchange rate and the level of prices. It may also have indicated that the policy makers' preference was beginning to accord a higher priority to controlling inflation. The negative impact on the central bank's own profitability of having to sterilise persistent payments surpluses may also have been an important consideration.

Thus when the rupiah came under attack in August 1997, the government chose not to defend it but to let it float. At an intellectual level, however, it was not truly committed to allowing market forces to determine the exchange rate, and when it saw the immediate large depreciation it panicked. On this occasion it chose to sacrifice its monetary targets in order to try to gain control over the exchange rate.

There was a sudden and large balance of payments deficit as a result of panicky capital outflow. Rather than allow the nominal exchange rate to continue to fall, the government imposed a severe reduction in the money supply, pushing up interest rates to very high levels in the hope of attracting capital back to the country. This strategy had worked on several occasions previously (Binhadi and Meek 1992, p. 115), but that was in the context of a quasi-fixed exchange rate policy. Now things were different: the markets had only just been told that the official policy was to float the rupiah, and they were not about to be swayed even by very high interest rates.

Monetary policy has subsequently oscillated wildly between extreme contraction and expansion as the government searches for a coherent approach to deal with the crisis. On the one hand, the economy is in deep recession, with the private sector unable to cope with extraordinarily high nominal interest rates. On the other, the government fears further devaluation of the currency if monetary tightness were to be relaxed. At the time of writing (April 1998) it appears to have opted for tight money (by means of setting high interest rates on SBIs), allowing market determination of the exchange rate. It remains to be seen if it will be able to withstand pressure from the business community to weaken this stand.

CONSEQUENCES FOR MICROECONOMIC POLICY IN THE BANKING SECTOR

For most of the period under consideration inflation has been a problem. The explanation, as suggested above, is that exchange rate policy has usually caused base money to increase too rapidly. Or, to put it another way, exchange rate targets have been incompatible with inflation targets. Rather than settling on a single nominal target so as to remove the inherent conflict, however, the perceived solution most often has been to impose various kinds of restrictions on the banking system – all of them counterproductive in terms of the ability of banks to serve the interests of their existing and potential customers.

Lending Controls on Banks

One form of restriction is loan ceilings. Lending controls on banks had been used as an anti-inflationary device during the 1960s, without success: inflation was as high as 635 per cent per annum in calendar year 1966. Nevertheless similar controls were reintroduced in April 1974 (Arndt 1974, p. 9) in response to persistent high inflation, and became an important element of the banking policy regime for the rest of the 1970s and early 1980s. They were predictably unsuccessful. Worse, at the microeconomic level they had the undesirable side-effects of encouraging ever widening bureaucratic intervention in the intermediation process, and of weakening competition between banks. As Chant and Pangestu (1994, pp. 228–9) put it:

> [T]he new system came to be used as a mechanism for the allocation of credit, with detailed ceilings by type of credit for each bank ... [T]he system of credit allocation determined the structure of the banking system because Bank Indonesia could set the shares assigned to any bank.

One plausible explanation for the central bank's enthusiasm for lending controls is that they implicitly transfer the blame for persistent inflation away from it to the commercial banks. Moreover, when the controls fail to bring down inflation, this can be used to argue for even more extensive controls, resulting in the accumulation of considerable power in the hands of those who administer them. Thus Bank Indonesia built up a large bureaucracy over several years whose job it was to devise increasingly complex loan ceilings differentiated not only by bank but even by sector. It was never clear how decisions were arrived at as to how much each bank was permitted to increase its lending; the ceilings appear to have been negotiated with the banks individually behind closed doors.

The loan ceilings tended to solidify banks' market shares rather than allowing them to evolve in accordance with individual banks' success in meeting their customers' requirements. There was no need to offer attractive deposit rates, since the loan ceilings meant there was no need for additional funds. Nor was there much incentive to look after borrowers, since the ceilings implied conditions of excess demand in which the banks could do without additional custom. In short, the ceilings contributed to poor service and to limiting the range of banking products. In consequence, the banking system of the 1970s and early 1980s left a great deal to be desired in terms of efficiency and responsiveness to customers.

Lending controls were abolished in a major package of banking reforms introduced in June 1983 (McLeod 1996, p. 8). Inflation had fallen in the early 1980s because the balance of payments surplus disappeared with falling oil prices, reducing the rate of monetary expansion. Falling oil prices also significantly reduced the government's revenues, resulting in a corresponding reduction in its ability to finance the investment needed to fuel economic growth. In these circumstances it was thought sensible for banks to expand their role in mobilising private sector savings and allocating them to firms for investment. With this new strategy, lending controls were clearly no longer appropriate.

The private banks in particular responded strongly to their new freedom, posting far more attractive deposit interest rates than before so as to attract more funds, and increasing their lending rapidly. Paradoxically – at least for the supporters of lending controls – inflation averaged less than 9 per cent per annum in the following five-year period, compared with 17 per cent during 1974–83, when loan ceilings had been in operation. In October 1988 a further deregulation package removed most constraints on the establishment of new banks and the expansion of branch networks. Again the private banks responded with vigour; deposit mobilisation proceeded apace, matched by a rapid expansion of lending.

By the early 1990s, with a recovery of oil prices and an increase in the level of private capital inflow, the balance of payments had again returned to surplus, causing base money growth to accelerate; inflation rebounded somewhat. At the same time, broad money (M2) and bank lending were growing even more rapidly as a result of the new freedom deregulation had brought to the banking system. Eventually, dogged by its continued failure to bring inflation within the target maximum of 5 per cent per annum outlined in the Five-year Development Plan (Government of Indonesia 1994, Book I, p. 147), Bank Indonesia once again fell back on blaming 'excessive' growth of bank lending, arguing that controlling inflation required direct control over the expansion of the commercial banks' portfolios. To this end, it adopted targets in the mid-1990s for the rate of growth of bank lending and for the closely related monetary aggregates, M1 (narrow money) and M2.

It is unclear in retrospect whether the government anticipated the rapid expansion in bank intermediation brought about by the reform packages of the 1980s. Official statements at the time suggested that the primary intention of the June 1983 package was simply to induce the then dominant state-owned banks to mobilise more deposits from the public, to reduce their reliance on Bank Indonesia refinancing facilities (Bank Indonesia 1984, pp. 1–2). An expansion of the scale of their lending activities does not seem to have been contemplated, and the private banks' potential response to deregulation seems hardly even to have been considered.

By contrast, the major thrust of the early literature on financial development (for example, McKinnon 1973) was that getting rid of financial repression (in Indonesia, mainly in the form of various restrictions on competition and expansion of the banking system) would permit a significant increase in intermediation. The possibility that this might have inflationary consequences does not seem to have been entertained – rightly – because it simply involved the transfer of spending power between entities, not an addition to total spending power.

To the extent that the authorities sought to control M1, M2 and lending indirectly, by controlling the expansion of base money, this would have been fairly harmless. That after all was the approach followed from 1983 until the early 1990s – a period in which the inflation management record far surpassed that of the 1960s and 1970s, with inflation being held fairly consistently to between 5 and 10 per cent per annum. In practice, the central bank fell back instead on its old policy of setting ceilings on loan growth for each of the banks. At first the banks were required to submit plans for business growth for the coming year, and heavy pressure was applied to persuade them to keep this growth within the limits set for aggregate banking growth.[7] Later, however, a system of fines was introduced for exceeding the growth limits set by the central bank. Different rates of expansion were determined for different banks, but as before the process was non-transparent.

Changing Reserve Requirements

A second form of control over the banking system, used throughout the period under consideration, was the imposition of reserve requirements – that is, requiring banks to hold reserves (base money) equal to some specified minimum percentage of their customers' deposits. This artificially increases the banks' demand for base money and offsets the inflationary impact of an equal amount of base money supplied to the system (as a consequence of exchange rate policy, for instance).

Reserve requirements are sometimes thought of as a safety measure, to ensure that the banks have sufficient liquid assets to be able to meet unanticipated cash outflows. In fact, of course, banks are well aware of the need to hold liquid reserves without being forced to do so. An alternative rationale sometimes proposed is that reserves provide a cushion of safety for depositors against losses incurred by the bank. In fact they do not. That function is served by the bank's equity capital, which can easily be dissipated as a result of bad management, regardless of the existence of reserves.[8]

From the microeconomic viewpoint, a regulatory reserve requirement is equivalent to imposing a tax on the intermediation process undertaken by banks, because funds mobilised from depositors have to be invested in non-interest-bearing liabilities of the central bank.[9] This tax tends to restrain the development of banking, since borrowers and lenders can avoid the tax by relying instead on informal finance (such as trade credit).[10]

A very high reserve requirement had been imposed on the banks during the Sukarno era (Bank Indonesia 1968, pp. 63, 260–61),[11] and this was maintained throughout the first decade of President Soeharto's New Order. Banks were required to hold reserves amounting to 30 per cent of 'current liabilities' (the precise definition of which changed from time to time). Following the re-emergence of inflation in the early 1970s, the reserve requirement inherited from the Sukarno regime was pushed even higher, by increasing the proportions of time and savings deposits required to be included in the measure of 'current liabilities'. The central bank also offered to pay interest on *excess* reserves deposited with it.[12] If we define 'base money' as *zero interest* monetary liabilities of the central bank, then this new approach can be interpreted as achieving a cut in base money by shifting some of the banks' reserves into an interest-paying deposit at the central bank.[13]

Somewhat surprisingly, the nominal required reserve ratio was cut to half its previous level (that is, from 30 to 15 per cent) at the end of 1977,[14] while the rate paid on excess reserves was cut from 10 to 6 per cent per annum. These changes were bound to have an inflationary impact, and although inflation continued its rapid decline from a peak of 47 per cent per annum in 1974 to only 7 per cent in 1978, it rebounded vigorously to 30 per cent in 1979.

Cutting the required reserve ratio to 15 per cent had less impact on the volume of intermediation than might have been expected because of the direct controls on expansion of bank loans discussed above, which meant that the banks could not fully utilise their reserves. Thus the average level of excess reserves jumped from 5 to 9 per cent – despite the now much lower interest rate offered – and then trended upwards to over 10 per cent during the next three years. The lack of a strong profit orientation on the part of the state banks may also have militated against more vigorous expansion of loan portfolios.

In the second major deregulatory package of October 1988, the required reserve ratio was again cut dramatically, this time to only 2 per cent. Bank Indonesia issued certificates of deposit to offset much of the monetary impact, while a new withholding tax of 15 per cent on deposit interest offset the potential impact on the volume of intermediation by banks.[15] But the desire to minimise (if not entirely remove) the distorting impact of reserve requirements was eventually overtaken by the same old urge to search for a solution in the commercial banking system to persistent inflation.

As mentioned already, strong balance of payments surpluses in the late 1980s and early 1990s were largely sterilised by the issue of SBIs and by increasing the government's deposits at Bank Indonesia. This allowed inflation to be kept under control – if not as low as the government would have liked. But the interest earned on rapidly increasing foreign exchange reserves (of the order of 3–4 per cent per annum on US dollars, for example) was far lower than the rates Bank Indonesia had to pay on its own certificates (typically around 12–13 per cent per annum), even after allowance for rupiah depreciation of around 4 per cent per annum. With a negative spread of about 5 per cent after depreciation on an amount of roughly US$11 billion, losses on this part of Bank Indonesia's portfolio would have been running at around US$550 million annually by the end of 1993.[16]

It is not surprising then that Bank Indonesia would seek other, less costly ways of accomplishing sterilisation. To avoid at least some of the interest expense of issuing SBIs, Bank Indonesia eventually moved to force the banks to hold more of its non-interest-bearing liabilities instead, in the form of required reserves. Thus the required reserve ratio was raised again to 3 per cent in February 1996 (Bird 1996, pp. 9–10).

At the same time the definition of reserves was changed to exclude the banks' holdings of cash, which previously had constituted more than half of the total. For this reason, the policy change was more significant than appeared at first sight. The result was to require an increase in the banks' deposits at the central bank from Rp2.3 trillion to Rp6.0 trillion. With the interest rate on SBIs at about 15 per cent per annum, this would have cut Bank Indonesia's annual interest outgoings by the not inconsiderable sum of about Rp550 billion (then roughly US$260 million). In April 1997 the ratio was raised further to 5 per cent. This caused an additional increase in banks' reserves of around Rp4 trillion; SBI rates were now of the order of 10 per cent per annum, suggesting a further annual saving to Bank Indonesia of some Rp400 billion (US$165 million).

At the microeconomic level, the effect was simply to increase the distortionary tax on bank intermediation, thus increasing the incentive of finance market participants to bypass banks in favour of other financing techniques. It should not be imagined that this tax is insignificant. Quick inspection of a small number of the larger private banks' financial statements for recent years shows annual personnel costs as a ratio of end of year deposits running at 1.5–2 per cent. If we assume that funds tied up as required reserves could otherwise be invested at a net return of around 16 per cent per annum, then the tax burden implied by a 5 per cent required reserve ratio is equivalent to roughly half of total labour costs (0.16 x 0.05 ÷ 0.015 = 53%; 0.16 x 0.05 ÷ 0.02 = 40%). In other words, the burden is as heavy as requiring the banks to add one employee for every two currently employed, but not allowing the new employees to do any work.

Controls on Foreign Borrowing by Banks

The amount of offshore borrowing that could be undertaken by Indonesian banks had been severely limited throughout most of the 1970s and 1980s. A new policy package introduced in March 1989 (Government of Indonesia

1989) to supplement the October 1988 package removed these controls and replaced them with a new prudential limit on banks' 'net open positions' – that is, the gap between banks' liabilities and assets denominated in foreign currencies, relative to their capital.[17]

It is not clear what purpose might have been served by the previous restriction on offshore borrowing. Indonesia has an open capital account,[18] and there are close links between Indonesian business and the financial centres of Singapore and Hong Kong in particular. Preventing the banks from bringing in as much capital as they needed to satisfy their borrowers' demands simply meant in practice that the larger borrowers went offshore themselves for funding – a kind of reverse protectionism, artificially reducing rather than enhancing local banks' ability to compete with foreign banks.[19]

The removal of this unnecessarily distorting restriction on banks' freedom to compete was soon overturned; the central bank reimposed the controls in 1991.[20] The pretext was the need to support the work of a newly established, high-level government committee, which had been given the responsibility of cutting back on Indonesia's foreign borrowing (Muir 1991, pp. 15–21). This was supposedly made necessary by Indonesia's increasing indebtedness to the rest of the world, which was said to pose a threat to the balance of payments because of the implied debt service burden.[21]

Before long, however, the newly restored controls came to be seen by the authorities as assisting in the fight against inflation. The balance of payments surpluses of the early 1990s were blamed on 'speculative' capital inflows, so controls on offshore borrowing by the banks could now be justified as a means of preventing unwanted monetary expansion. This was a rather forlorn strategy, since the more fundamental open capital account policy remained intact. Firms that normally would have used domestic banks to intermediate foreign funds simply went directly to offshore banks, or tapped the foreign capital market by issuing bonds.

In both cases, the specialised intermediation role of the domestic banks was significantly weakened, and this turned out to have unanticipated negative consequences. The fact that firms bypassed domestic banks meant that there was no ready source of data on the amount and maturity of offshore borrowing, and this hampered policy makers' attempts to deal with the foreign debt problem when the rupiah suddenly fell in 1997–98.

Tightening Licensing of Bank Branches

The government's tendency to shift blame for persistent inflation to the commercial banks – rather than sheeting it home to its own insistence on maintaining incompatible macroeconomic policies – has also resulted in a tightening of branch licensing procedures, slowing the physical expansion of the banking system. Yet the relaxation of branch licensing in 1988 had brought immense benefits to the general public and to small business, by increasing their access to banks. Some 126 new private banks were established over the next nine years, including 33 foreign joint ventures, and new branches seemed to spring up on every street corner. No less than 4,609 new branches were added, increasing the total from 1,728 in 1988 to 6,337 in 1997; the number of savings deposit accounts grew from 24 million to 56 million.

Notwithstanding the obvious benefits of this flourishing of the banking sector, it was announced in 1996 that Bank Indonesia and the Department of Finance were to become 'more selective' in the licensing of new branches with a view to avoiding 'unhealthy competition' between banks (*Bisnis Indonesia*, 28 June 1996). The Governor of the central bank was reported as acknowledging 'that in certain areas, there were too many bank offices', but it was not explained how this could be other than beneficial to the interests of the general public. Nor was there any reference to the vast expansion of the use of the banking system by the general public following the freeing up of the branching process in the 1988 reforms.[22] To the extent that there are problems now in the banking industry, there is little evidence to indicate that these have anything to do with the expansion of branch networks.

Explicit Government Guarantees for All Domestic Banks

The drastic fall of the rupiah that immediately followed the government's decision to float it on 14 August 1997 marked the commencement of a deep economic crisis that as yet shows little sign of abatement. After nearly two months of steadily deteriorating economic conditions the government called on the International Monetary Fund (IMF) for assistance. The first significant measure undertaken as part of the initial IMF package of remedial measures was to close down 16 banks abruptly at the end of October. The reason for this move, apparently, was that they were believed to be insolvent. It appears also that they had a history of flouting certain prudential regulations, including those regarding excessive lending to related parties.

It is unfortunate that the central bank had not moved in this direction long before. The prevalence of banks lending excessively within their own group was well known – indeed, a principal shareholder in one closed bank insisted that his bank had only been following what was common practice in the whole banking community– but there had been a lack of political will to enforce the regulations. Although a regulatory response was therefore long overdue, in retrospect this was not a good time for it. There should have been a greater effort to prepare the public before moving in this manner,[23] notwithstanding the government's promise to guarantee deposits up to a level of Rp20 million per depositor.[24]

The unwanted impact of the bank closures was to raise serious concerns on the part of depositors and other creditors about the remaining banks – even the state banks, with their perceived implicit government guarantee. There was a rush to withdraw deposits, to shift them to state or foreign banks (or offshore) or even to hold them as cash. To stem the outflow of deposits, the government was eventually forced to offer a blanket guarantee to depositors and other creditors of all domestically owned banks.

By April 1998 the banks were still in great peril. Commentators have been quick to blame them for ignoring prudential regulations, and the central bank for its failure to enforce them, implying that this has been one of the main causes of the present crisis. And indeed, Bank Indonesia's approach to prudential supervision left much to be desired (Habir 1994, pp. 177–9). Its system for rating the soundness of banks was so poorly conceived that even a bank that had lost *all* its capital could still be rated 'sufficiently sound' if its performance in other respects was satisfactory! This may provide an explanation for why the aforementioned 16 banks had not been closed down earlier.

Nevertheless, to argue in this manner is again to misplace the blame. The drastic and entirely unexpected fall in the value of the rupiah is the fundamental source of the banks' woes – not because they were directly exposed to exchange rate risk, but because many of their borrowers had foreign currency loans which they could no longer service when the rupiah fell. Even banks that played by the prudential rules, maintaining adequate capital and avoiding highly concentrated lending, have suffered for this reason.

There has been criticism of the banks, too, along the lines that they lent too much to property developers that had no natural currency hedge, since their future revenues were in rupiahs. This is a superficial view that ignores the fact that banks also had large exposures in the form of importers' letters of credit that failed as a result of the devaluation. Letters of credit are standard bread and butter business for even the best-managed banks; they are an essential feature of Indonesia's trade links with the world economy, not instruments for reckless excess. Put simply, the banks cannot and should not be blamed for the fact that the rupiah has lost 70 per cent of its value.

Huge Increase in Minimum Capital Requirements for Banks

The government seems hell-bent on a total restructuring of the banking system. Unfortunately, its strategies are disastrously misconceived. Following its closure of the 16 private banks in October 1997, the government announced at the end of the year that it would merge four of the seven state-owned banks. The merger was to be complemented by stripping out their bad loans and selling them to a new state-owned entity set up especially for the purpose. The intention was that the new entity would concentrate on the loan recovery process, while the remaining megabank would be free to concentrate on the more mundane tasks of collecting deposits and generating new loans. While no observer of the Indonesian banking system doubts that there are very serious weaknesses in the state banks, the willingness of the government and many commentators to believe that these problems can be overcome by merging them is astonishing.

The rationale seems to be the belief that 'bigger is better', but while there is often much to be said for the takeover of a weak bank by a strong one, the notion that a strong bank can be created by merging several banks – all of whose portfolios are in a parlous state – seems fanciful. Merging banks does not make their bad loans disappear, nor does it improve the ratio of aggregate capital to aggregate bad loans.

The private banks have also been placed under increasingly heavy government pressure to undertake mergers among themselves. This pro-merger push culminated in the announcement in February of a huge increase in the minimum capital requirement for banks, from only Rp50–150 billion (depending on whether the bank has a foreign exchange licence) to Rp1 trillion, to be met by the end of 1998. Similarly large increases were to be phased in over the next two years. The intention clearly was to force them to merge, since very few would be able to secure such enormous new equity injections.

Merging just two companies is a difficult enough process in normal times, let alone attempting multi-firm mergers when there is crisis all around. If this extreme pro-merger policy is sustained it will create an overwhelming new set of management distractions, such as determining new organisational structures, harmonising disparate management information systems, deciding which branches and other buildings to keep and which to dispense with, dealing with major workforce dislocation and so on. Moreover, the policy will force mergers between groups of not just two or three banks, but many.[25]

This is likely to prove a practical impossibility, yet there is nothing to indicate that the government has thought through the implications of the likely inability of banks either to raise sufficient additional capital or to merge. Will it, for example, force such banks to close? There are undoubtedly some small banks that have been well managed and that have observed all the prudential regulations. The implication is that they are now to be punished for the crime of being small.[26]

The National Banking Rehabilitation Agency

A third government initiative for dealing with the problems of the banks was also announced in February 1998: the establishment of a National Banking Rehabilitation Agency (NBRA)[27] responsible for restoring the health of presently unsound banks – both private and state owned – after which it would be wound up. The agency is empowered to take over the management of such banks; to purchase their bad loans and other impaired assets for subsequent sale to third parties; and to arrange for them to be merged with other banks, taken over, or sold to new shareholders. The government is contemplating issuing bonds to finance these activities.

In early April, NBRA froze the operations of a further seven private banks and took over another six private and one state bank. By contrast with the 16 banks closed in October, this new group comprised some of the largest private institutions, which together accounted for a substantial portion of total bank assets. The very large loans each had received by way of temporary assistance from Bank Indonesia were likely to be converted to government equity, effectively turning them into new state-owned banks, at least for the time being.

It appears that the Boards of Commissioners and Directors of each bank have been purged, as though they were all collectively responsible for the present condition of their respective banks. As always, the banks and their managers make convenient scapegoats to draw attention away from the more fundamental cause that is the subject of this chapter,[28] but the banking system can hardly afford to lose such a large proportion of its top managerial talent at this time of extreme difficulty. To add insult to injury, these individuals have been replaced mainly by present and former managers of various state banks, seemingly regardless of the fact that the state banks as a group have an appalling record of poor management over many decades, needing to be saved from bankruptcy on many occasions by further injections of capital by the government.[29] It seems extraordinary that the government would want to draw managerial 'saviours' exclusively from this particular pool.

CONCLUSION

The immense achievements of the last 15 years in restructuring the banking sector along market-oriented lines are now in real danger of obliteration. The inherent conflict between the government's exchange rate and inflation targets has been primarily responsible, first, for steady erosion of the sensible deregulatory reforms of the 1980s, and second, for the all-out assault now under way that is likely to leave Indonesia with a banking system little better than that which existed in the 1970s. If sound macroeconomic policies have been credited with providing the stable foundation for rapid growth in the past, the inherent shortcoming in those policies described in this chapter will come to be credited with the implosion of the banking sector now occurring, from which it will take years to recover.

NOTES

1. Brief details of the history of the state banks are contained in Bank Indonesia (1968, pp. 50–54).
2. McLeod (1996) provides a detailed discussion of the evolution of bank sector policies in the period prior to the current crisis.
3. Under the previous Sukarno regime, there had been an attempt to control the nominal exchange rate while having an extremely expansionary monetary policy (or rather, just allowing money growth generated by budget deficits to run out of control). This ended in disaster in the mid-1960s, with hyperinflation, the exhaustion of international reserves and negative growth.
4. The appropriateness of this move remains controversial. In the author's view, the OPEC-induced boost to oil exports was only valuable to Indonesia if it enabled a decrease in the production of tradeables and a corresponding increase in production of non-tradeables; a loss of competitiveness was precisely what was needed to reallocate productive resources in the required direction.
5. The usual practice is to use trade shares by destination or source, so as to maintain roughly constant competitiveness of the country in question among its trading partner economies taken as a whole.
6. In Indonesia the term 'balanced budget' is interpreted to mean that government expenditures, including debt amortisation, are covered by revenues plus the proceeds of foreign borrowing. Maintaining a 'balanced budget' has been one of the major constants of the Soeharto regime. In practice this has meant that the government has always financed its budget deficits by borrowing offshore, rather than borrowing from the central bank. For this reason the budget has rarely been a source of money creation, and so has rarely contributed to inflation.
7. As the Governor of Bank Indonesia put it, 'Lending plans should take into consideration the national monetary targets' (Djiwandono 1995, p. 3; author's translation).
8. Of course, if the reserve requirement is set at a very high level, the risk to depositors arising from bank lending is reduced, since risk-free reserves crowd out risky assets in the banks' portfolios.
9. Revenue from the tax of course flows to the central bank in the first instance.
10. Other forms of formal finance also gain a competitive advantage over banks if they are not subject to reserve requirements, but this factor was of little significance during the period in question.
11. The requirement was introduced in 1960, apparently as a reaction to liquidity difficulties experienced by banks in 1959 when the government introduced contractionary measures to try to control inflation.
12. The interest rate was not market determined, but at 10 per cent per annum it certainly provided an attractive option to the then dominant state banks, which at the time were being forced to lend at similar – and sometimes even lower – rates.
13. The present day equivalent is the issue of interest-yielding SBIs.
14. The effective reserve requirement on time deposits was less than 15 per cent, because less than 100 per cent of such deposits was to be included as 'current liabilities' in the reserve ratio calculation. The portion that was included also varied across bank ownership groups. For example, at the beginning of 1978 state banks had to include two-thirds of time deposits,

making their effective ratio 10 per cent, whereas private banks had to include only one-third, making their effective ratio 5 per cent.

15. An interesting aspect here is the diversion of the implicit tax on intermediation collected by the central bank to the Department of Finance.

16. This estimate cannot be verified, as Bank Indonesia ceased publishing its profit and loss statement in its Annual Reports in 1992/93.

17. The net open position (NOP) limitation has been interpreted by some observers as a near substitute for the previous direct control on the volume of offshore borrowing by banks (see, for example, Chant and Pangestu 1994, p. 233). In fact, the latter constrains the amount of capital inflow in the form of funds intermediated by banks, whereas the NOP merely seeks to prevent banks from taking an unmatched currency position in such intermediation. Under the NOP constraint, banks may bring in as much foreign funds as they like, provided they on-lend them predominantly in the same currencies. The aim is therefore to prevent the banks from speculating too heavily on exchange rate movements, not to stop them from bringing funds into the country.

18. The commitment to an open capital account has been another major constant of economic policy in the Soeharto era.

19. Some observers have interpreted this to mean that smaller borrowers with no reputation in, or links to, the international finance market were starved of funds as a result of this restriction. In reality, the fact that larger firms could turn to overseas markets meant that domestic rates did not rise to the extent they would have under full financial autarky. Small firms could borrow as much as they wanted domestically, at going rates.

20. Bank Indonesia Directors' Decree No. 24/52/KEP/DIR, dated 29 November 1991.

21. There was also a political motivation for reimposing the controls (McLeod 1996, p. 24).

22. Expressions of concern about 'unhealthy competition' have often been used elsewhere, of course, to justify the imposition of controls that promote the interests of existing firms in the industry in question.

23. The central bank monitored the banks' financial condition and compliance with the regulations, and from time to time assigned each bank a soundness rating. But it deliberately chose not to share these ratings with the general public.

24. In March 1998 the government decided to pay out domestic creditors in full, although amounts in excess of Rp100 million were frozen as two-year time deposits at the state banks, at well below the market interest rates.

25. There are now about 138 private banks, and their aggregate reported shareholders' funds were only Rp25 trillion as of February 1998. In the absence of new equity this would be enough to support only 25 banks under the new minimum requirements. On average this will require groups of about five or six banks to merge – perhaps several more in the case of smaller banks. The reader may imagine the difficulty of carrying out mergers on such a scale within such a short period of time.

26. For an example, see Tripathi and McBeth (1998).

27. The agency is usually referred to as the Indonesian Bank Restructuring Agency, but this is not an accurate translation of its Indonesian title, Badan Penyehatan Perbankan Nasional.

28. This is not to deny, of course, that some of those pushed out were very likely guilty of deliberate infringement of the prudential regulations.

29. Anon. (1971, p. 25) notes that the government of the day was in the process 'of rehabilitating ... Bapindo' (the state-owned Indonesian Development Bank). Grenville (1977, p. 28) briefly mentions episodes involving two other state banks, Bank Negara Indonesia in 1946 and Bank Bumi Daya in the early and mid-1970s, which prompted the government to replace the President Directors and some Executive Directors of each bank. He quotes an anonymous but prescient banker who was under no illusion that state bank losses would be avoided in the future: 'This is a changing of the guard, and the palace remains'. The most recent case also involved Bapindo (McLeod 1996, pp. 22–3).

6. Dollarisation and Financial Sector Developments in Vietnam

Suiwah Leung and Ngo Huy Duc

INTRODUCTION

Dollarisation refers to the phenomenon whereby the residents of a country (other than the United States) hold US dollars as a medium of exchange and as a store of value. This phenomenon is asymmetrical in that US residents do not normally hold the currency of the other country. The extent of dollarisation can be considered in terms both of the *volume* of US dollars circulating in the country (usually expressed as a ratio of the domestic currency) and the *propensity* for domestic residents to switch to US dollar holdings in response to expected changes in macroeconomic variables such as the inflation rate, interest rates and exchange rates.

In countries with significant dollarisation, the effectiveness of domestic monetary policy is limited since the authorities can control only part of the money supply. Moreover, for any given budget deficit, the printing of money to finance the deficit has to occur at a more rapid rate, resulting in increased inflation. Therefore, once inflationary expectation is entrenched, it reduces the purchasing power of the domestic money stock and imposes an implicit tax (known as inflation tax) on holders of domestic money, inducing them to substitute into US dollars. This process of dollarisation means a dwindling of the domestic money holdings and hence a whittling away of the inflation tax base, necessitating higher rates of inflation to finance the same budget deficit.

In this sense dollarisation is analogous to very mobile short-term capital flows. While it may be desirable for residents to be able to hold an additional financial asset in the form of US dollars, dollarisation also has the potential to trigger macroeconomic instability. It could, of course, be argued that in the presence of dollarisation, governments will be less likely to print money to finance budget deficits because of the increased danger of macroeconomic destabilisation. In developing and transitional economies with under-developed government bond markets, however, such fiscal discipline would require a degree of political will that is unlikely to be forthcoming. In particular, in the context of the Asian financial crisis, lack of trust in the government's political will, associated with a high degree of dollarisation and the potential for macroeconomic destabilisation, could result in an increased risk premium being required by foreign investors. This would make the country more vulnerable to changes in investor sentiment.

This chapter examines the evidence for dollarisation in Vietnam, and for a feedback effect on inflation. We discuss first how economic liberalisation and developments in Vietnam's financial sector have led to a rapid increase in the volume of dollars held in the country. We then estimate econometrically the propensity of Vietnamese residents to substitute into dollars before examining the impact of dollarisation on inflation.

ECONOMIC LIBERALISATION AND DOLLARISATION, 1985–95

In the decade prior to 1985, with the exception of the Vietnam War period in the South, there were no significant holdings of foreign currency in Vietnam. Trade was conducted predominantly with the former Soviet bloc on a barter basis; a detailed bilateral agreement was drawn up every year identifying the goods and commodities to be exchanged. The so-called Soviet convertible rouble (each one equalling five domestic roubles) was used as the unit of accounting, and there was no incentive for foreign trading firms to diversify or optimise their portfolio holdings.

Table 6.1 shows that this situation began to change in 1986, with the expansion in foreign currency holdings becoming particularly pronounced in 1989. The table also shows that Vietnam's inflation rate reached triple digits between 1986 and 1988, after which it remained quite volatile until 1993. These changes coincided with a period of economic liberalisation in Vietnam, during which budget constraints on state-owned enterprises were tightened and an incipient domestic private sector emerged. Firms and households were encouraged to maximise their profits and utilities, and hence focused their attention on the efficiency of payments as well as on maximising the value of their assets for any given degree of risk. The holding of US dollars could, under certain circumstances, be both efficient and optimal for these households and firms.

In addition to giving firms and households the incentive to hold US dollars as a means of payment and store of value, economic liberalisation brought about certain institutional changes that made it easier for them to hold US dollars. First, with the changes in trade and foreign investment patterns that followed the collapse of the former Soviet Union, firms and house-

Table 6.1 Monetary Survey, 1986–93

	1986	1987	1988	1989	1990	1991	1992	1993
Foreign currency deposits (billion dong)								
in Vietnam	1	29	242	2,089	3,583	8,354	8,213	7,406
abroad	1.44	10.15	99	110.7	272.7	388.6	390.5	449.4
Total foreign currency deposits								
in billion dong	2.44	39.15	341	2,200	3,856	8,743	8,604	7,855
in US$ million	135.6	111.9	113.7	536.5	565.6	719.9	815.1	751.7
as % of net foreign assets	–	19	120	487	233	130	81	140
as % of M2 (inclusive of foreign currency deposits)	2	8	13	29	33	43	31	24
as % of exports	27	18	16	41	33	35	33	25
as % of imports	12	9	8	32	32	34	32	22
Inflation rate (general retail price) (%)	487.3	301.3	308.2	74.3	36.4	82.7	37.7	8.3

Sources: General Statistics Office of Vietnam (1991), *Economy and Finance of Vietnam 1986–90*, Hanoi; General Statistics Office of Vietnam (1992), *Economic Conditions of Vietnam 1986–91: A System of National Accounts*, Hanoi; General Statistics Office of Vietnam (1995), *Statistical Yearbook*, Hanoi; IMF (various issues), *International Financial Statistics*, Washington DC; International Economic Data Base, Australian National University, Canberra; World Bank (1994), *Vietnam: Public Sector Management and Private Sector Incentives*, Washington DC; authors' estimates.

holds began to use US dollars to make international payments. Second, the three-tiered exchange rate regime was unified in 1989, bringing about an effective five-fold devaluation in the official exchange rate. This made the holding of US dollars less risky, as they could be changed into dong at an official rate that was not too different from the parallel market rate. Third, new financial regulations meant that firms and households could legally maintain foreign currency deposits at a commercial bank and receive a positive real rate of interest on such deposits.

It is therefore not surprising that the hyperinflationary episode of 1985–88, together with the large devaluation of the dong in 1989, brought about a discrete upward shift in US dollar holdings. What is surprising is that these holdings – as a percentage of the money supply and as a share of international reserves – have remained high in spite of a slowdown in the inflation rate, indicating a significant transactions motive for holding US dollars. The US dollar continues to be the preferred medium for transactions because of the very small denominations of dong notes (the highest denomination equalling US$5) and because the Vietnamese lack familiarity with the use of credit cards and cheque accounts. As Vietnam's financial sector and payments system develop, the transactions motive can be expected to diminish.

Another factor in dollarisation in Vietnam is the prevalence of smuggling activities, which are transacted predominantly in dollars. Government trade statistics show that in 1994 Vietnam's exports were worth US$3.6 billion and its imports US$5.0 billion. United Nations Conference on Trade and Development (UNCTAD) figures using data from Vietnam's trading partners show exports to have been worth US$4.5 billion and imports US$6.2 billion in the same year. The total volume of illegal foreign trade was therefore almost equivalent to 25 per cent of the total volume of legal foreign trade. In many Latin American countries with significant dollarisation, smuggling has been recognised as a factor in the use of US dollars in the domestic economy.

Economic liberalisation and the opening of the economy to trade and investment with the West have also had the effect of bringing back the savings of Vietnamese living abroad. A significant quantity of these remittances was brought into the country illegally in US dollars, adding to the supply of dollars in the economy since 1989.

Since as early as 1988, various administrative controls have been used to curb the use of dollars in the economy. In 1988 the aim of exchange control was to encourage the inflow and discourage the outflow of foreign exchange. This was achieved by requiring firms to place foreign currency in a bank account from which withdrawals for certain purposes (for example, the importation of inputs) could be made. Households were also encouraged to deposit their foreign currency in bank accounts paying interest of 6–6.5 per cent per annum. This was considerably higher than the interest paid on the holdings of firms. Firms could, however, hold unlimited amounts of foreign currency in their accounts, and for them the use of foreign currency in transactions was legal.

With the tightening of exchange controls in 1994, firms were required to sell to the government all foreign currency above a limit set by the State Bank. All domestic transactions had to be realised in dong and the number

Table 6.2 Ratio of Foreign Currency Deposits to M2 in Selected Asian and Transitional Economies (%)

	1990	1991	1992	1993
Vietnam*	33.0	43.0	31.0	24.0
Indonesia	14.3	20.3	19.1	17.8
Korea	0.6	1.3	1.0	0.6
Mongolia	2.3	6.1	7.5	37.6
Albania	2.1	1.3	23.8	20.7
Bulgaria	12.9	38.4	25.3	n.a.
Hungary	5.4	5.4	n.a.	n.a.
Poland	31.5	24.7	24.8	28.8
Romania	2.9	3.9	17.9	n.a.

Note: *The figures for Vietnam include foreign currency deposits abroad.

Source: World Bank (1994), *Vietnam: Financial Sector Review: An Agenda for Financial Sector Development*, Washington DC; authors' estimates.

of firms authorised to use foreign currency was greatly reduced. Visitors to Vietnam were required to exchange their foreign currency for dong. However, two years after this ruling the US dollar was still in wide use as a means of payment. It appears that the new regulation may simply have driven dollars out of official channels rather than reduced its use significantly.

Table 6.2 uses the ratio of foreign currency deposits to M2 (money base plus bank deposits) to compare dollar holdings in Vietnam with those in some other Asian and transitional economies. It can be seen that according to this measure dollarisation is higher in Vietnam than in most other countries listed in the table.

This is consistent with the relatively low degree of financial deepening found in Vietnam by the World Bank (1997, p. 50). This report estimated that the ratio of total bank deposits to GDP is only 16.3 per cent in Vietnam, compared with 50.2 per cent in China and 43.4 per cent in the Philippines. The ratio of domestic currency in circulation to bank deposits, on the other hand, is very high (53.9 per cent, compared with 16.1 per cent in China and 13.2 per cent in the Philippines). Therefore, a decade after *doi moi* [economic renovation], Vietnam is still a 'cash' economy and confidence in the domestic banking system is weak.

THE PROPENSITY TO HOLD US DOLLARS, 1990–94

The discussion so far has equated dollarisation with the *level* of US dollars in the Vietnamese economy. This concept is insufficient – partly because it is impossible to measure with any degree of accuracy the actual stock of US dollars circulating in a developing economy such as Vietnam; and more importantly because it does not address the behavioural question of the *propensity* of Vietnamese residents to switch to US dollar holdings in response to changes in the macroeconomy that affect the relative risk-adjusted returns on different assets. In this section we use econometrics to estimate the degree of substitution into dollars in Vietnam from 1990 to 1994.

The basic form of the estimating equation is

$$\log(F/M) = \alpha + \beta x \qquad (6.1)$$

where F represents the nominal stock of foreign money; M represents the nominal stock of domestic money; and x is the inflation differential between Vietnam and the rest of the world determining the expected rate of depreciation of the Vietnamese dong.[1] Assuming that total holdings of domestic and foreign money $(F + M)$ remain unchanged at given levels of real income and interest rates, then a positive β would mean that an increase in expected depreciation of the dong would result in greater holdings of foreign money and reduced holdings of domestic money. Thus the sign and size of β capture the degree of substitution, or propensity to substitute US dollars for dong.

Added to Equation (6.1) is a time trend, T, which captures the inertia of the dollarisation process, and a dummy, DT, for the change in slope of the time trend after January 1992. The dummy captures structural change in the demand for foreign and domestic monies, F/M, after Decision No. 337/HDBT, which gave the State Bank of Vietnam sole control of the sale and purchase of foreign currency and the authority to determine foreign exchange rates. Equation (6.1) was then incorporated into a partial adjustment model to obtain the final estimating equation of the form

$$\log(F/M)_t = \alpha + \beta x_t + \gamma T + \delta DT + \phi \log(F/M)_{t-1} + \varepsilon \qquad (6.2)$$

where ε is the disturbance term, and DT equals T for all observations after January 1992 and zero otherwise.

Two alternative definitions of money are employed: M1 (narrow money), which includes cash in circulation and demand deposits; and M2, which consists of M1 plus time/savings deposits (excluding foreign currency deposits). The foreign currency stock F is proxied by deposits denominated in foreign currency; that is, US dollar deposits (expressed in dong) of the non-bank sector in Vietnam. Since the actual stock of US dollars in Vietnam – as in many other developing countries – is impossible to measure with any degree of accuracy, US dollar bank deposits are used as a proxy on the assumption that they vary in proportion to changes in the actual stock of US dollars in Vietnam.

As with many other studies in the field, the choice of proxy for x, the expected rate of depreciation of the domestic currency, presents a major challenge. There are additional difficulties in the case of Vietnam as the dong is not fully convertible and there is no futures market for it. Therefore, following the work of Rojas-Suarez (1992) and El-Erian (1988), the actual change in the black market exchange rate of the US dollar against the dong is used as a proxy for the expected change in the value of the dong. That is, $x = \log(E_t/E_{t-1})$, where E is the price (expressed in index form) of the US dollar in terms of the dong at the black market rate.

The Research Institute of Market and Price in Hanoi provided data on black market exchange rates. Other data were obtained from the State Bank of Vietnam and the International Monetary Fund (IMF), with cross-checks being conducted to ensure consistency among the various sources of data. Monthly series for the period December 1990 to December 1994 were used in the estimation.

Equation (6.2) was estimated using the ordinary least squares (OLS) estimation procedure, and Table 6.3 reports the main results.[2] The main conclusions to be drawn from the table are as follows.

* There is strong evidence for the presence of dollarisation in Vietnam. The coefficient of dollarisation (β) is significant at the 5 per cent level. If the expected rate of depreciation of the dong increases by 1 absolute percentage point (say, from 40 to 41 per cent), F/M will increase by about 0.6 per cent (say, from 1 to 1.006) within a one-month period. If $F = M$, this may be thought of as a 0.3 per cent increase in F and a 0.3 per cent decrease in M. That is, on average 0.3 per cent of domestic money is substituted by foreign money for each 1 per cent increase in the expected rate of depreciation of the dong.
* The strong and rapid substitution into US dollars in response to an increase in expected depreciation of the dong indicates that the 'store of

Table 6.3 Estimation of Dollarisation Coefficient

	$\log(F/M1)_t = \alpha + \beta x_t + \gamma T$ $+ \delta DT + \phi \log(F/M1)_{t-1} + \varepsilon_t$	$\log(F/M2)_t = \alpha + \beta x_t + \gamma T$ $+ \delta DT + \phi \log(F/M2)_{t-1} + \varepsilon_t$
x	0.605*	0.576*
t-statistic (P-value)	2.203 (0.033)	2.263 (0.029)
T	0.020**	0.023**
t-statistic (P-value)	3.481 (0.001)	4.008 (0.000)
DT	−0.035**	−0.034**
t-statistic (P-value)	−3.991 (0.000)	−4.280 (0.000)
$\log(F/M)_{t-1}$	0.478**	0.549**
t-statistic (P-value)	3.961 (0.000)	5.137 (0.000)
R^2 adjusted	0.952	0.941
LM test χ^2 12 d.f.	12.632	12.290
(P-value)	(0.396)	(0.423)
RESET test F^1 43 d.f.	3.206	1.303
(P-value)	(0.080)	(0.260)
J-B test χ^2 2 d.f.	3.761	6.733 *
(P-value)	(0.153)	(0.035)
CUSUM, CUSUMSQ	Passed	Passed

Notes:
* denotes significance at 5 per cent level.
** denotes significance at 1 per cent level.
d.f. denotes degree of freedom.
LM test is a test for serial correlation up to order 12.
RESET is Ramsey's test for mis-specification using the square of the predicted dependent variable.
J-B test is the Jacque-Berra test for normality of the disturbance term.
CUSUM and CUSUMSQ are tests for the stability of the estimated parameters.

increase in expected depreciation of the dong indicates that the 'store of value' motive for holding US dollars is significant in Vietnam.

- As pointed out earlier, Vietnam's banking sector is underdeveloped and the degree of financial deepening low by regional standards. This is also indicated by the fact that the estimated results are very similar for both M1 and M2, implying that the economy is still predominantly cash based and that savings deposits in banks are a relatively small component of the money supply.
- The speed of adjustment in the stocks of money held is also reasonably fast, with between 48 and 55 per cent of desired change being realised within a one-month period.
- The dummy coefficient for institutional change is highly significant (at the 1 per cent level) but relatively small in absolute magnitude. Clarifying the powers of the State Bank and giving it sole authority to determine exchange rates may have increased confidence in the dong, leading to less dollarisation. On the other hand, a unified exchange rate reduces the risk of holding US dollars. The counteracting effect of these two forces may have accounted for the very small coefficient observed in the institutional variable.

HAS DOLLARISATION LED TO HIGHER INFLATION?

We have shown that the short-run response to increases in the expected rate of depreciation of the dong is a significant and large increase in dollarisation. Given that expected depreciation is related to the inflation differential between Vietnam and the rest of the world (proxied by the US inflation rate), then if dollarisation brings about higher inflation in Vietnam, there could well be a vicious circle in which inflation leads to increased expected depreciation, leading to increased dollarisation, which feeds in turn into increased inflation. This process has the potential to be very destabilising, making the economy highly vulnerable to currency and financial crises. It is therefore important to examine the nature and magnitude of the impact of dollarisation on inflation in Vietnam.

It is generally agreed that the Vietnamese government finances part of its budget deficit through inflation tax. One of the effects of dollarisation is that the government has to accept a loss of inflation tax revenue, as dollarisation implies a contraction in holdings of the domestic currency and hence a shrinkage in the inflation tax base. To generate a given amount of inflation tax, therefore, domestic money needs to increase more rapidly, resulting in a higher domestic inflation rate. In other words, domestic monetary growth depends positively on the rate of change in foreign versus domestic money holdings (F/M). This can then be translated into higher rates of inflation as follows:

$$\log(P_t/P_{t-1}) \equiv \Delta \log P_t = \alpha + \beta \Delta \log FM_{t-2} + \gamma \Delta \log y$$
$$+ \delta DI + \phi \Delta \log P_{t-1} + \varepsilon_t \qquad (6.1a)$$

Equation (6.1a) postulates that current period inflation $(\Delta \log P_t)$ is dependent on a constant (α); changes in the stock of foreign versus domestic currency holdings in the previous two periods $(\Delta \log FM_{t-2})$; changes in real income $(\Delta \log y)$; structural change in 1992 proxied by a dummy variable (DI); the inflation rate in the previous period $(\Delta \log P_{t-1})$; and a disturbance term (ε_t).[3]

The equation was estimated for monthly series from December 1990 to December 1994. During this time, there was generally a downward trend in nominal interest rates on dong deposits at banks (from about 4 per cent to 1.7 per cent monthly). Because interest rates are determined by the State Bank rather than the market, they were not specifically included in the estimating equation. However, it is expected that the interest rate effect would be picked up by the constant term (α), which is therefore expected to be positively related to the inflation rate in the current period.

As foreign to domestic money holdings (FM) increases, the shrinkage in the domestic money base implies a higher rate of money supply growth (and therefore a higher inflation rate) to finance constant (or expanding) budget deficits in subsequent periods. Thus β is expected to be positive.

An increase in real income (y) leads to increased transactions demand for domestic money, and γ is therefore expected to be negative.

As discussed earlier, the powers of the State Bank, and thereby the effectiveness of stabilisation measures, were enhanced in 1992; δ is therefore expected to be negative.

The Augmented Dicky–Fuller (ADF) test shows that all variables are stationary, justifying the use of the standard OLS estimation procedure. As before, two measures of domestic money supply, M1 and M2, were used in the estimation. The following conclusions can be drawn from the results, which are presented in Table 6.4.

- There is a feedback mechanism from dollarisation to inflation. Other things being equal, a 1 per cent increase in the ratio $FM1$ results, on average, in a 0.047 per cent increase in the monthly inflation rate two months later. The coefficient is higher for M2. Since the period under study was characterised by relatively moderate but somewhat volatile inflation rates (ranging from 5.3 to 82.7 per cent per annum), it can be expected that both the speed and magnitude of response would be greater in a higher inflation environment.

Table 6.4 Estimation of the Impact of Dollarisation on Inflation

	$\Delta \log P_t = \alpha + \beta \Delta \log FM1_{t-2} +$ $\gamma \Delta \log y + \delta DI + \phi \Delta \log P_{t-1} + \varepsilon_t$	$\Delta \log P_t = \alpha + \beta \Delta \log FM2_{t-2} +$ $\gamma \Delta \log y + \delta DI + \phi \Delta \log P_{t-1} + \varepsilon_t$
α	0.023**	0.023**
t-statistic (P-value)	4.260 (0.000)	4.550 (0.000)
$\Delta \log FM_{t-2}$	0.047*	0.060*
t-statistic (P-value)	2.029 (0.049)	2.625 (0.012)
$\Delta \log y$	−0.105**	−0.100**
t-statistic (P-value)	−3.740 (0.001)	−3.657 (0.001)
DI	−0.014**	−.014**
t-statistic (P-value)	−2.820 (0.007)	−2.973 (0.005)
$\Delta \log P_{t-1}$	0.342	0.309
t-statistic (P-value)	3.044 (0.004)	2.943 (0.005)
R^2 adjusted	0.544	0.571
LM test χ^2 12 d.f.	13.744	13.401
(P-value)	(0.317)	(0.341)
RESET test F^3 38 d.f.	2.691	2.122
(P-value)	(0.060)	(0.114)
J-B test χ^2 2 d.f.	0.292	0.350
(P-value)	(0.864)	(0.839)
CUSUM, CUSUMSQ	Passed	Passed

Notes:
* denotes significance at 5 per cent level.
** denotes significance at 1 per cent level.
d.f. denotes degree of freedom.
LM test is a test for serial correlation up to order 12.
RESET is Ramsey's test for mis-specification using the squared, third and fourth power of the predicted dependent variable.
J-B test is the Jacque-Berra test for normality of the disturbance term.
CUSUM and CUSUMSQ are tests for the stability of the estimated parameters.

- The importance of output growth in Vietnam for the short-run control of inflation is underlined by the highly significant and negative coefficient between inflation and change in industrial output. Similar results were reported by Edwards (1983) for Latin American countries experiencing persistently high inflation and dollarisation.
- The favourable effect on inflation of the decision to reinforce the State Bank's control over foreign exchange is confirmed.

CONCLUSIONS

This chapter has argued that dollarisation, whether measured in terms of the volume of US dollars circulating in the economy or in terms of the propensity of the people to change their dong into US dollars, is significant in Vietnam. Economic liberalisation since 1989 has increased the volume of US dollars in the economy as well as the desire to hold dollars. In particular, we have shown that on average, for each 1 per cent increase in the expected depreciation of the dong, there is a 0.3 per cent shift out of dong and into US dollar holdings, and that this shift occurs very quickly – within the space of one month.

There is significant and rapid feedback between dollarisation and inflation in Vietnam. On average, for each 1 per cent increase in foreign currency deposits relative to domestic currency holdings, there is a 0.05–0.06 per cent increase in the inflation rate two months later.

Given that increases in the domestic inflation rate relative to world inflation are likely to increase the expected rate of depreciation of the domestic currency, a significant and rapid response between dollar holdings and inflation could mean that once inflation is entrenched in the economy, there would be a vicious circle of increased expected depreciation leading to increased dollarisation, leading in turn to increased inflation and increased expected depreciation. Thus the presence of dollarisation could make the Vietnamese economy highly vulnerable to currency and financial crises.

Repeated attempts to control dollarisation through administrative measures (in 1994 and more recently in 1998) have had limited success. Indeed, these measures could well drive US dollars out of the official banking system into the informal sector, as well as having negative effects on foreign investment. Given the very rapid speed at which expected devaluation results in dollarisation, and dollarisation leads to inflation in Vietnam, there is a genuine need to establish confidence in the government's political will to limit budget deficits and build a strong financial sector. An important policy implication is therefore that the government should assiduously avoid monetising the budget deficit. Once the credibility of government stabilisation measures and confidence in the banking sector and local currency have been established, then there is every possibility of building a virtuous circle of reduced dollar holdings, lower inflation and a reduced expected rate of depreciation of the dong, leading in turn to further de-dollarisation and so on. In this way a resilient financial sector could contribute significantly to stabilisation and viable long-run growth in Vietnam.

NOTES

1. Appendix 1, which shows the theoretical derivation of this equation from a transactions cost model of currency substitution, is available from the authors on request.
2. Appendix 2, giving an analysis of the econometric properties and justifications for using OLS, is available from the authors on request.
3. Appendix 3, which is available from the authors on request, gives a formal derivation of Equation (6.1a).

7. Borrower Transaction Costs and Segmented Markets: A Study of the Rural Credit Market in Vietnam

Tran Tho Dat

One of the legacies of rapid economic growth in many developing countries is increased income inequality, particularly between the urban and rural areas. Vietnam is no exception, and the need to redress this imbalance has led to an enormous amount of credit being injected into the rural sector through an evolving system of formal financial institutions (World Bank 1995). However, given the ceiling on formal interest rates and the excess demand for formal sector credit that this generates, formal sector lenders are forced to rely on interest rate substitutes to ration credit. An important substitute comes in the form of transaction costs imposed on borrowers. These include, for example, application fees, travelling expenses to get to the bank, gifts and entertainment expenses for bank officials, and lost work days as a result of delays in loan processing.

On the other hand, as pointed out by McLeod in Chapter 5, reform of the domestic financial sector in Indonesia brought significant benefits, including an increase in the number of bank branches and better access to credit from the formal sector on the part of ordinary Indonesians. Reform of Vietnam's financial sector should therefore result not only in improved financial intermediation and enhanced growth and investment, but also greater access to bank credit on the part of small borrowers in the countryside.

To substantiate the assertion that financial deregulation in Vietnam could improve the access of small borrowers to formal credit, the author undertook a survey in the Binhluc district of Vietnam in 1996.[1] Based on data from the survey, this chapter discusses and then quantifies transaction costs in Vietnam's rural credit market. It then shows that the existence of such costs divides the market into formal and informal segments, with the small borrowers resorting to informal finance because of the high transaction costs per unit of borrowing facing them in the formal sector of the market.[2] It is also shown that the level of transaction costs is negatively related to the interest rates being charged.

This would seem to indicate that 'cheap' loans provided by the government and aid donors and targeted at the rural poor do not, in fact, reach those for whom they are intended. Because of the high per unit transaction costs of these loans, the very small borrowers tend to self-select out of the formal credit market. Furthermore, removing ceilings on interest rates could induce the banks to lower their transaction costs and hence improve access to formal sector credit for small borrowers in Vietnam's rural areas. A corollary of these findings is that genuine income support programs for the rural poor could better be pursued as welfare programs rather than as 'cheap loans' via the formal financial system.

THE CONCEPT OF BORROWER TRANSACTION COSTS

Transaction costs play an important role in credit allocation and the structure of the rural financial market, as shown in past studies.[3] They can be considered to be those costs incurred in carrying out a transaction other than the cost of the good or service itself. Broadly speaking, they may include search costs, selection costs, contract negotiation costs, monitoring costs and any residual costs associated with the settlement of broken or amended contracts. More specifically, they can be defined as those costs incurred in formalising and executing contracts (Graham, Schreider and Leon 1996, p. 82).

In the financial market, transaction costs refer to the resources required to transfer one unit of funds between participants (borrowers and lenders). According to Cuevas (1984), they are a measure of 'friction' in the functioning of financial markets. There are specific reasons why financial transactions generate significant costs. First, the essence of such a transaction lies in the characteristic that it is completed only when the borrower finally discharges the loan; consequently financial transactions involve uncertainty. In the process of finding suitable borrowers, lenders have to collect and analyse information to assess the capacity and willingness of borrowers to repay the loan. At the same time, borrowers searching for appropriate lenders have to demonstrate their creditworthiness. This is especially important in the rural financial markets of developing countries, where information on the creditworthiness of customers is restricted and costly. Second, participants in financial transactions have to negotiate the terms and conditions of the contract and monitor its execution. The level of transaction costs among participants is influenced by the efficiency of financial markets, which in turn depends on financial regulations, the internal efficiency of banks and other financial intermediaries, and the interaction of demand for and the supply of credit (Puhazhendhi 1995, p. 4).

Transaction costs are incurred by both borrowers and lenders. Borrower transaction costs, our main concern, include all non-interest expenses that borrowers incur in the course of arranging a loan.

Quantification of Borrower Transaction Costs

The essential difference between formal and informal lenders in the district in which we carried out our rural household survey – Binhluc in the Red River Delta – is that the former operate under the regulation of the State Bank of Vietnam while the latter do not. Under this classification, formal institutions in the survey area consist of the District Vietnam Bank for Agriculture (VBA) and a number of Popular Credit Funds; informal lenders comprise relatives and friends, traders, moneylenders and rotating savings and credit associations (ROSCAs). The most important source of formal credit is the VBA.

Since formal sector lending rates are subject to ceilings below the market clearing rate in the area in which we carried out our study, the bank cannot afford to charge a premium for extra risk or hire additional personnel to conduct risk-reducing activities. It therefore has to devise ways to ration excess demand while still selecting lower-risk borrowers from among the loan applicants. One of the rationing mechanisms adopted by the bank is to implement a complex delivery system through which it can sort and screen potential borrowers. At least four kinds of borrower transaction costs were observed in the district covered by our survey, as follows.[4]

1. *Loan charges* through application fees collected by the lender (over and above interest payments); service fees collected by local officials or commune/village leaders; and service fees related to collateral certification.
2. *Travel expenses* incurred to obtain loans. Bad roads and poor infrastructure meant that it took a long time for borrowers to complete all the necessary paperwork and have documents signed by various authorities in accordance with bank requirements. The most common means of transportation was bicycle. The distance from borrowers' homes to the bank ranged from one to fifteen kilometres, averaging 5.7 kilometres. Lack of understanding of lending regulations contributed to the frequency of visits. The number of trips required to transact a loan ranged from one to five, averaging two.
3. *Costs to attract bank officials' attention.* Because of the ceiling on interest rates, the bank seems to have perceived itself to be doing loan applicants a favour in processing their applications. Borrowers – who had to deal with several layers of bureaucracy when negotiating a loan – commonly offered bank officials gifts of tea and cigarettes, and in many cases effectively had to pay for an official to make a 'field trip' to assess the application. In addition, because of the variety of lending schemes on offer, some offering

more attractive terms and conditions than others,[5] rent-seeking by bank officials in the form of implicit or explicit demands for gratuities, gifts and bribes was not uncommon. Since it was felt that borrowers might be reluctant to disclose the amount spent on bribes and gifts, our survey asked respondents to report instead total cash expenditures incurred in obtaining a loan, net of interest payments and application fees.

4. The most significant transaction cost incurred by borrowers was *the time involved in applying for the loan*. The bank required considerable documentation in support of loan applications, and there were usually long delays between the filing of an application and the rendering of a decision by the bank's loan officers.[6] When borrowers were asked how long they had to wait between first applying for a loan and actually receiving it, the answers ranged from 7 to 35 days. On average it took one week to obtain approval for loans below 10 million dong; ten days for loans above 10 million dong; and one month for loans above 20 million dong (as these required approval from the VBA at the provincial level).

Delays in obtaining a loan imposed costs on the applicant in terms of forgone opportunities. Interviewees were asked to state the number of workdays actually missed in order to apply for a loan as distinct from total waiting time. To determine the opportunity cost of this time, it was essential to calculate the cost of each lost workday. Borrowers were therefore asked to recall payments made to hire replacement labour while the applicant attended to the loan, or to evaluate the amount of income forgone because the applicant needed to take time off work. If the borrower was unable to provide such information, the prevailing market wage rate for male workers in the borrower's occupation in the village was used to estimate the cost of each lost workday (Ahmed 1982, p. 84). The rate prevailing in the area covered by our survey was the land levelling wage rate.

The frequency distribution of loans by total transaction costs and its two components – cash outlays and the cost of lost workdays – is shown in Table 7.1. It can be seen that 51 per cent of borrowers incurred cash costs of 26–50,000 dong and 3 per cent cash costs of 101–125,000 dong. The average for the sample was about 50,000 dong, accounting for 57 per cent of total transaction costs. The two components of cash outlays incurred by borrowers in the process of applying for and receiving a loan were application fees, and travel and other expenses, which accounted respectively for 20 and 38 per cent of total transaction costs. About 90 per cent of borrowers incurred costs of 26–50,000 dong and 8 per cent costs of 51–75,000 dong in lost work time. The average cost for the sample was 36,640 dong, accounting for 42.5 per cent of total transaction costs. Although not shown in Table 7.1, our research found that about 21 per cent of the time lost was spent travelling to

Table 7.1 Distribution of Loans by Transaction Cost of Borrowing from the Formal Sector

Transaction Cost	Application Fees (1)	Travel and Other Expenses (2)	Cash Outlays (3) = (1) + (2)	Cost of Lost Workdays (4)	Total Transaction Costs (5) = (3) + (4)
0–25,000 dong					
No.	69	33	8	2	–
(%)	(88.46)	(42.31)	(10.25)	(2.56)	–
26–50,000 dong					
No.	9	36	40	70	3
(%)	(11.54)	(46.15)	(51.28)	(89.74)	(3.85)
51–75,000 dong					
No.	–	6	23	6	27
(%)	–	(7.69)	(29.49)	(7.69)	(34.62)
76–100,000 dong					
No.	–	3	5	–	31
(%)	–	(3.85)	(6.41)	–	(39.74)
101–125,000 dong					
No.	–	–	2	–	10
(%)	–	–	(2.56)	–	(12.82)
Over 125,000 dong					
No.	–	–	–	–	7
(%)	–	–	–	–	(8.97)
Sample average					
thousand dong	17.01	32.76	49.77	36.64	86.41
(%)	(19.64)	(37.82)	(57.46)	(42.54)	(100)

Note: – indicates zero.

and from the bank, 29 per cent in the bank and the remaining 50 per cent in carrying out procedures required by the bank. The distribution of loans by total transaction costs shows that about 74 per cent of borrowers had costs of 51–100,000 dong and about 9 per cent costs in excess of 125,000 dong. On average the prospective formal sector borrower had to pay 86,410 dong in addition to interest charges – without knowing whether or not the loan application would be accepted. In practice, however, it is noted that borrowers were usually informed of the probable decision at an early stage of negotiations, so the risk cost was not as high as it might appear. Table 7.1 indicates that prospective borrowers had to have about 50,000 dong on hand to pay out-of-pocket expenses. Those who did not have this amount available had to forgo the formal credit market.

Since there has been no previous study of transaction costs in the rural credit market in Vietnam, the estimates of borrower transaction costs given in this study are compared with those obtained for other countries (Table 7.2). All four studies shown in the table – of Bangladesh (Ahmed 1982), Bolivia (Ladman 1984), the Philippines (Abiad, Cuevas and Graham 1988) and Vietnam – are based on field surveys at the farm level and document the explicit (cash outlays) and implicit (cost of lost workdays) non-interest costs incurred by borrowers in the process of securing and repaying their loans. Borrowers in the Philippines incurred the greatest cash outlays and the least lost workdays – 81.1 and 18.9 per cent of total borrower transaction costs respectively – while borrowers in Bangladesh incurred the least cash outlays

Table 7.2 Components of Borrower Transaction Costs in Selected Countries (%)

	Cash Outlays	Cost of Lost Workdays
Bangladesh	51.7	48.3
Bolivia	69.7	30.3
Philippines	81.1	18.9
Vietnam	57.5	42.5

Sources: Abiad, Cuevas and Graham (1988, p. 13); Ahmed (1982, p. 133); Ladman (1984, p. 115); author's survey.

*Table 7.3 Average Borrower Transaction Costs from Formal Sector
         by Loan Size*

Loan Size (dong)	Cash Outlays (thousand dong)	Cost of Lost Workdays (thousand dong)	Total Transaction Costs (thousand dong)	Ratio of Transaction Costs to Loan Size (%)
Below 0.5 million	31.00	12.50	43.50	9.67
0.5–1 million	28.00	28.00	56.00	6.22
1–2.5 million	37.35	37.06	74.41	4.03
2.5–5 million	55.67	37.24	91.35	2.10
5–10 million	55.17	40.00	107.57	1.26
10–20 million	53.70	45.00	142.50	0.71
Over 20 million	71.43	60.00	145.00	0.43
Sample average	49.77	36.64	86.41	1.65

(51.7 per cent) and the most lost workdays (48.3 per cent). Vietnam and Bolivia fall between these extremes on both counts.

Table 7.3 presents a breakdown by loan size of the average transaction costs of borrowing from the formal sector. It can be seen that although total transaction costs are higher for larger loan sizes, they are lower per unit of dong borrowed. When we view transaction costs as a proportion of the loan amount received, the general pattern in the last column of the table supports the hypothesis that transaction costs reflect economies of scale. Small borrowers are therefore penalised by a 'tax' on borrowing at rates proportionally greater than those paid by larger borrowers. While transaction costs make up a sizeable portion of small loans – about 9.7 per cent in the case of loans under 0.5 million dong – they comprise only 0.43 per cent of loans over 20 million dong.

We now compare our estimates of transaction costs with those obtained for selected countries, based on Abiad, Cuevas and Graham's (1988) summaries of the findings of several studies (Table 7.4). If Bangladesh is

Table 7.4 Comparison of Borrower Transaction Costs for Selected Countries

	Bangla-desh	Ecua-dor	Hon-duras	Pan-ama	Peru	Philip-pines	Viet-nam[a]
Transaction costs as % of loan amount							
Sample average	21.7	2.8	3.0	5.2	1.2	3.1	1.65
Small loans	29.4	5.3	5.9	5.7	3.9	4.2	9.67
Transaction costs as % of interest rate							
Sample average	180.8	22.9	23.1	46.4	4.0	17.4[b]	6.45
Small loans	245.0	47.7	45.4	50.9	13.0	25.0	38.37

Notes:
[a] In the case of Vietnam small loans are those below 0.5 million dong.
[b] In their study, Abiad, Cuevas and Graham (1988, p. 31) provide two figures: one for the period before and one for the period after the deregulation of interest rates in the Philippines in around 1985. The figure shown here has been adjusted to cover the entire period encompassed by the study, and is therefore not the same as the figures provided by the authors.

Sources: Abiad, Cuevas and Graham (1988, p. 31); author's survey.

excluded because of its extreme values, transaction costs as a percentage of the loan amount range from a low of 1.2 per cent in Peru to 5.2 per cent in Panama.[7] Similarly, when transaction costs are measured as a proportion of interest rates, Peru has the lowest rate (4 per cent) and Panama the highest (46.4 per cent). If the Philippines figure is considered to represent the mid-point, then transaction costs in Vietnam fall in the lower half of the range.

In general, the level of transaction costs on small loans is two or three times higher than that for the sample average. Although transaction costs as a percentage of loan amount are only a little higher in Vietnam than in Peru based on the sample average, they are far higher in the case of small loans. Indeed Vietnam charges more for small loans as a percentage of loan amount than all other countries except Bangladesh. This comparison of transaction costs for small loans should shed much light on the burden of implicit charges on small borrowers.

Table 7.5 shows borrower transaction costs for loans from the formal and informal sectors. The transaction costs for loans from moneylenders, traders

Table 7.5 Average Borrower Transaction Costs for Formal and Informal Sectors (thousand dong)

	Applica-tion Fees	Travel & Other Expenses	Cash Out-lays	Cost of Lost Work-days	Total Tran-saction Costs	Ratio of Transaction Costs to Loan
	(1)	(2)	(3)=(1)+(2)	(4)	(5)=(3)+(4)	(%)
Formal lenders	17.01	32.76	49.77	36.64	86.41	1.650
Relatives/friends	–	14.11	14.11	4.81	18.92	1.120
Moneylenders	–	–	–	0.11	0.11	0.004
Traders	–	–	–	0.19	0.19	0.053
Other	–	–	–	0.02	0.02	0.004

Note: – indicates zero.

and other informal sources are very low and comprise a negligible proportion of the loan size. Informal lenders do not charge application fees; travel and other expenses are very low; and the cost of lost workdays is minimal. Such lenders utilise local information in screening potential borrowers and can monitor loans at low cost because of their proximity to their clients. Often relying on long-established credit ties, informal lenders enjoy a higher probability of repayment at a lower cost than formal lenders, who lack accumulated information on new clients and are located at a distance. It is worth noting, too, that although in transitional economies like Vietnam and China loans from relatives and friends are usually interest-free (Feder, Lau, Lin and Luo 1989, p. 514), implicit interest payments in the form of free labour, other forms of help and gifts are common, resulting in a higher transaction cost ratio for such loans than is the case for other informal sources.

THE EFFECTIVE INTEREST RATE ON LOANS

One way to look at the effect of borrower transaction costs on the cost of rural credit is to estimate the effective cost of credit to borrowers. Since most borrower transaction costs are incurred before receiving the loan, we assume here for simplicity that all such costs are incurred before and at the time of obtaining the loan. These costs can then be deducted from the loan amount to arrive at the net value of the loan received. The effective interest paid by borrowers will be measured as the difference between the total repayment that is due on maturity of the loan and the net amount borrowed. The effective rate (e) on the net loan received is then

$$e = (1 + r) \left(\frac{L}{L - TC}\right)^{\frac{1}{n}} - 1 \qquad (7.1)$$

where r is the nominal interest rate; n is the loan term (periods); e is the effective interest rate (per cent per period); L is the loan amount; and TC is transaction costs.

Table 7.6 shows average effective monthly rates of interest for different loan sizes in the formal market and in various segments of the informal market. In general the average effective rate decreases as the size of the loan increases, especially in the case of the formal market. For the smallest loans the rate is as high as 5.08 per cent per month, and for the largest loans it is as low as 2.06 per cent. Comparing rates in the two markets, we can see that in the formal market the average effective rate for the sample is 2.66 per cent per month. This is lower than the rate in all segments of the informal market except relatives and friends. However, the formal market imposes a higher effective rate than the informal sector for loans below 0.5 million dong; a lower effective rate applies only to larger loans (those above 0.5 million dong). Partitioning of demand will occur at the loan volume at which farmers are indifferent among different lenders – that is, at which the effective cost of borrowing from alternative sources is equal. In the study area, the calculation of effective rates of interest indicates that partitioning of the credit market will occur at a loan size of 0.5–1 million dong. Changes in the partitioning of the market will depend on changes in borrower transaction costs and/or in the lending rates of each lender. If borrower transaction costs in the formal sector were reduced, partitioning of the market would occur at a smaller loan size, and more small borrowers would seek credit from the formal sector, *ceteris paribus*.

DETERMINANTS OF BORROWER TRANSACTION COSTS

At least three studies have examined the determinants of borrower transaction costs: Ahmed (1982), Abiad, Cuevas and Graham (1988) and Puhazhendhi (1995). Ahmed estimated the determinants of borrower transaction costs for Bangladesh using a single equation in which loan amount is an explanatory variable. However, as pointed out by Cuevas and Graham

Table 7.6 *Effective Interest Rates on Loans from Various Sources by Loan Size (%/month, no. of transactions)*

Average Loan Size (dong)	Formal Sector (%)	(no.)	Moneylenders (%)	(no.)	Traders (%)	(no.)	Others (%)	(no.)	Relatives/Friends (%)	(no.)
Below 0.5 million	5.08	2	4.33	21	4.99	16	4.19	33	0.82	14
0.5–1 million	4.09	5	4.21	7	4.50	1	3.94	8	0.90	14
1–2.5 million	2.87	17	4.04	14	n.a.	n.a.	2.10	1	0.43	15
2.5–5 million	2.50	36	4.63	13	n.a.	n.a.	n.a.	n.a.	1.78	1
5–10 million	2.13	14	3.00	1	n.a.	n.a.	n.a.	n.a.	0.18	1
10–20 million	1.96	2	n.a.	n.a.	n.a.	n.a.	n.a.	n.a.	n.a.	n.a.
Over 20 million	2.06	2	n.a.	n.a.	n.a.	n.a.	n.a.	n.a.	n.a.	n.a.
Sample average	2.66	78	4.29	56	4.96	17	4.09	42	0.72	45

Note: n.a. indicates not available.

106

(1985), transaction costs must be considered part of the total loan price, and hence the appropriate model is a system of simultaneous equations in which transaction costs and loan amount are endogenous variables. Abiad, Cuevas and Graham (1988) and Puhazhendhi (1995) tested this approach for the Philippines and India respectively. We apply this system of simultaneous equations to Vietnam to estimate the determinants of borrower transaction costs.

Borrower transaction costs are hypothesised to be determined by the following factors.

1. Since the bank offers a number of schemes with various interest rates in the survey area, nominal interest rates are considered to be an important factor affecting the transaction costs incurred by borrowers. The lower the interest rate, the greater the benefit of obtaining the loan, hence the more the borrower will be willing to pay. Gifts and bribes are typically proportional to the amount of the preferential loan. In addition, since the procedures used to determine who is eligible for preferential loans are more complicated than those for normal loans, the time taken in obtaining such loans will be longer, and the opportunity cost of lost workdays and other related expenses will be greater.
2. Although the cost of carrying through a loan application is not essentially dependent on the amount applied for, some parts of transaction costs do differ. The larger the loan amount applied for, the more the borrower will have to pay in stamp duty and fees. Also, in the case of large loans, the bank tends to be more careful and to require additional documentation. As a result, the time and other costs incurred by borrowers of larger loans will be greater.
3. Borrower transaction costs may be affected by a borrower's previous credit relationship with the bank or influence over bank personnel. Borrowers who have a prior relationship with the bank can be expected to incur lower transaction costs than those who do not since they will understand the bank's requirements better. It can also be expected that for repeat borrowers with a good credit rating, the bank will simplify its loan procedures. Borrowers who have a close relationship with bank personnel or hold an influential position in the community can be expected to exert their influence to reduce the time and other costs involved in obtaining a loan.[8]
4. Borrower transaction costs are affected by the institutional arrangement used in the credit delivery system; that is, whether the loan is obtained by the individual or through the mediation of a group.
5. Finally, the proximity of the borrower's residence to the bank is expected to affect borrower transaction costs.

In light of these considerations, the borrower transaction costs function is specified as follows:

$$\ln TC = \alpha_0 + \beta_1 \ln r + \beta_2 \ln L + \eta_1 INFLU + \eta_2 PRE$$
$$+ \rho ARR + \mu \ln DIS \qquad (7.2)$$

where:

TC = borrower transaction costs (thousand dong);

r = nominal interest rate (per cent per month);

L = loan amount applied for (thousand dong);

$INFLU$ = dummy variable for influence (1 if the borrower is considered to be influential, 0 if not);

PRE = dummy variable for a prior relationship with the bank (1 if the borrower has a prior relationship with the bank, 0 if not);

ARR = dummy variable for the institutional arrangement used in obtaining the loan (1 if the borrower obtained the loan as an individual, 0 if the borrower obtained the loan through a group); and

DIS = distance from borrower's residence to the bank (kilometres).

The loan demand equation is specified on the basis of the hypothesis that the demand for credit is determined by:

1. the cost of borrowing, comprising the interest rate charged and transaction costs;
2. the financial strength of the borrower, including household assets (the home and other financial assets), and the area of land recognised by land use rights – these variables are used as a measure of the household's wealth and resource endowment and as an indicator of its liquidity requirements for production;[9] and
3. the availability and use of credit from informal sources.

The loan demand equation is specified as

$$\ln L = a_0 + b_1 \ln TC + b_2 \ln r + c_1 \ln ASSET$$
$$+ c_2 \ln FARM + d INFOR \qquad (7.3)$$

where:

$ASSET$ = value of borrower's assets (thousand dong);

$FARM$ = area of land recognised by land use rights (*sao*); and

$INFOR$ = dummy variable for borrower's use of credit from informal sources (1 if the bank borrower has obtained credit from informal sources, 0 if not).

The two-stage least squares method is applied to quantify the influence of these factors on loan demand and borrower transaction costs, based on cross-sectional data from our survey of 75 formal borrowers making 78 transactions. The parameter estimates and *t*-statistics are reported in Table 7.7. The basic statistics of the variables used in this regression are summarised in Appendix Table 7A.1. The correlation matrices for variables in the transaction cost and loan demand equations are shown in Appendix Tables 7A.2 and 7A.3 respectively.

The model passes all diagnostic tests. The F-tests indicate reasonable explanatory power of the model for the survey data. Although the coefficients of determination (R^2) are low in both equations (0.45 in the loan demand equation and 0.38 in the transaction cost equation), this is not unusual for studies using cross-sectional data.

In the loan demand equation, the following two determinants of loan demand are found to be statistically significant: transaction costs incurred by the borrower; and the value of the borrower's assets. As the borrower's up-front transaction costs increase, the borrower will rationally choose to borrow more from the bank so that the total cost of borrowing per unit of dong borrowed declines. The positive sign for the *ASSET* variable, as expected, shows that loan demand is greater for households with more assets. As mentioned earlier, physical assets such as houses are the most common form of collateral for formal loans in the study area. The greater the value of assets available to use as collateral, the larger is the loan that can be applied for.

The interest rate charged on loans has an unexpected sign, although the variable is not statistically significant. This result is surprising. A possible explanation lies in the design of the bank's lending activities, according to which smaller loans usually have lower interest rates. In the area in which we carried out our survey, loans for the poor carried the lowest rate. Our conversations with poor borrowers revealed that they applied for small loans first because they were risk averse, and the activities typically financed through formal loans (cropping and animal husbandry activities) did not require much capital; and second because they felt that an application for a larger loan would stand a good chance of being rejected.

Although the area of land owned by the borrower (*FARM*) has the expected sign, it is not statistically significant. This suggests that formal sector loans are typically used for purposes other than buying inputs for cropping activities. This is consistent with the results of the Vietnam Living Standards Survey, which indicate that the majority of loans for farm inputs come from private credit sources and cooperatives (World Bank 1995, p. 73).

*Table 7.7 Estimation of the Transaction Costs Function (number of
observations = 78)*

Right-hand-side Variable	Jointly Dependent Variable			
	Loan Demand (ln$L$)		Transaction Costs (lnTC)	
	(estimate)	(t-value)	(estimate)	(t-value)
CONST	−14.3632***	−3.7878	3.3011***	5.3777
ln$L$			0.1888**	2.4356
lnTC	3.1460***	4.8096		
ln$r$	0.6796	1.0507	−0.3613*	−1.7595
ln$ASSET$	0.7969***	2.9161		
ln$FARM$	0.0088	0.0427		
INFOR	0.0052	0.0288		
INFLU			0.0220	0.1786
PRE			−0.0342	−0.5683
ARR			0.0343	0.2574
lnDIS			0.0555	1.2830
R^2	0.4466		0.3846	
F-value	11.6218		7.3949	
Diagnostic tests	χ^2		χ^2	
Functional form	0.4896		0.0365	
Normality	0.4922		0.3805	
Heteroscedasticity	0.0081		0.8715	

Note: * indicates significant at the 10 per cent level; ** indicates significant at the 5 per cent
level; *** indicates significant at the 1 per cent level.

The use of informal credit (*INFOR*) is not significant in relation to loan
demand from the formal sector. However, the positive sign of the coefficient
implies that informal credit is a complement to rather than substitute for formal sector credit.

Let us turn now to the transaction cost equation. All coefficients except
INFLU have the expected sign. Two of the six variables in the transaction

cost equation are found to be significant in determining the level of transaction costs: nominal interest rate; and loan amount applied for. The larger the loan amount applied for, the higher is the magnitude of transaction costs. In contrast, the lower the interest rate on the loan, the higher are the transaction costs. Since all the dependent and independent variables are measured in logarithms (except the dummy variables), the regression coefficients are interpreted as elasticities. *Ceteris paribus*, a 10 per cent increase in the nominal interest rate from, say, 2 per cent to 2.2 per cent, reduces transaction costs to borrowers by 3.6 per cent. A 10 per cent increase in loan amount applied for would increase transaction costs by 1.9 per cent.

The variable *INFLU*, which has an unexpected sign, is not significant in our regression. The explanation for this may be that the influential receive favours from bank officers mainly in the form of preferential loans at lower interest rates.[10] In exchange for these cheaper loans, borrowers are expected to offer gifts and gratuities, the cost of which is likely to offset the reduction in transaction costs gained from the use of influence.

The results show that borrowers who had a prior credit relationship with the bank did not incur significantly lower transaction costs than those who did not. This would appear to indicate that the bank relies on current information about the financial strength of borrowers rather than accumulated information on the credit record of loan applicants, and therefore that it lacks experience in making appropriate use of such information.

Although the *ARR* variable has a positive sign, indicating that group borrowing contributes to a reduction in borrower transaction costs, the relationship is not significant. The group borrowing schemes that emerged in the study area in 1995 still play a minor role – only about 6 per cent of total loans outstanding in 1995 were transacted by groups (Binhluc District VBA Branch 1996). Of the 78 transactions with the formal sector in our sample, only eight were undertaken through groups. Our interviews with group members revealed that borrowing through groups is likely to reduce the time spent with the bank seeking a loan, but that this is offset by the increased time spent with the group, especially in the case of newly established groups. The net result is that group borrowing does not contribute significantly to a reduction in the opportunity cost of time for borrowers. Since the cash outlay component of borrower transaction costs is nearly the same for both individual and group borrowing, total borrower transaction costs do not differ significantly between the two.

We now compare our results with those obtained for the Philippines and India, where the simultaneous equations model was also used to estimate the transaction costs function. In the Philippines, Abiad, Cuevas and Graham (1988, p. 15) estimated transaction costs and loan demand functions using two-stage least squares, based on data from a household survey consisting of

176 bank borrowing households in six predominantly rural agricultural areas. The results of the estimations reveal two factors to have been significant: type of bank; and distance to the bank. The bank dummy variable is positively related to borrower transaction costs, indicating that transaction costs are higher for rural than for non-rural banks.[11] The coefficient of the distance variable, which is measured in terms of travelling time to and from the bank, has a positive sign, indicating that borrowers who live further from the bank have significantly higher transaction costs.

The study by Puhazhendhi (1995, p. 62) for India focuses on quantifying the cost-effectiveness of credit flow through a new channel in which the rural poor have better access to the intermediation of non-governmental organisations (NGOs) and self-help groups (SHGs), based on a survey of 150 households. Two variables are significantly related to transaction costs: type of bank (dummy); and NGO/SHG intermediation (dummy). As in the case of the Philippines, the results indicate that borrowing through non-rural (commercial) banks lowers borrower transaction costs. Group lending with the intermediation of NGOs/SHGs lowers transaction costs significantly by reducing the time individual borrowers must spend at bank premises and eliminating cumbersome documentation procedures.

In our study area, where the VBA dominates the formal sector credit market, the bank dummy is not included in the regression. Although group lending through SHGs is positively related to transaction costs, indicating that group lending contributes to a reduction in transaction costs, the relationship is not statistically significant. This raises doubts as to the effectiveness of group lending in reducing transaction costs, although it may be that there are barriers to this type of lending in Vietnam that inhibit its effectiveness. Since the number of loans through group lending schemes was not sufficiently large, a more conclusive answer to this question cannot be provided here.

It is interesting to observe, however, the significant relationship found in our study between transaction costs, loan amount applied for and interest rates. The larger the loan amount applied for, the higher is the magnitude of transaction costs. In contrast, the lower the interest rate, the higher are the transaction costs. These results are also consistent with the findings of Ahmed (1982) for Bangladesh and Cuevas (1984) for Honduras.[12]

SUMMARY AND CONCLUSIONS

Based on data collected from a household survey in Binhluc in Vietnam, the chapter has quantified borrower transaction costs and analysed their role in explaining the quantitative structure of the rural credit market. The determinants of borrower transaction costs have also been examined.

The results indicate that, in order to pursue a formal sector loan, borrowers must have about 50,000 dong available for up-front cash outlays. Those who do not have sufficient funds available to cover these out-of-pocket expenses will preselect out of the formal sector market. This is an important constraint on borrowing by the poor in the formal sector.[13] It has also been shown that among borrower transaction costs, the cost of lost workdays and travel plus other expenses (entertainment, gifts and so on), at 42.5 per cent and 37.8 per cent respectively, make up the two largest parts.

Borrower transaction costs were found to be an important factor in discouraging small borrowers from taking out formal sector loans. While these costs make up a substantial part of total borrowing costs for the smallest borrowers (9.7 per cent of the loan size), they play a negligible role for the largest borrowers (0.4 per cent of the loan size). This confirms the findings of a variety of studies in developing countries. We calculated the effective cost of borrowing from different sources, taking into account both the explicit interest rate and transaction costs. One of the main conclusions drawn is that small borrowers will rationally choose to borrow from informal lenders rather than from the formal sector. The partitioning of the credit market occurs at a loan size of 0.5–1 million dong, at which the effective cost of borrowing from the informal and formal markets is the same. If borrower transaction costs from the formal market were reduced, the market partition would change and more borrowers would be willing to borrow from the formal market.

In the district in which our survey was conducted, the borrower transaction costs observed are likely to be underestimated relative to the level of such costs elsewhere in the country. In remote and mountainous areas with poor roads, borrower transaction costs are likely to be far higher, especially for ethnic minorities who are more isolated from the formal sector. Distance to the bank, poor information flows, and lack of awareness and understanding of loan regulations in the formal sector all contribute to higher borrower transaction costs.[14]

The level of borrower transaction costs is determined by two factors: nominal interest rate; and the loan amount applied for. The insignificance of a prior credit relationship with the bank suggests that the VBA in Binhluc lacks experience in processing information on repeat borrowers. We found that the lower the nominal interest rate, the higher are borrower transaction costs. In the survey area, lower nominal interest rates are often attached to loan funding provided by donors and the government for a particular purpose, such as planting a specified crop, the purchase of machinery or aid to poor farmers. Such loan targeting imposes additional transaction costs on borrowers in complying with the particular eligibility requirements. Borrowers who obtained 'cheap' loans incurred higher non-interest payments. Some could not even afford the cash outlay involved and had to self-select out of the credit programs targeted at them. The estimation of the transaction costs function by the two-stage least squares method indicates that a 10 per cent increase in the nominal interest rate from 2 per cent to 2.2 per cent involves a 3.6 per cent decrease in borrower transaction costs.

It is worth noting that an optimum outcome can be obtained in a segmented market where informal lenders have cost advantages over formal lenders in lending to small borrowers; such an outcome cannot be obtained under an interest rate ceiling, however. If the bank did not place a ceiling on interest rates, the higher rates that would ensue would eliminate or at least reduce excess demand for loans. The bank might then consider simplifying its procedures for obtaining formal sector loans, and reducing or waiving some of its charges (such as application and service fees). This would contribute to a reduction in travel and other opportunity costs for the borrower, whose cash outlay threshold would decline. Consequently, the partition of the market would change in favour of smaller borrowers. The mere injection of credit through the VBA and other formal financial institutions, unaccompanied by an appropriate interest rate policy, has failed to make formal sector credit available to a large portion of the rural population or to create a healthy rural financial market.

NOTES

1. Sample design and the socio-economic characteristics of sample households are discussed in more detail in Tran (1996).
2. The most common explanation for constrained access to formal sector credit among the rural poor is the small size of loans and the lack of collateral (see, for example, Tran et al. 1992, p. 39; Tran and Nguyen 1998, p. 40). However, these studies did not examine in depth why small borrowers did not seek loans from the formal sector.
3. See, for example, Ahmed 1982; Ladman 1984; Cuevas 1984; Cuevas and Graham 1984, 1985; Abiad, Cuevas and Graham 1988; Puhazhendhi 1995.
4. The procedure for borrowing can be summarised as follows. The applicant for a VBA loan must make an appointment with the bank official responsible for the commune/town. This is not easy when the official has no office in the commune/town and is very mobile. After seeing the bank official, the applicant fills out an application form and a paper describing the proposed 'business production project'. The bank official then conducts an on-site visit to evaluate the feasibility of the project. If it is considered feasible, the applicant is asked to fill out another form to certify his or her property and/or land use right, requiring at least three signatures from authorities at different levels of the commune/town. Finally, the bank official arranges for the successful applicant to come to the bank and receive the loan.
5. Under the VBA's loan targeting policy, loans can be subject to a range of interest rates. The bank argues that differentiating interest rates according to the use to which the loan will be put is a way to achieve the government's social objectives. It therefore offers lower rates on loans to finance fixed assets, loans to encourage longer-term investment in agriculture and loans to the poor.
6. The survey found considerable inefficiency in bank practices. There was much overlap of

paperwork and procedures, and in practice bank officials paid little attention to the forms that had been filled out.

7. As Abiad, Cuevas and Graham (1988, p. 31) point out, Bangladesh's unusually high transaction costs as a proportion of both loan amount and interest rate can be attributed to the very small loan sizes and relatively low nominal interest rate prevailing in that country. For example, whereas the average loan size is US$130 in Bangladesh and the explicit interest rate is 12 per cent per annum, in Vietnam the comparable figures are about US$500 and 25.2 per cent per annum respectively.

8. Borrowers were asked whether they had an established relationship with the bank's officers or held a community position. As some borrowers may have been reluctant to disclose such information, we double checked their answers with other farmers in the community.

9. In Vietnam the government owns the land, and farm households hold land use rights rather than owning the land outright. According to the Land Law promulgated in 1993, however, land use rights may be transferred, mortgaged, rented, exchanged or inherited.

10. An examination of the correlation matrix of the independent variables (Appendix Table 7A.2) shows a low correlation among all variables except *INFLU* and $\ln r$, which have a correlation of –0.66. However, conventional wisdom suggests that such a correlation is not high enough to create a multicollinearity problem.

11. The dummy variable for type of bank is equal to 1 for rural banks and 0 for non-rural banks. Non-rural banks include commercial banks, private development banks, cooperative rural banks, land bank cooperatives, the Philippine National Bank and the Development Bank of the Philippines.

12. A study carried out by Cuevas in Honduras in the early 1980s found that a 1 per cent increase in the nominal interest rate in a subsidised credit program would lead to a 1 per cent decline in borrower transaction costs (Graham, Schreider and Leon 1996, p. 90).

13. Average annual income per household in Binhluc district in 1995 was 560,000 dong (Binhluc District Statistical Office 1996).

14. Of 150 household heads interviewed during the survey, two did not know that there was a formal lender in the area, and 37 knew of but did not understand the lending regulations of formal lenders.

Appendix Table 7A.1 Statistical Summary of Variables Used in Equations
(7.2) and (7.3) (number of observations = 78)

Variable	Mean	Standard Deviation	Variance	Minimum	Maximum
ln*TC*	4.4176	0.2897	0.0839	3.7377	5.0434
ln*r*	0.7753	0.1782	0.0318	0.4055	1.0296
ln*L*	8.2462	0.9526	0.9075	5.9915	11.5129
INFLU	0.1410	0.3503	0.1227	0	1
PRE	0.3590	0.4828	0.2331	0	1
ARR	0.8974	0.3054	0.0932	0	1
ln*DIS*	1.5832	0.6496	0.4220	0.0000	2.7081
ln*ASSET*	10.2450	0.3214	0.1033	9.7981	11.7753
ln*FARM*	1.9163	0.4371	0.1911	0.6931	2.7726
INFOR	0.6667	0.4745	0.2251	0	1
ln*TCFIT**	4.4176	0.1888	0.0356	3.8093	4.8234
ln*LFIT**	8.2642	0.6537	0.4273	6.5966	9.7255

Note: *Indicates the fitted value in the first stage regression of ln*TC* and ln*L* on all independent variables in Equations (7.2) and (7.3).

Appendix Table 7A.2 Correlation Matrix of Variables Used in Equation (7.2)

	ln*r*	ln*L* (ln*LFIT*)	ln*DIS*	*INFLU*	*PRE*	*ARR*
ln*r*	1.00					
ln*L* (ln*LFIT*)	−0.30 (−0.44)	1.00 (1.00)				
ln*DIS*	0.01	0.16 (0.35)	1.00			
INFLU	−0.66	0.39 (0.57)	0.09	1.00		
PRE	−0.20	0.23 (0.34)	−0.03	0.23	1.00	
ARR	−0.22	0.46 (0.68)	0.18	0.14	0.16	1.00

Appendix Table 7A.3 Correlation Matrix of Variables Used in Equation (7.3)

	ln*r*	ln*TC* (ln*TCFIT*)	ln*ASSET*	ln*FARM*	*INFOR*
ln*r*	1.00				
ln*TC* (ln*TCFIT*)	−0.42 (−0.65)	1.00 (1.00)			
ln*ASSET*	−0.09	0.16 (0.24)	1.00		
ln*FARM*	−0.05	−0.13 (−0.15)	0.10	1.00	
INFOR	0.06	−0.12 (−0.19)	−0.05	0.07	1.00

PART THREE

East Asian Export-oriented Industrialisation and Vietnam's Strategic Directions

8. Industrialisation in ASEAN: Some Analytical and Policy Lessons

Hal Hill

INTRODUCTION

Although somewhat overshadowed by Japan, the Northeast Asian newly industrialising economies (NIEs) and, more recently, the China colossus, during the 30 years from 1966 the four high-growth ASEAN economies – Indonesia, Malaysia, Singapore and Thailand – grew more quickly than almost any other group of countries. In the early 1960s, with the exception of Singapore, the process of industrialisation had barely commenced. What little manufacturing activity there was consisted primarily of simple resource processing industries and factories producing a limited array of basic consumer goods for the domestic market. Manufactured exports were minuscule, there were few large modern industrial plants, and the presence of multinational enterprises (MNEs) in manufacturing was very limited beyond what had been established in and remained from the colonial era.

Prior to the current foreign exchange and financial crises, all four economies had emerged as significant industrial powers. Annual industrial growth rates of 8–10 per cent or more had been sustained for nearly three decades, far-reaching structural changes had occurred, and perhaps most important of all, all four had achieved internationally oriented industrialisation. Industrial growth has been rapid, exceeding developing country averages by 50–100 per cent in the 1970s and by a much larger margin since 1980. The share of the manufacturing sector in output has more than doubled in both Indonesia and Malaysia, and nearly so in Thailand. All four economies have now passed a key turning point in the long sweep of economic development in that manufacturing output exceeds that of agriculture. (The absence of such structural change in the – until recently – slower-growing Philippine economy is by contrast striking.) Manufacturing employment has also grown, at a slower pace owing to rising capital intensity. There has been a spectacular increase in export orientation. In 1970, in all but Singapore, manufactures constituted less than 10 per cent of merchandise exports; in

Indonesia they were virtually non-existent. By the mid-1990s, manufactures had become the major engine of export growth, even in the resource-rich economies of Indonesia and Malaysia (and also in the Philippines), contributing at least half and more commonly two-thirds of the total.

These four countries are of course highly diverse, and have little in common other than geographic proximity, high growth and a commitment (in varying degrees) to openness. The ratio of GDP per capita from the highest to the lowest is 25:1 (or, in purchasing power parity terms, 8:1). Their populations range from over 200 million to less than 3 million. Exports as a share of GDP vary from about 180 per cent to 25 per cent. There are also great differences in their history, institutions, policy-making structures, foreign investment environments and natural resource endowments. Owing to this combination of great diversity and rapid growth, the ASEAN industrialisation experience holds enormous policy and analytical lessons for the region. These four countries constitute an ideal laboratory for the examination of a number of important issues related to the determinants and sustainability of rapid industrialisation in developing countries. The purpose of this chapter is to explore some of these lessons. I focus in successive sections on the issue of industrial policy and a selective versus a neutral incentives regime, strategies towards foreign investment and technological development, the various paths towards export orientation, the sources of growth debate – Krugman's (1994) famous 'perspiration versus inspiration' equation – the changing size distribution of industry, and the question of seller concentration and the case for some sort of competition policy. The first half of the chapter is concerned primarily with policy issues and the latter half more with outcomes and structures, but all sections combine elements of both. The exposition is necessarily highly condensed. The reader is referred to the references for more detailed information.[1] No empirical material is included.[2]

Two points need to be emphasised at the outset. First, among developing countries, industrial growth and economic growth almost invariably go hand in hand. I know of no developing country that has achieved rapid and sustained industrial growth in the absence of a high rate of GDP growth. The converse generally applies as well, apart from special instances of economies that are highly dependent on mining or services. Thus the explanations for rapid industrial growth are to be found in those factors which underpin high rates of economic growth: sound macroeconomic management, international orientation, observance of property rights and judicial independence, and investments in human capital and physical infrastructure. This study is not concerned with these general factors, but rather takes them as given and focuses instead on the specifics of a range of industrial policy issues.

Second, the four high-growth ASEAN economies now look far less attractive as a model to emulate than they did a year ago. Indonesia is experiencing its most serious economic crisis since Independence; Thailand has negative growth for the first time in over three decades. Economic growth has also slowed significantly in Malaysia, the Philippines and even Singapore. The crisis has also resulted in a sharp slowdown in industrial growth. However, its origins have little to do with industrialisation and industrial policy but lie rather in the macroeconomic and financial realm: rapidly rising short-term foreign debt in the context of fixed (or quasi-fixed) exchange rates (tied to the appreciating US dollar), and poorly managed financial systems. Other factors have exacerbated these problems: the absence of a regional locomotive, given the parlous state of the Japanese economy; and, in Indonesia, the stand-off between the government and the International Monetary Fund (IMF), combined with domestic political factors.

INDUSTRIAL POLICY

What role has industry policy – defined here as a deliberately non-neutral incentives regime – played in ASEAN's rapid industrialisation? This is one of the most extensively debated development policy issues, much of it focused on Northeast Asia, but now also engaging ASEAN.[3] At the risk of oversimplification, two contending paradigms have emerged. According to one, the major contribution of governments has been in getting the 'fundamentals' right: macroeconomic stability, predictable and stable policy regimes, improved physical infrastructure and education, a reasonably adequate system of property rights and legal infrastructure, and increasing openness to international commerce. An alternative paradigm accepts some or all of the above prescriptions,[4] but argues that it is an insufficient recipe for industrial success. This school rejects an emphasis based primarily on economic liberalism and static comparative advantage. It argues that Korea, Taiwan and Japan owe their success to selective industrial policies – targeting industries, 'picking winners', and deliberately 'getting prices wrong' through fiscal incentives, subsidised credit, import protection and direct investment. In the words of one widely cited author: 'not only has Korea not gotten relative prices right, it has deliberately gotten them "wrong". Nor is Korea an isolated case. It is part of a general group of ... late industrializers' (Amsden 1989, pp. 139–40).

ASEAN is a fertile area for testing these competing theories. The primary focus here is on Indonesia, Malaysia and Thailand.[5] These three economies have industrialised rapidly, and their governments, particularly in Indonesia, have intervened extensively at the industry level. Superficially at least, therefore, the ASEAN evidence might be interpreted as supporting the notion that selective industrial policies have contributed to their success.

However, on closer examination such an argument receives little empirical support. For the arguments of the interventionist school to be convincing, it is obviously insufficient merely to point to the coexistence of selectivity and rapid growth. There has to be a demonstration of causality, and the research emerging on this topic finds little evidence of this kind. The standard tools of industrial policy have been employed in all three economies, although over time deliberate policy-induced distortions have declined. Interindustry variations in protection have been considerable, especially in Indonesia. A large state enterprise sector is present in all; again Indonesia stands out, as does Malaysia to a lesser extent. Subsidised credit and interest rate controls have existed in these three countries for at least some of the past 25 years. Fiscal incentives have also been employed. Moreover, official policy pronouncements give the impression of coherence, in the sense that governments have stated their intention to develop specific industries (for example, automobiles) or sectors such as heavy and technology-intensive industry.

The issue here is whether policy implementation has matched the official statements, and whether it is possible to discern any development impacts from these interventions. Establishing cause and effect in this area is of course difficult: the causal mechanisms are still not well understood; there are likely to be long lags in the relationships; and detailed micro-level information is required to address the question definitively. On the first general question, it is clear that industrial policy has lacked coherence. The political economy of industrial policy in ASEAN has yet to be written, but contending policy schools in all three countries have pulled in different directions. Ministries of Finance and central banks have been concerned primarily with macroeconomic stability and have propounded market-oriented microeconomic strategies. They have usually exerted enough influence to keep advocates of selective industrial policy in check, especially during periods of economic difficulty. The interventionist groups, moreover, have rarely spoken with one voice. Typically, they have comprised a diverse group of interests, ranging from those with a genuine industrial promotion mission to brazen rent seekers.[6]

The record of industrial policy in these three countries is therefore quite unlike even the idealised model of Northeast Asia. Promotional measures in ASEAN have been prone to abuse, implementation has been sporadic and often short-lived, and there has been little systematic attempt to prescribe conditionality, in the sense of linking incentives to tightly defined performance criteria. It is therefore hardly surprising that studies that have examined the relationship between interindustry variations in government assistance (for example, through protection and credit subsidies) and subsequent (lagged) performance, according to a variety of measures, have found little evidence of causality. In the case of Indonesia, a survey of selective policy instruments introduced or extended in the 1970s and early 1980s – protection, credit subsidies, state enterprises – detected very little evidence of such a strategy having 'worked' according to a range of subsequent performance criteria (Hill 1996). Similarly, Warr's (1995) study of several policy correlates of export performance in Thailand over the period 1970–89 revealed a remarkably consistent picture of negative coefficients for all variables and time periods. In the case of Malaysia, it is very difficult to find any evidence in support of the proposition that the government's promotion of heavy industry over the period 1978–86 promoted efficient industrial growth (Athukorala and Menon 1997).

The economic crisis has weakened still further the case for an interventionist industrial policy. Attempts to finance uneconomic, highly politicised industrial projects through a shaky financial system, or through foreign borrowings with implicit government guarantees, have contributed to the current difficulties. Moreover, senior technocrats in charge of macroeconomic policy have been distracted from their primary policy responsibilities in their efforts to oppose such grandiose projects. This has been particularly evident in Indonesia in recent years, as these officials have sought without much success to contain the excesses of both Minister (now President) Habibie's ambitious high-tech projects, and the ever expanding business empires of President Soeharto's children (extending now to his grandchildren).

Thus theory, empirical evidence and the political economy of industrial policy making all provide little support for the notion that a selective incentives strategy has contributed to the region's rapid, internationally oriented industrialisation. Rather, the limited attempts to quantify the interindustry effects of micro-level interventions in ASEAN support the 'fundamentals' camp, in the sense that these countries have industrialised extremely rapidly without a coherent industry policy. Moreover, there is evidence to suggest that growth has been more efficient and rapid during periods of policy liberalisation. The link between liberalisation and economic performance is, of course, extremely difficult to verify empirically, as even the huge World Bank project on the subject demonstrated,[7] but there is a strong and positive association between the rate of total factor productivity (TFP) growth and a more liberal trade regime.

THE ROLE OF FOREIGN INVESTMENT AND TECHNOLOGY

Policies on foreign investment and technology development are also central to the debate over industrial strategy and policy. They are closely linked, in the sense that foreign direct investment (FDI) is one of the principal means of acquiring new technologies. But they also raise different analytical and policy issues: FDI policy relates to broader questions of openness (discussed in the conclusion), while much of the literature on technology policy is concerned with the appropriate role of the state in overcoming market failure, and therefore relates more closely to the discussion in the previous section. With this in mind, the two topics are treated separately here.

FDI Policy

The role of FDI in the ASEAN economies, and perceptions about that role in the host economy, has changed dramatically over the past quarter-century. In the mid-1970s, for example, only Singapore had an unambiguously open stance (although Malaysia, too, was generally quite open); in early 1974 a tour of ASEAN capitals by the then Japanese Prime Minister provoked a violent response in some of them. In the 1990s, if there is a concern about FDI, it is more likely that the host economy is attracting *insufficient* foreign capital. The pendulum has swung completely and decisively, as governments recognise that FDI, in concert with appropriate domestic policies, is an effective means of acquiring new technologies and promoting exports. Nowadays, one rarely hears high-level support for the once popular Korean model (on which see, for example, Kim 1997), which included a restrictive approach to FDI as a means of developing indigenous technological capability. The China factor – the need to compete with what is now, by a large margin, the developing world's largest recipient of FDI – has become an important additional element in the swing of the pendulum.

There will undoubtedly be nationalist opposition to the inevitable increase in foreign ownership in the region in the wake of the current crisis, as financial institutions and firms recapitalise their operations through injections of foreign equity. But with the possible exception of Indonesia, the principal policy issue in these countries is whether host economies should adopt a neutral or proactive strategy towards FDI. Major business conglomerates in the region are now more confident of their capacity to negotiate with MNEs, and for the first time all countries have emerged as outward investors – Singapore on a large scale.

Singapore's FDI policies are often held up as a model for how developing countries might manage the MNE presence, and it is therefore useful to summarise the main features.[8]

• All sectors are open to foreign firms, except for a small number of instances where, on national security or strategic grounds, it is clearly stated to the contrary.

- One hundred per cent foreign ownership and generous numbers of senior expatriate personnel are permitted in almost all circumstances.
- Policy consistency, in the sense of the absence of major policy swings, is a very high priority.
- The Economic Development Board plays an activist role in promoting the advantages of the country internationally, and in ensuring that foreign firms encounter minimal disruption during start-up and the early operational phase.
- Fiscal incentives are employed liberally and aggressively, often on a firm-specific basis, as one means of ensuring that the returns for Singapore-based companies are (on a risk-adjusted basis) competitive with the best internationally.
- The government seeks to extract the benefits of FDI through the establishment of joint venture technology and training programs, and a range of other initiatives.
- Once firms are established, they are subject to a clear but 'hard' regime in which there would be no scope for tax evasion, corruption, avoidance of labour regulations and Central Provident Fund commitments, or import protection.

The approach in the other three countries has gradually come to resemble that of Singapore more closely. Initially their investment boards were ambivalent in the management of their twin roles of promotion and regulation, with the result that neither was effectively achieved.[9] In the 1990s, the crucial difference is that the more open trade regimes have removed most of the 'tariff bargaining' that was a frequent feature of import substituting MNE entry in the 1970s. The shift towards export orientation has therefore not only attracted internationally efficient foreign capital, but also altered the political economy of investment regulation.

Fiscal incentives remain in some countries, but they have been de-emphasised. Indonesia, for example, abolished them completely in 1984, in the context of sweeping taxation reforms. By the late 1980s it was attracting record FDI inflows without having to offer costly and corruption-prone incentives. Singapore has admittedly retained such incentives, but this is in the context of a completely open economy and a ruthlessly incorruptible bureaucracy. In any case, it is not obvious that such an incentives regime is essential, as compared to the alternative of Hong Kong-style uniformly low rates without concessions. Hong Kong's superior record in the growth-accounting exercises referred to above constitutes prima facie support for this proposition.

Technology Policy

As noted, technology policy and strategies relate more closely to the issue of government intervention to overcome market failure. In particular, it is argued that markets will underinvest in most forms of education, training, and research and development (R&D). Since these are crucial ingredients for rapid economic development, so the argument goes, governments have a role to play, both at a general level and in quite industry-specific domains. This school of thought adopts an intermediate position between the orthodox neoclassical prescription and the more interventionist approach.[10] It shares with the former a concern about the consequences of extensive import protection, credit subsidies and an inefficient state enterprise sector. But it has more in common with the latter group in its willingness to advocate a larger government role in the provision of education, in playing a catalytic role in technological development and, in certain tightly defined instances, in fostering infant industry growth.

The issue is of particular relevance to the three lower-income ASEAN countries. All have experienced a first round of labour-intensive, export-oriented industrialisation which, building on low labour costs, was propelled by a combination of competitive exchange rates, reforms that placed export-oriented industries at least on a near free-trade footing, and a reasonably adequate international transport and communications infrastructure. However, rising wages, most obviously in Malaysia and Thailand, are shifting these countries' comparative advantage out of labour-intensive industries, notwithstanding large-scale labour immigration. Their challenge is to compete downwards with lower-wage countries such as China, and upwards with the much stronger technological base of the NIEs. While the ASEAN record in the provision of primary education has been good, it is much weaker in the areas of secondary, tertiary and vocational education, in industry-level R&D institutes and in firm-level R&D activity.[11] Governments in some countries, especially Indonesia, have generally defined 'technology policy' as synonymous with a 'great leap forward' in hugely ambitious and uneconomic high-tech projects. The state-owned Indonesian aircraft firm, IPTN, is a case in point. Its investment over the past two decades, conservatively valued (pre-crisis) at US$3 billion, has yet to meet any form of market test, while the project has drained much more worthy investments – ranging from primary education and health care to industrial extension programs – of much needed funds (Hill and Thee 1998). Such an approach is seemingly ignorant of the fact that clever and nimble supply-side interventions can enhance efficiency if – as in Taiwan, for instance (Lin 1998) – they are implemented in the context of an open, well-managed economy with a strong education system. Moreover, the intellectual approach underpinning these large projects neglects the fundamental lesson of all the best studies of technological development, that it is a long-term, gradual and evolutionary process.[12]

Technology can of course be imported, through FDI and skilled labour inflows, and this is already occurring on a large scale. However, local absorptive capacities need to develop commensurately, and this is not yet happening quickly. Private sector R&D and training is very limited, in part because firms are unable to appropriate the returns from such investment in an environment where labour mobility is very high. Government research institutes, with a few exceptions, are poorly funded and weakly linked to the private sector. In such an environment there is a case for government intervention to 'kick start' the process of private sector R&D, by funding dynamic, private sector-driven research institutes, by fostering the development of effective cooperative institutions at the industry level to overcome the appropriability problems of free-riders, and through carefully structured fiscal incentives. Thus far, only Singapore has made substantial progress in these areas. Within the space of a decade, its R&D expenditure as a percentage of GDP has risen from something like the middle-income norm (about 0.3 per cent) in the mid-1980s to close to the Organisation for Economic Cooperation and Development (OECD) average (1.5 per cent). The other three countries, while effective macro managers, have a much poorer record of innovative micro-level management.

Thus the evidence on 'state and market' in ASEAN's industrial success is mixed. There is little persuasive evidence to demonstrate that governments have achieved rapid, efficient growth through selective industrial policies seeking systematically to direct the allocation of resources towards industries which have later become internationally competitive. Rather, much of the benefit of this selective intervention – whether in the form of protection, state enterprises or subsidised credit – has been captured by vested interests intent on personal enrichment. At the same time, paradoxically, with the exception of Singapore, governments have tended to underinvest in areas where markets do not operate effectively, failing to deliver certain types of support infrastructure which is needed to promote an efficient industrial sector. This record is all the more puzzling when it is recalled that Indonesia, Malaysia and Thailand have all developed reasonably effective agricultural extension services in which government played an important role in facilitating the rapid introduction and dissemination of new agricultural technologies.

ALTERNATIVE PATHS TOWARDS EXPORT ORIENTATION

This chapter works within a framework which assumes that an open trade regime is welfare enhancing, and that unilateral liberalisation is preferable to partial, conditional or discriminatory liberalisation. A strong case can be made that the ASEAN experience provides empirical support for this proposition, but that is the subject of another paper. The question here is whether, since all but Singapore have erected (sometimes substantial) trade barriers, the ASEAN record, and in particular that of the high-growth three (Indonesia, Malaysia and Thailand), sheds any light on the merits of alternative paths to import liberalisation and export orientation. Four issues are addressed in this section.

First, as in East Asia more generally, trade liberalisation has generally been introduced first of all for the export sector. That is, apart from Singapore, a dual trade regime has operated in which exporters have been placed on some sort of quasi-free-trade footing, at least as it affects their raw material and capital good imports. Countries as diverse as Korea and Indonesia have been able to achieve rapid export growth while maintaining substantial import protection through such devices. They have been introduced in countries in which governments are unwilling or politically unable to introduce first best trade reforms. Sometimes, though not always, they have been used as a transitional device en route to more general liberalisation.

The most popular instrument has been export processing zones, which proliferated from the early 1970s. These zones usually allow firms to import on a duty free basis subject to the requirement that their entire output is exported. Some are geographically separate and have special provision for infrastructure (and possibly also pricing). (For analytical purposes, obviously, Singapore may be treated as a single export processing zone.) Other regulations may also be relaxed, including labour laws and restrictions on foreign ownership. Their success, as measured in the realm of the second best, is mixed (see Warr 1989). Malaysia has exploited them effectively, in the context of a generally open economy, an able bureaucracy and a location strategy that linked these zones to the country's good international transport infrastructure.[13] Its timing was also fortuitous, in the sense that the establishment of its zones coincided with the rapid global growth of internationally integrated electronics production, dominated by a few MNEs who placed a premium on low-wage production sites providing good infrastructure and allowing 100 per cent foreign ownership. By contrast, the Philippine zones have performed poorly, owing to injudicious site selection and inappropriate infrastructure pricing. Another point of contrast between the two countries was that in Malaysia the zones have been accompanied by progressive, unilateral import liberalisation and a relatively open capital account; neither has been present in the Philippines until recently.

The zones have not been such an important feature of export-oriented industrialisation in Indonesia and Thailand. Both countries have set up zones, but duty drawback schemes for exporters have been more commonly employed. Owing to the fact that these two countries have reasonably strong and clean Ministries of Finance, which have administered these arrangements, the duty drawback schemes have generally worked efficiently. Their attraction is their simplicity. They do not involve the establishment of a separate bureaucracy, as is generally the case for the zones, and there is not the temptation for governments to either over or underprice physical infrastructure. Firms are also free to locate wherever they wish, thus minimising the possibility of poor site selection. Conversely, the zones probably offer some institutionalised protection to investors. Zones are less subject to the whims of the bureaucracy, in the manner which occurred, for example, in Indonesia in the early 1990s when, following personnel changes, that country's drawback scheme became more cumbersome and corrupt. It is probably also politically easier for governments to insulate firms in such zones from labour regulations and ownership restrictions, and their presence provides some reassurance for foreign investors. For example, in spite of its much higher wages, Malaysia has been more successful in attracting export-oriented, labour-intensive electronics foreign investment than either Indonesia or Thailand. This has almost certainly been mainly because it has managed its zones so effectively, and because of its less restrictive approach to FDI.

Second, and not surprisingly, the ASEAN record does not provide any support for an optimal tariff (or export tax) argument. Government attempts to exert international market power through export prohibition or taxation have been uniformly disastrous. The best-known Southeast Asian example has been the long-established rice export tax in Thailand, which was abolished only in 1986 (Warr 1997). Indonesia has introduced a range of export restrictions, of which the ban on the export of logs is the most prominent; other controls have affected rattan, leather, coconuts and livestock. The Philippine government in the 1970s and 1980s established export controls over a range cash crops, the most important of which affected coconuts (Bautista and Gonzales 1992). By contrast, the traditionally open economies of Malaysia and Singapore have largely eschewed such controls. The results of these interventions, predictably, have been a combination of one or more of the effects anticipated by standard political economy theory. Market power has proved to be largely illusory, certainly in the medium to longer term, as close substitutes have been available (for example, other types of cooking oil in the case of copra, and other building materials in the case of timber). Rent dissipation has been widespread, owing to massive corruption in the timber industry and serious problems of inefficiency in downstream processing industries, as illustrated by the experience of the Indonesian industry (Lindsay 1989).

The third issue relates to partial trade liberalisation through preferential trading arrangements within ASEAN. ASEAN, which was established in

1967, is unquestionably the most successful and durable example of economic and political cooperation in the developing world. However, its success derives fundamentally from each government pursuing growth-promoting policies at home. To be sure, the institution has played a crucial political role in fostering harmony and cooperation in a region where, until recently, suspicion and tension were common. But there is no evidence that the various attempts at formal economic cooperation have played any role in this success. The first initiatives, following the 1976 Bali summit, included a very limited preferential trading arrangement, some joint venture industrial projects and measures to stimulate private sector cooperation. These petered out within a decade, and were followed in 1992 by the introduction of the ASEAN Free Trade Area (AFTA).

In principle AFTA is discriminatory, in the sense that it offers concessions only to its members. Nevertheless, in practice thus far these concessions have been informally 'multilateralised', reflecting the preferences of the major reform-oriented policy makers in the region, and also the administrative difficulties associated with weak and corruption-prone customs services in distinguishing between imports from free-trade Singapore that are from within and outside the region. It is possible that, at some later stage in its implementation, AFTA could manifest itself in mildly discriminatory practices, especially for some politically sensitive items. However, even if this were to occur, the effects would almost certainly be trivial. Over 70 per cent of intraregional trade passes through Singapore, for which the principle of free trade is non-negotiable; a further 10 per cent separately involves Malaysia, which is nearly free trade. Moreover, as unilateral liberalisation proceeds in all countries, the margins of preference implicit in any such discriminatory arrangements would become very small. Finally, of course, it needs to be emphasised that there is no evidence – based either on theory or on empirical research on the region – to provide any empirical support for the proposition that preferential trading arrangements would have contributed to accelerated economic growth. Nor is there any support for a second best, 'political economy' hypothesis that regional trade liberalisation is preferred on the grounds that it is politically easier to introduce than unilateral liberalisation. If anything, the ASEAN experience tends to support the converse, in the sense that technocratic reformers have been able to move more quickly on a unilateral basis than have Ministers of Trade in sometimes drawn-out and convoluted regional negotiating sessions.[14]

The ASEAN countries also shed some light on the political economy of trade reform.[15] For historical reasons, in the 1960s the governments of Malaysia, Singapore and Thailand inherited a commitment to open frontiers, from which there have been few serious departures in the past 30 years. Both Malaysia and Thailand flirted with modest import protection in the late

1970s and in the 1980s, but in both countries disappointment with the results and the evident success of liberal economic policies tipped the balance in favour of the reformers. Indonesia's experience has been quite different, however. As with FDI, the policy pendulum swung sharply towards liberalism in the late 1960s, but during the oil boom period significant barriers to international commerce were reintroduced. It took the sudden decline in oil prices in the mid-1980s to reverse the trend towards protectionism. The technocratic reformers were able to convince President Soeharto that major liberal reforms were essential if economic growth was to be restored and Indonesia was to avoid serious external debt problems. The result was a series of decisive microeconomic reforms that, delivered in the context of good macroeconomic and exchange rate management, quickly revived economic activity. Once the process got under way, moreover, it developed its own momentum. In the words of the key architect of the reforms, Former Coordinating Economics Minister Professor Ali Wardhana (as quoted in Soesastro 1989, p. 854), it was able to 'win over a new constituency for further reform'.

Thus the ASEAN experience is consistent with that of the Northeast Asian economies. Once high growth becomes deeply rooted, it becomes almost impossible to reverse the trend towards further liberalisation. Communities demand continuously rising living standards, and there is an understanding of the link between growth and openness which delivers these improvements. The process is further strengthened by the fact that liberalisation exposes the unreformed sectors of the economy, rendering vulnerable the recipients of such special treatment. It is possible that serious political turbulence, for example in the transition to the post-Soeharto era in Indonesia, could derail this seemingly inexorable process. It is also true that nepotism and corruption remain widespread in all but Singapore. But in the long sweep of history, these challenges should not obscure the underlying trend towards liberalism and openness.

One final, if obvious, observation concerning the path to export orientation is warranted. Good macroeconomic management has underpinned economic success in all four countries. Monetary and fiscal policy has usually been conservative, and international capital accounts have been either open or – as indicated by the absence of black markets for foreign exchange – not subject to serious disequilibrium. The resulting good outcomes are revealed in inflation rates that, with the partial exception of Indonesia, have consistently been among the lowest in the developing world.[16] Investors have enjoyed a stable and predictable macroeconomic environment, and exchange rates have never experienced severe misalignment. It is difficult to establish a close relationship between, for example, inflation and growth rates, at least below certain 'threshold' inflation levels (perhaps in the range 15–25 per cent). Above such a threshold a negative relationship begins to appear, and in addition there is increased risk of hyperinflation developing. However, these empirical difficulties notwithstanding, there is no doubt that in general good macroeconomic management has been one of the key factors explaining East Asian economic success, and that the four Southeast Asian economies conform to this record.[17]

SOURCES OF GROWTH

The debate over the various growth-accounting estimates goes to the heart of the origins and sustainability of Southeast Asian economic growth. This topic shot to international prominence with the provocative 'inspiration versus perspiration' formulation by Krugman (1994). Krugman employed TFP analysis to argue that there was nothing 'miraculous' about rapid East Asian development, using as an example the case of Singapore. The record, he maintained, could be explained essentially by a primitive, Stalinist model of factor accumulation. That is, the growth was accounted for principally by the expansion of inputs, with very little unexplained residual in the equations, suggesting low or even negative TFP growth. If Krugman is correct, the implications are far-reaching: the Southeast Asian success would then have to be seen primarily in terms of a capacity to achieve high rates of saving and labour force growth which, once haven fallen to 'average' levels, would see the spectacular growth rates likewise subside.

Since the pioneering work of Jorgenson and others (see, for example, Jorgenson and Griliches 1967), economists have decomposed growth into its major elements: labour, capital and a residual perhaps misleadingly called TFP. Recent studies have generated more sophisticated estimates, which allow not only for the quantitative expansion of factor inputs but also qualitative improvements, notably in the case of labour to allow for human capital expansion. Capital stock estimates have been improved and data series have become more reliable, although quality improvements have been more difficult to incorporate, other than simply as market-price estimates.[18] Improved estimates of factor inputs have in turn reduced the magnitude of TFP growth, since the unexplained residual is thereby smaller.

It is useful to look at the TFP estimates for Southeast Asia, bearing these caveats in mind. A large number of studies have been undertaken in the past decade, as the database has improved and as interest in the topic has grown. A number of features of these data deserve emphasis.[19] First, in international perspective, the four high-growth Southeast Asian countries, Singapore excepted, have generally achieved TFP growth that is above the average for developing countries (Bosworth, Collins and Chen 1995; Nehru and

Dhareshwar 1994). So much of the literature has focused on the Young (1994) and Krugman Singapore–Hong Kong comparison that the broader East Asian achievement is frequently overlooked. The second feature of these estimates is that their range is very large. Even for the same country and time period, the differences are frustratingly significant in a number of cases. This alone emphasises the empirical difficulties inherent in such exercises, and warns against using these data in anything other than a highly cautious manner.[20] Probably the most useful comparisons can be made for numbers generated by the same project, on the assumption that with a common methodological framework one can at least be confident that differences cannot be attributed to variations in assumptions and databases.

Notwithstanding the latter observation, there are systematic differences in TFP growth over time in each country. It will be useful to examine Singapore and the other ASEAN countries separately, since so much of the international debate has focused on the former country. In Indonesia, in the 1970s TFP growth was positive but modest, presumably reflecting the influence of a sudden return to high growth of investment and GDP in response to the oil boom. During the recession of the 1980s it fell – though not apparently in non-oil manufacturing – before rising again during the period of export-oriented development. A similar trend is evident in Malaysia, except that the acceleration since the mid-1980s has been even more pronounced. The Philippine record mirrors its overall economic performance. During the 1970s TFP grew at a rate comparable to its neighbours, although its manufacturing performance was poorer. In the first half of the 1980s its record was disastrous, and has shown little evidence of recovery since. Thailand has not recorded such sharp swings in TFP growth, presumably reflecting the absence of major variations in its policy regime. Here too there has been strong growth since the mid-1980s. The conclusion from these country studies is that TFP growth moves broadly in line with that of GDP. It appears in addition that liberalisation and international orientation have resulted in faster TFP growth, consistent with the notion that such a strategy promotes greater efficiency. This is illustrated by a comparison of the TFP–GDP growth differentials in Malaysia, Thailand and Indonesia (in the latter, at least for non-oil manufacturing) in the 1970s and since the mid-1980s.

Singapore occupies a special position in this analysis. It was central to Krugman's provocative analysis, and it is the only country among the high-growth four for which negative numbers have occurred quite frequently. However, to compare its record with some sort of Soviet-style input accumulation model is far-fetched. It is one thing to point out that some other economies have achieved comparable GDP growth rates with lower savings and/or labour force growth rates, suggesting the possibility of some sort of 'oversaving', possibly linked to the country's compulsory saving arrangements. However, it is quite another to imply that such growth is sustained only through factor accumulation. The principal difference between Singapore and the Soviet model is that the former's completely open economy ensures that its investments are internationally efficient, unlike the latter case where exposure to international markets revealed that much of its tradeables economy was not internationally competitive.

There are two additional reasons for caution in drawing too much from the Singapore data. First, part of the reason why Singapore's high savings have generated lower returns than the other NIEs is that it has invested much more in public goods that do not generate an immediate, quantifiable return – its housing is generally better, and its public infrastructure (parks, roads, airport) is of higher quality. According to these quality of life indicators, therefore, Singapore scores more highly. Second, TFP growth appears to have accelerated sharply since the mid-1980s, according to all series, to levels which are at least comparable with those of other East Asian countries. Over this period, TFP growth has been maintained even as labour force growth has approached zero and savings rates have plateaued. The reasons for this sudden increase in TFP growth are difficult to discern, and probably reflect, at least in part, analytical weaknesses in the concept and measurement of TFP. It may also in part be the result of rapid restructuring over this period, including the shift into higher value added activities.

Thus, in sum, while it is true that Southeast Asian countries have achieved high savings rates, their TFP performance has also generally been impressive, and so the empirical basis for the assertion that growth has primarily been the result of 'perspiration' is misleading. It is also important to emphasise the nexus between TFP growth and liberalisation, which has been clearly evident over the past decade.

THE SIZE DISTRIBUTION OF INDUSTRY

The size distribution of industry is an important issue for a number of reasons. There are public policy issues, such as how well markets operate in remote rural areas where many small and medium-sized enterprises (SMEs) are located, and whether there is any case for special SME assistance. There are also interesting industrial organisation issues associated with the explanation of international differences in the size structure of industry and of changes in this structure over time.[21]

First, the industrial organisation issues. Taking employment of up to 200 workers as the cut-off point, SME firms in ASEAN constitute at least 85 per cent of all industrial establishments. They employ a sizeable proportion of the industrial workforce, in the range 30–60 per cent, and they generate between one-fifth and one-third of total output. One surprising feature of the data is that there does not appear to be any systematic correlation between SME shares and per capita GDP. It might be expected that there would be an inverse relationship, on the assumption that smaller units become relatively less important as incomes rise. This is to some extent the case with employment shares. But even here the Malaysia–Philippines rankings do not conform to the predicted pattern, and the rankings are quite different for output shares, with the two lower-income countries, Indonesia and the Philippines, also having the lowest SME shares.

More reliance can be placed on the comparison of shares for the medium-sized firms, with a workforce of 50–199 employees. There is no obvious explanation for these differences, but two tentative hypotheses might be advanced. The first has to do with differences in industrial structure, a factor of particular relevance to Indonesia. Owing to its natural resource endowments and to government policy, Indonesia has a larger share of capital-intensive (mainly resource-based) industries than would be expected on the basis of its per capita income.[22] A second possible explanation is that Indonesia and the Philippines have traditionally been the most regulated and protected economies of the five. It might also be argued that the policy regime has depressed the share of SMEs, to the extent that high levels of protection have encouraged the development of scale-intensive activities (such as the automotive industry).

The general presumption in much of the SME literature is that these firms become less important over the course of industrialisation (Anderson 1982). The only ASEAN country for which comprehensive time series data are available on the size distribution of manufacturing, spanning more than two decades, is Singapore. Over the course of that country's rapid industrialisation, there has been a clear shift to units of large scale. From 1965 to 1992, the share of firms with 300 or more employees doubled in the case of value added and more than doubled in the case of employment. For the two smaller groups (firms with 1–49 employees, and those with 50–199 employees), by contrast, shares contracted sharply and by 1992 were well under one-half the 1965 figures for both employment and value added. The sharpest changes in size distribution occurred in the period 1965–75. After 1975, the value added and employment shares of the largest group (300+ employees) was virtually constant.

How might this pattern – of rapid changes in 1965–75 followed by fairly stable shares – be explained? One intuitively plausible explanation is that the early period coincided with Singapore's major push into labour-intensive, export-oriented industrialisation, which saw the establishment of large plants in electronics, textiles and other activities. The SME sector did not shrink absolutely, but its share fell quickly because most of the new plants were in the 300+ group. Once this transitional phase was over, there was no great difference in expansion rates among the various size groups, suggesting that, as the industrial structure upgrades to a more human capital-intensive phase, there continues to be a role for the SME group, and particularly the larger SMEs. These conclusions are at best speculative, but they do suggest that SMEs are not necessarily marginalised by the process of factory sector industrialisation, and the data are also consistent with evidence from other high-income East Asian economies. The biggest shake-out may occur in the initial stages, in the transition from cottage to factory-based organisation.[23]

In analysing trends in size distribution, it is important to understand not just the aggregate trends, but also the dynamics of these changes. From the point of view of both efficiency and equity, it matters a lot whether, for example, a trend towards agglomeration occurs because SME firms are displaced by, or themselves grow into, larger units. It is rarely possible to answer such a question at the macro level because detailed firm-level records are not available. However, a recent analysis of such data from Indonesia over the period 1977–91 sheds light on this issue (Aswicahyono, Bird and Hill 1996). Two sets of size distribution data are computed. The first follows the conventional approach and classifies firms by their size in the year of enumeration, while in the second firms are classified by their size in the base year – 1975 (the year the data set commences) or, if later, the year the firm commenced operations. The second data set reveals a good deal of dynamism on the part of smaller firms, as shown by the fact that the share of the 20–99 group is consistently higher in the 'initial year' series. In the current year series, there is no significant change in the distribution, other than a gradual increase in the middle group. In other words, smaller firms appear to be 'graduating', in contrast to popular (and populist) perceptions that they are struggling to survive.

The policy approach to SMEs in ASEAN has changed over the past decade, based on the gradual realisation that, for all the government rhetoric concerning their importance, public policies have often actually discriminated against them.[24] Trade policies have been biased against SMEs to the extent that they have offered above average protection to large scale-intensive industries. Fiscal incentives have had a similar effect when, as is often the case, they apply only to investments of a certain minimum size. Interest rate ceilings have often affected SMEs adversely, since banks cannot recoup the higher per unit administrative costs of dealing with such firms. Complex regulatory regimes, which are frequently fixed cost in nature, add an additional cost penalty for SMEs. In the country with the most pervasive regime, Indonesia, there may be a 5–8 per cent cost penalty for SME firms according to as yet unpublished research. The evidence from ASEAN and elsewhere is that SME programs that are not in some respects 'market friendly' have not been successful, in the sense of promoting efficient industrial development. Examples include enforced subcontracting schemes, reservation schemes, and general requirements or exhortations that large firms assist smaller units in some way. Indonesia has developed the most comprehensive set of programs in this area, generally with little success. Conversely, its government has also introduced successful and innovative programs in finance, which have both reduced costly subsidies and enabled small borrowers to obtain better access to formal credit markets (Patten and Rosengard 1991). Another illustration of the scope for simple reform facilitating the development of a more efficient and accessible capital market has been highlighted in the research on Thailand demonstrating the nexus between clear land titles, the credit market and agricultural productivity (Feder et al. 1988).

Nevertheless, considerable policy challenges remain in this area. Agencies charged with responsibility for SME development still tend to take a 'welfare' rather than an 'efficiency' approach, with a continuing emphasis on reservation schemes, cooperatives, bureaucratically driven 'partnerships' and the like. Such an approach ignores the major lessons from the best studies of SME development, which point to common ingredients where these firms have been successful.[25] These generally include some local skill or craft base, combined with good physical infrastructure, competitive exchange rates and injections of foreign technological expertise (often of a simple nature, such as fashion trends in international markets, or export market channels). Governments do play a *general* role here, as noted, and they could do more through an efficiently operating industrial extension scheme. But more commonly, as in the Indonesian case studies referred to in the endnote, these are 'accidental cases of industrialisation'; not infrequently, the crucial foreign linkages have been harassed rather than supported.

INDUSTRIAL CONCENTRATION AND COMPETITION POLICY

These two related issues are becoming increasingly important in the three lower-income countries. They never rate a mention in the completely open Singapore economy, for the obvious reason that, with the possible exception of a very few internationally oligopolistic industries, the issue of concentration is of no great importance if all sectors are fully tradeable and there are no barriers to international trade. As a corollary, obviously, the trade regime constitutes the most effective tool of competition policy.

The commercial landscape in Southeast Asia has changed dramatically over the past 30 years.[26] In the 1960s there were very few corporations of international size, apart from a handful of MNEs and state-owned conglomerates. Now there at least 50 such corporations which are large by Asian, if not yet international, standards. Studies of these business entities reveal much about the region's growing internationalisation and business competence; they also reveal a good deal about business–government relations. Region-wide generalisations about these large business groups are hazardous, owing to the diverse business and political climates. Most of the groups are highly diversified across sectors, and their primary facility lies in a capacity to identify projects, combine packages of finance and skills (often imported), and negotiate through the bureaucratic and political minefields necessary to commence business. Many groups evolved from trading, plantation or banking operations, although by the 1990s 'new money' was as well represented as old. Ethnic Chinese groups, alongside a new breed of well-connected indigenous entrepreneurs, dominate the landscape. Links with governments (especially in Indonesia, and Malaysia outside the export processing zones) and MNEs have been very important. Stock markets have become a significant means of financing their operations, and for periods in the 1990s portfolio capital inflows exceeded FDI.

We lack detailed data on seller concentration for all four economies, but the general picture is clear enough. The most complete information is for Indonesia (see Bird 1998, on which this paragraph relies), and its experience approximates developing country norms (see, for example, Kirkpatrick, Lee and Nixson 1984, Chapter 3). Seller concentration is high in Indonesia, with more than half of manufacturing output originating in industries in which the four-firm concentration ratios (that is, the four largest firms' share of the industry's output) are at least 40 per cent; concentration ratios in excess of 70 per cent are quite common. While these figures primarily reflect the influence of industrial infancy and scale, there is as yet no clear downward trend. Even during the period of trade liberalisation from 1985 onwards, while there was a slight decline, it was not statistically significant. Similar comments apply to the trade adjusted concentration ratios.

Continuing high levels of concentration have triggered a debate in several countries on the merits of some form of competition policy. Proposals have included a wide range of measures, including price surveillance and control, more elaborate institutional mechanisms such as some form of trade practices commission, and the unusual approach suggested by an Indonesian Minister for Investment that existing firms in highly concentrated industries be prohibited from expanding their productive capacity except for export. However, much of the discussion has lacked analytical focus. Moreover, proponents of increased intervention generally make little reference to the link between competition and trade policy (except that, paradoxically, many of them oppose trade liberalisation or consider it irrelevant), and they overlook the fact that restraints on trade are often caused directly or indirectly by governments.

The experience in both Indonesia and Thailand illustrates these propositions. In Thailand, as Wisarn (1996) points out, successive governments have maintained or introduced various excess profit and anti-monopoly regulations, with mixed results and erratic implementation. In quite a few cases the regulations have actually had little to do with competition policy. As he notes (p. 8), 'the [anti-monopoly] Act has been implemented mainly as an administrative instrument to maintain price stability ... rather than as an instrument to promote fair competition and anti-monopoly practices'. There has not been any detailed analytical research on the impact of these regulations, and although they are being implemented with less vigour over time, they remain on the statute books and could easily be resurrected by zealous officials.

In Indonesia, some form of competition policy has been advocated since the early 1980s, and the government is now actively considering new policy initiatives in this area. The political economy agenda which drives this debate is complex, and has little in reality to do with competition policy as the term is normally understood. Two key elements underpin this agenda. The first is that the term 'monopoly' is often discreet code for the highly privileged business activities of members of the extended family of President Soeharto. Several of these people have built up vast business empires in the space of just 10–15 years on the basis of the country's highly personalistic commercial practices, which often bypass the usual checks and balances.[27] For example, they have secured firm-specific import protection and credit access; they have been able to circumvent regulations relating to local content and service provision; they have been awarded huge government contracts in a highly non-transparent manner; and they have been able to acquire shares in several partially privatised, very large state enterprises without any formal tendering process.[28] Direct criticism of these business arrangements is not possible, and so instead public criticism focuses more generally on monopolies. But it is clear that advocates of reform in this instance are concerned about the issues of transparency, non-preferential treatment and pluralistic political structures, rather than some elaborate bureaucratic construct to promote competition policy.

The second agenda in the debate derives from bureaucratic power interests within the government. Deregulation may have become the principal economic policy slogan in Indonesia over the past decade, but most of the technical departments have been reluctant to surrender the authority which generates lucrative rents. One therefore has to confront the paradox that senior policy makers are advocating the introduction of more, not fewer, regulations to promote competition, while at the same time presiding over a regulatory environment that actively discourages trade. Anyone who reads the Jakarta press will quickly gain an approximate understanding of the magnitude of the problem. A recent example concerned export procedures, when a very senior official in the Ministry of Industry and Trade revealed to a parliamentary hearing in July 1996 that an exporter is liable to pay about 4,400 levies imposed by various tiers and departments of the government. This number, moreover, referred only to *official* levies; the number of illegal levies is unknown but considerable. With extraordinary figures such as this, the estimate by the country's Chamber of Commerce and Industry that these sorts of levies could amount to 27 per cent of production costs becomes a credible, if wildly approximate, figure.[29]

The problem is therefore more likely to be 'government failure' rather than 'market failure', and the solution is a complete overhaul of the government's administrative structures and procedures, combined with continuous import liberalisation. In such an environment, the establishment of some sort of competition commission is more likely to exacerbate than solve the problem, in addition to the lucrative opportunities it would present to the country's fledgling commercial law industry. There may be a case for some form of government surveillance in genuinely non-tradeable sectors such as wholesale and retail trade and utilities. But this is a low priority compared to the pressing task of bureaucratic reform. It also needs to be added that the problem is more serious in Indonesia than in neighbouring countries, owing to its traditionally less open economy and its deeply entrenched problems of corruption.

CONCLUSION

Several points need to be emphasised by way of summary. First, the four Southeast Asian countries achieved continuous and rapid industrialisation, combined with far-reaching structural change, for about 30 years through to the mid-1990s. The dimensions of this record, in terms of industrial structure, increased internationalisation and rising productivity, have been analysed in this chapter.

Second, this rapid industrial growth is explained primarily by the same general factors that have underpinned high growth in the region, including openness to the international economy, sound (pre-crisis) macroeconomic management, investments in physical and social infrastructure, and reasonably good equity records. There is little in the way of sector-specific explanations for this high growth. As a corollary, the recent slowdown in industrial growth has its origins in macroeconomic and financial policies, and has little to do with the specifics of industrial policy.

Third, the case for a selective industry policy, in the sense of governments attempting to pick industry or firm-specific 'winners', is a weak one. Rather, if anything, the Southeast Asian experience illustrates the adage that 'while governments are not very good at picking winners, losers are often good at picking governments'. Governments are critical to the achievement of rapid industrialisation, but their major contribution has been in getting the fundamentals right. There is scope for micro-level intervention where markets do not work efficiently, particularly in such areas as information flows, market intelligence in the early stages of export orientation, and the adoption of new technologies. But these interventions will be successful only in a competitive commercial environment where the costs of mistakes are quickly evident, and where a reasonably competent, corruption-free bureaucracy is in place.

NOTES

1. There is an extensive general literature on industrialisation in ASEAN. Country studies include Ariff (1991), Jomo (1993) and Athukorala and Menon (1997) on Malaysia; Medhi Krongkaew (1995) on Thailand; Lim and Associates (1988, Chapter 9) on Singapore; and Hill (1997a) on Indonesia. The Philippine experience is comprehensively examined in Medalla and Associates (1995). Two more general, though dated, references are Ariff and Hill (1985) on ASEAN industrialisation through to the mid-1980s, and the comprehensive assessment of East Asia by Hughes (1988).
2. A set of comparative tables covering these topics is available on request from the author.
3. The literature on this subject is now very large. An example of the orthodox approach, modified by the constraints imposed by its authorship, is World Bank (1993). Smith (1995) provides a comprehensive survey of the East Asian literature from a largely neoclassical perspective. Influential East Asian case studies among the interventionist school include Amsden (1989) on Korea, Johnson (1982) on Japan and Wade (1990) on Taiwan. Hughes (1988) provides an important airing of competing views in the debate.
4. Indeed, this school arguably takes achievements in these areas too much for granted, and downplays the fact that, with limited high-level bureaucratic resources available, a more activist strategy may be implemented at the cost of diminished performance in the core areas.
5. Singapore is a special case because of its almost completely open boundaries, although there is an emerging, but unconvincing, literature that it owes its success in part to extensive intervention in the form of state ownership and selective fiscal incentives.
6. Consider, for example, the following assessments, echoed by many other writers in the region, of industrial policy in Malaysia and Thailand respectively:

   [T]he weakness of a non-specialised bureaucracy subordinated to vested 'political' interests has combined with a strong rentier class based in the dominant Malay political group to prevent the emergence of an efficient, 'deepening' industrial policy (Edwards and Jomo 1993, p. 333).

   ... Thailand's sectoral policies ... have become a means to distribute economic rents, rather than the promotion of industrial and technology enhancement ... For a long time, tariff policy has been Thailand's only industrial policy (Mingsarn 1992, pp. 1–10, 1–47).

7. See Papageorgiou, Michaely and Choksi (1991), and in particular the review of this seven-volume project by Greenaway (1993).
8. For a useful summary, see Low et al. (1993).

9. In the words of Helen Hughes (1993, p. 15): 'Until the 1980s, the role of the ASEAN member country Investment Boards, other than of the Economic Development Board of Singapore, was to ration access to domestic monopolistic markets created by protection, fiscal, credit and other incentives'.
10. Lall (1992, 1996) exemplifies the approach of this school.
11. The 'diamond' approach, employed by Dobson (1997) and others, illustrates effectively the technological bases of countries in comparative international perspective. Graphically, the Y-axis presents R&D expenditure as a percentage of GDP and educational enrolment ratios, while the X-axis shows the stock of FDI as a percentage of GDP and the percentage of trade with OECD economies.
12. See Hobday (1995) for a recent East Asian case study.
13. It might also be noted that the location of these zones around Penang and more recently Johor has not only been wise from an efficiency viewpoint but has also enabled the country to avoid some of the chronic capital city congestion evident in most other East Asian capitals.
14. Recent surveys of ASEAN economic cooperation which discuss some of these issues in more detail include Chia (1996) and Pomfret (1996).
15. See Hill (1997b) for more discussion of the issues examined in this paragraph.
16. The average inflation rate in the four countries over the period 1961–91 was: Indonesia, 12.4 per cent; Malaysia, 3.4 per cent; Singapore, 3.6 per cent; and Thailand, 5.6 per cent. By contrast, the figure for all low and middle-income economies was 61.8 per cent (World Bank 1993, p. 110).
17. The best recent general analysis of macroeconomic management in East Asia is provided by Corden (1996), which was originally prepared as a background paper for the World Bank's (1993) 'miracle' study. A more detailed treatment of the issues is provided by Little, Cooper, Corden and Rajapatirana (1993) in their 18-country comparative study, which included two of the four countries examined in this chapter – Indonesia and Thailand.
18. The issue of quality improvements, incidentally, highlights one of the major analytical conundrums, namely that if all factor inputs are measured comprehensively, both quantitatively and qualitatively, there should not in fact be any unexplained residual. Moreover, it is difficult empirically to estimate TFP independent of factor accumulation, since technical change generally takes place in the form of embodied factor augmentation.
19. A tabular summary of the estimates is available on request from the author. Chen (1997) provides a convenient recent summary.
20. A particular concern, argued forcefully in a recent paper by Harberger (1997), is the highly aggregated nature of most of the estimates, many of which are computed simply for the whole economy without any sectoral disaggregation. Even where sectoral estimates are presented, the data may be misleading in an economy experiencing rapid structural change owing to problems of aggregation.
21. There is a large literature on this subject. The best general survey for East Asia as a whole is Berry and Mazumdar (1991).
22. Conversely, this factor cannot be the whole story: while the resource-poor Philippines also has a low value added SME share, resource-rich Malaysia has a high share.
23. For example, over the period 1955–86, there was surprisingly little change in the size structure of manufacturing in Japan (Go 1992, pp. 329–31).
24. Bruch and Hiemenz (1984) were among the first to document these 'perverse interventions' in the Southeast Asian context in some detail. More recent discussion is provided by the country studies in Meyanathan (1994).
25. Two excellent recent case studies from Indonesia are Cole (1998) on Bali's garment exporters and Schiller and Martin-Schiller (1997) on the furniture industry in the Central Javanese city of Jepara.
26. See Lim (1996) for a general survey.
27. Another strand of criticism is directed at the ethnic Chinese community who, while numbering less than 3 per cent of the population, dominate much of its modern commerce and industry. The issue of government patronage here is more complex. While most large Sino-

      Indonesian conglomerates have close ties to the government, this is often motivated as much by the need for political protection as it is by the desire to receive government largesse.
28. These cases are extensively documented in the 'Survey of Recent Developments' in many past issues of the *Bulletin of Indonesian Economic Studies*.
29. These figures are reported in the *Jakarta Post* (11 July 1996), which in an accompanying editorial not inappropriately commented that anyone interested in exporting from Indonesia 'may want to ask themselves if they have the strength and stamina to overcome the frustration they will encounter from mounting bureaucracy'. Numerous reports by business organisations and the World Bank provide detailed examples of this kind.

9. Developing with Foreign Investment: What Can Vietnam Learn from Malaysia?

Prema-chandra Athukorala

Following the opening of the economy to international trade and foreign investment in 1987, Vietnam has experienced large inflows of foreign direct investment (FDI). Annual FDI inflows have risen very quickly, from about US$60 million in 1988 to nearly US$2 billion in 1996; since 1992 they have exceeded inflows of official development assistance (ODA) by a large margin. Though these numbers look impressive in absolute terms, they hide the fact that Vietnam has so far failed to capture the full developmental impact of FDI. First, the volume of FDI is still low both by international standards and in relation to the many intrinsic advantages – in particular, market size, geography and a rich human capital base – Vietnam enjoys as a potential location for international production. Second, there is reason to suspect that the net national gains from these modest inflows may be far less than the numbers suggest. The bulk of foreign investment is in joint ventures with state-owned enterprises (SOEs) involved in import substitution production in a sheltered domestic market. Moreover, despite immense potential to thrive through international specialisation in labour-intensive products and processes with FDI participation, export-led industrialisation has yet to take off in Vietnam.

What explains Vietnam's lack-lustre performance in promoting FDI? Can it simply be treated as a reflection of Vietnam's latecomer status and/or the special challenges associated with the transition from a centrally planned to a market economy? Alternatively, can the explanation be found in the half-hearted nature of policy reforms? The purpose of this chapter is to shed light on these and related issues through a paired case study of Vietnam and Malaysia. Malaysia provides an interesting comparator for the analysis. It is an example of a country in the region that has achieved rapid growth and dramatic structural transformation through export-led industrialisation with FDI participation. Moreover, the Malaysian experience is often referred to in the current Vietnamese policy debate on FDI to justify selective policy intervention, in particular the use of SOEs as a vehicle for mobilising FDI. Of course no two countries are alike, and it is hazardous to generalise from one country's case to another. But the paired case study approach also provides a valuable opportunity to develop a rich understanding of the conditions, processes and outcomes relating to the design and implementation of a national policy on foreign investment.

The chapter is structured as follows. The following section gives an overview of the Malaysian experience. The next compares Vietnam's performance with that of Malaysia. A prognosis of relative performance is then presented with emphasis on the role of policy. A final section summarises the main conclusions and draws policy inferences.

FDI AND EXPORT-LED INDUSTRIALISATION IN MALAYSIA

Malaysia is among the few developing countries that have successfully mobilised FDI to achieve economic growth through export-led industrialisation. By the mid-1970s Malaysia was already a favoured location for assembly activities in the global electronics industry. The subsequent years witnessed a rapid expansion in the involvement of multinationals from the 'conventional' source countries (in particular the United States) in the electronics industry, and the entry of export-oriented firms from neighbouring newly industrialising economies (NIEs) into light consumer good industries. The timing of investment liberalisation in 1985–86 coincided with economic changes in Japan and the East Asian NIEs – including the post-Plaza Accord appreciation of exchange rates, the loss of General System of Preferences privileges, and rising domestic wages – which caused many of their manufacturers to seek low-cost production sites offshore. Consequently, the inflow of FDI has been very rapid over the past decade. Between 1982–87 (averaged) and the mid-1990s, FDI inflows increased almost eight-fold, from US$844 million to US$7 billion (Table 9.1). Malaysia, together with its five East Asian neighbours – China, Singapore, Thailand, Indonesia and Hong Kong – was among the eight largest developing country recipients of FDI in the mid-1990s.

Until the late 1960s, multinational enterprises (MNEs) in Malaysian manufacturing were largely concentrated in import substitution production, in areas such as food and beverages, chemicals and pharmaceuticals. Their involvement in export production was limited to some processing activities linked to primary production sectors. The rapid expansion of export-oriented FDI since the early 1970s has brought about a dramatic transformation in the product structure of MNE participation. From about the mid-1980s,

Table 9.1 Inward Flows of FDI, 1981–96 (US$ million)

	1982–87[a]	1988	1989	1990	1991
Developed countries	52,757	131,313	168,488	169,777	114,001
Developing countries	14,752	27,772	27,376	33,735	41,324
Developing Asia	6,273	14,980	15,416	19,803	20,775
Hong Kong	1,014	2,627	1,077	1,728	538
South Korea	253	871	758	788	1,180
Taiwan	306	959	1,604	1,330	1,271
China	1,362	3,194	3,393	3,487	4,366
Malaysia	844	719	1,668	2,333	3,998
Indonesia	282	576	682	1,093	1,482
Philippines	96	936	563	530	544
Singapore	1,605	3,655	2,773	5,575	4,879
Thailand	287	1,105	1,775	2,444	2,014
Vietnam[b]	2	8	4	120	220
					(165)
Bangladesh	1	2	–	3	1
India	89	91	252	162	141
Pakistan	86	186	210	244	257
Sri Lanka	42	46	20	43	48

Notes:
– = negligible; n.a. = not available.
[a]Figures for 1982–87 are annual averages.
[b]Based on data compiled by the Ministry of Planning and Investment. Figures in brackets are alternative estimates produced by Jun et al. (1997).

production for the domestic market has become secondary to using Malaysia as a base for manufacturing for the global market. The share of projects with an export orientation of 50 per cent or more increased from 24 per cent of total approved projects in 1984–85 to over 85 per cent by the mid-1990s. This structural shift in MNE participation is clearly evident in the data on the output and employment composition of foreign production reported in Table 9.2. The share of semiconductors and electronics alone in total value added amounted to over 35 per cent in 1992, up from 19 per cent in 1974. There has

Table 9.1 (continued)

	1992	1993	1994	1995	1996
Developed countries	114,002	129,302	132,758	203,168	n.a.
Developing countries	50,376	73,135	87,024	99,670	n.a.
Developing Asia	27,174	46,481	53,619	65,033	n.a.
Hong Kong	2,051	1,667	2,000	2,100	2,235
South Korea	727	588	809	1,776	2,325
Taiwan	879	917	1,375	1,470	1,572
China	11,156	27,515	33,787	37,849	40,180
Malaysia	5,183	5,006	4,348	5,800	7,045
Indonesia	1,777	2,004	2,109	4,348	n.a.
Philippines	228	1,025	1,457	1,500	n.a.
Singapore	2,351	5,016	5,588	8,210	9,446
Thailand	2,116	1,726	640	2,068	2,336
Vietnam[b]	260	832	1,048	1,520	1,803
	(333)	(923)	(1,631)	(2,236)	(1,838)
Bangladesh	4	14	11	125	n.a.
India	151	273	620	1,750	n.a.
Pakistan	335	354	422	419	719
Sri Lanka	123	195	166	56	120

Sources: Data for Vietnam for 1990–96 are IMF estimates obtained from Jun et al. (1997). Data for Vietnam for other years and other countries for all years are from UNCTAD (1994, 1996), *World Investment Report*, supplemented by IMF (1996), *International Financial Statistics*.

also been a significant increase in the relative importance of new product areas, such as non-electrical machinery, consumer electronics and professional and scientific equipment. By contrast, the shares of traditional import substitution product sectors – such as food, beverages and tobacco, iron and steel, and chemicals – have declined over the years. By the late 1980s FDI inflows had shifted from production for the domestic market to using Malaysia as a base for manufacturing for the global market. The share of projects with an export orientation of 50 per cent or more increased from 24 per

Table 9.2   Malaysia: Composition of Value Added and Employment of MNE Affiliates in Manufacturing (%)

ISIC Code	Commodity	Value Added			Employment		
		1974	1988	1992	1974	1988	1992
31	Food, beverages & tobacco	25.1	18.5	7.0	10.7	6.0	2.9
32	Textiles, clothing & footwear	2.9	7.1	6.1	14.4	12.6	10.1
33	Wood products	1.6	1.6	2.6	3.0	3.8	5.0
34	Paper & paper products	3.1	1.0	1.1	3.1	1.1	1.0
351–54	Chemicals	11.6	6.8	5.9	7.0	2.5	1.9
355–56	Rubber & plastic goods	18.4	11.0	7.6	15.9	8.8	8.3
36	Non-metallic mineral products	3.1	2.1	1.8	2.9	2.2	1.5
37	Basic metal products	4.7	1.7	1.8	2.8	1.1	1.7
381	Fabricated metal products	4.9	1.5	2.5	6.9	1.5	2.7
382	Non-electrical machinery	4.9	4.5	7.0	6.3	2.4	4.4
383	Electrical machinery	19.3	38.7	51.7	26.5	50.0	52.8
38329	Semiconductors & electronics	19.3	29.7	34.9	26.5	32.6	33.1
384	Transport equipment	0.4	1.1	0.7	0.5	0.5	0.8
385	Professional & scientific equipment	0.0	2.4	2.7	0.0	3.7	3.9
390	Other manufactures	0.0	1.8	1.4	0.0	3.9	3.0
3	**Total**	100.0	100.0	100.0	100.0	100.0	100.0
	(US$ million)	1,477	5,764	15,193			
	(thousand)				99.2	216.6	470.1

Note: ISIC = International Standard Industry Classification.

Sources: Department of Statistics (1974, 1988, 1992), *Survey of Manufacturing Industries,* Kuala Lumpur. Data for 1974 are from the published survey report; unpublished data for 1988 and 1992 were provided by the Department of Statistics.

cent of total approved projects in 1984–85 to about 82 per cent by 1988–89. The proportion of projects with an export orientation of 80 per cent or more increased from one-fifth of the total in 1984 to about three-quarters in 1989.

The growing presence of MNEs in export-oriented manufacturing has dramatically transformed Malaysia's export structure. In the early 1970s, the share of manufactures in total merchandise exports amounted only to about

10 per cent.[1] Since then, manufactured exports have emerged as the most dynamic element in the export structure, accounting for over 75 per cent of total exports since the early 1990s. From 1994 onwards, Malaysia has been the developing world's sixth largest exporter of manufactures (with a total export value of over US$45 billion), after the 'Four Dragons' (Taiwan, South Korea, Hong Kong and Singapore) of East Asia and China. In the 1970s resource-based manufacturing – food, beverages, tobacco, wood products and basic metals – loomed large in the structure of manufactured exports. The transformation of the export structure in line with emerging patterns of the international division of labour gathered momentum in the late 1980s. At first Malaysia found market niches in clothing, footwear and simple (highly labour-intensive) assembly operations in electronics and electrical goods, and diffused technology consumer goods. In recent years, the export composition has begun to diversify into final products based on mature technology, such as radios, TVs, cameras and computers.

There are no direct estimates of the share of MNE affiliates in total manufactured exports. However, a simple comparison of data on the export and output shares of foreign firms shows that they provided over three-quarters of Malaysia's total manufactured exports in the mid-1990s. The (almost completely foreign-owned) electronics industry alone contributed over 60 per cent of total manufactured exports in 1995. Malaysia's efforts in attracting FDI to the electronics industry have been so successful that since the early 1980s it has been the largest developing country exporter (and a major world exporter) of electronic components, particularly integrated circuits.

The employment outcome of export-led industrialisation has been impressive. In the mid-1980s the unemployment rate in Malaysia was as high as 8 per cent; by 1995 it had declined to only 2.8 per cent. Most of the new employment opportunities have come from the rapidly expanding manufacturing sector. The direct contribution of manufacturing to the total employment increment between 1987 and 1994 was as high as 60 per cent, with MNE affiliates playing a pivotal role in this outcome. The share of MNEs in total manufacturing employment varied in the narrow range of 29–35 per cent during 1968–80. It then declined to an average level of 28 per cent in the first half of the 1980s, reflecting the state-led push for heavy industrialisation under Prime Minister Mahathir's 'Look East Policy' (see below). Following the market-oriented policy reforms implemented in response to the macroeconomic crisis of the mid-1980s, the employment share of MNEs has increased consistently to reach 45 per cent in 1992. In the same year the employment share of SOEs had declined to less than 3 per cent.

With the rapid expansion of export-oriented manufacturing, the structure of manufacturing production associated with MNEs has become more labour intensive. Reflecting this development, the share of the multinationals in

Table 9.3 Vietnam: Contribution of MNE Affiliates to Total Manufacturing Production and Employment (%)

ISIC Code	Industry	Value Added			Employment		
		1974	1988	1992	1974	1988	1992
31	Food, beverages & tobacco	45.5	32.8	28.9	18.6	14.6	15.6
32	Textiles, clothing & footwear	23.3	38.5	44.8	31.2	34.5	39.7
33	Wood products	6.1	8.5	17.8	5.9	10.7	17.3
34	Paper & paper products	21.2	8.1	10.2	14.3	7.8	11.4
351–54	Chemicals	71.7	16.7	22.7	52.8	28.2	30.9
355–56	Rubber & plastic goods	54.2	37.8	40.9	37.2	28.4	34.3
36	Non-metallic mineral products	20.1	73.4	14.2	11.7	66.1	17.4
37	Basic metal products	57.2	18.2	21.4	32.6	18.7	32.7
381	Fabricated metal products	46.2	17.2	25.4	38.1	13.5	27.9
382	Non-electrical machinery	50.1	56.7	69.7	34.2	32.5	56.3
383	Electrical machinery,	88.0	82.3	87.1	80.7	82.2	86.7
38329	Semiconductors & electronics	88.0	87.9	90.5	80.7	85.7	89.5
384	Transport equipment	5.4	11.0	6.5	4.2	6.9	11.7
385	Professional & scientific equipment	0.0	100.0	99.4	0.0	100.0	98.8
390	Other manufactures	0.0	78.4	45.1	0.0	74.5	66.6
3	**Total**	32.9	37.3	44.5	28.2	37.2	45.4

Source: As for Table 9.2.

total manufacturing employment has been rising much faster than their share of output (Table 9.3). This pattern is particularly noticeable in non-metallic mineral products, basic metal products, fabricated metal products and miscellaneous manufacturing.

Growing opportunities for non-agricultural work, particularly in export-oriented manufacturing industries, have contributed to a reduction in poverty and increase in overall living standards in Malaysia. Unskilled labour – the most widely distributed factor of production – is now so scarce that its price (real wage rate) is rising, resulting in an overall reduction in poverty. The increase in the number of two-income households has also helped raise household incomes, while underpinning the importance of women in the workforce. These changes are in large part due to the rapid expansion in demand for low-skilled labour generated by labour-intensive export-oriented manufacturing activities (Rasiah 1995; Athukorala and Menon 1997).

VIETNAM'S EXPERIENCE

Data on FDI flows to Vietnam are of dubious quality (Kokko 1997; Riedel and Comer 1997). The approvals data contained in official reports are believed to be highly unreliable because a large number of projects (perhaps over two-thirds) are never implemented (Kokko and Zejan 1996). The only data series on realised FDI available for the entire post-reform period is that compiled by International Monetary Fund (IMF) staff from the aggregate statistics provided by the Ministry of Planning and Investment (Table 9.1). Recently, Jun et al. (1997) have generated an alternative series for the period 1991–96 through a scrutiny of individual project records maintained by the Ministry (see notes to Table 9.1). While Jun et al.'s estimates of the level of annual investment are on average 22 per cent higher than those of the IMF, both reveal a similar pattern of investment over time. The two series indicate that annual FDI inflows to Vietnam have risen very rapidly over the past seven years, from around US$200 million in the early 1990s to nearly US$2 billion by 1996. Since 1992 FDI inflows have exceeded all other forms of financial inflows, including ODA (Kokko 1997). However, Vietnam's performance as an FDI recipient remains poor compared to other countries. Annual FDI flows to Vietnam in the mid-1990s amounted to only one-fifth of average annual flows to Malaysia during 1982–87. In 1988–96, the sum of total FDI inflows to Vietnam was a mere 2.3 per cent of total inflows to China (Table 9.1).

Unlike in Malaysia, where manufacturing has been the major area of attraction to FDI, in Vietnam an increasing proportion of licensed FDI has been directed to the construction and services sectors. The share of FDI directed to manufacturing has declined, from 91per cent in 1988 to 53 per cent in 1991 and 42 per cent in 1994 (Table 9.4). Within manufacturing, much of the investment has been in production for the domestic market. According to rough estimates provided in a recent UNDP study, only about a quarter of FDI capital in the industrial sector is intended mainly for export production (UNDP 1996, as quoted in Kokko 1997, p. 15).

Data on Vietnam's recent export performance reflect the import substitution bias of FDI participation in domestic manufacturing. Despite some noteworthy increases in the shares of clothing and footwear, Vietnam's export structure is still dominated by primary commodities (Table 9.5). Even in clothing and footwear, its recent performance does not match that of

Table 9.4 Vietnam: Industry Distribution of Licensed FDI, 1988–94 (%)

	1988	1991	1994
Primary sector	1.4	11.5	4.9
Agriculture, forestry & fishing	0.0	1.8	3.2
Mining & oil exploration	1.4	9.7	1.7
Manufacturing	91.2	53.4	42.2
Food, beverages & tobacco	79.4	34.5	11.2
Textiles & clothing	5.3	4.2	8.6
Other manufacturing	6.5	14.7	22.4
Construction & services	7.4	35.1	52.9
Hotels & restaurants	5.2	28.8	48.1
Transport & communication	1.4	3.2	1.0
Other services	0.8	3.1	3.8
Total	100.0	100.0	100.0
(US$ million)	84.6	65.1	62.5

Source: Kokko and Zejan (1996), Table 2.

countries like Sri Lanka, Mauritius and Bangladesh, let alone that of more established exporters such as Thailand and Indonesia. The disaggregated export data show clearly that FDI has not as yet brought about a significant increase in MNE-dominated, labour-intensive assembly activities in vertically integrated global industries, such as electronics and electrical goods and motor spare parts (SITC 7). For the past 15 years this has been the most rapidly expanding area of activity for MNEs in their developing country locations (Krugman 1995). Contrary to some optimistic observations (for example, Truong and Gates 1996, p. 13; Dollar 1996, p. 183), there is no evidence to believe that FDI has yet begun to restructure Vietnamese manufacturing in line with the country's comparative advantage in international production. In 1994–96, firms with foreign capital participation (foreign affiliates) accounted for about 18 per cent of total manufactured exports (7 per cent of total exports) from Vietnam (Jun et al. 1997, Appendix Table 1b).

A striking feature of foreign investment in Vietnam is its heavy concentration in SOEs, which account for over two-thirds of the country's industrial production. A large proportion of inward FDI – perhaps as much as three-

Table 9.5 Vietnam: Structure of Exports, 1985–96* (%)

	1985	1990	1991	1992	1993	1994	1995	1996
Primary products (0–4)	90.2	88.7	83.7	73.3	65.3	62.4	65.1	63.3
Manufactures (5–8)	7.7	10.4	16.2	26.0	34.2	37.1	34.6	36.4
Chemicals (5)	0.2	0.3	0.2	0.6	0.5	0.4	0.5	0.4
Resource-based manufactures (6)	5.1	5.0	5.0	5.7	6.2	6.2	6.4	7.1
Machinery and transport equipment (7)	0.3	0.4	0.3	0.7	2.0	1.3	1.4	1.5
Miscellaneous (8)	2.1	4.7	10.6	19.0	25.5	29.2	31.2	31.7
Textiles and clothing	1.4	3.8	9.6	9.9	10.7	13.2	15.6	15.9
Footwear	0.6	0.7	0.6	0.8	2.2	2.8	5.4	7.3
Unclassified	1.2	0.9	0.1	0.7	0.5	0.5	0.3	0.3
Total	100.0	100.0	100.0	100.0	100.0	100.0	100.0	100.0
(US$ million)	350	1,282	1,650	2,227	3,130	4,187	5,449	7,255

Note: *Standard International Trade Classification (SITC) code of commodity categories is given in brackets.

Source: International Economics Data Base, Australian National University.

quarters – has been realised in joint ventures with SOEs (Kokko 1997, p. 3). To the extent that such investment is in activities made financially attractive by protection and other forms of government patronage, the net national gain is likely to be much less than the reported figures suggest – and could even be negative. Moreover, the process of channelling FDI to SOEs can be expected to create strong constituencies against future liberalisation reforms. These enterprises are not only large and powerful, they are also intimately connected with various levels of political decision making, and in a position to use their political influence to oppose trade liberalisation or other reforms that may reduce their privileges (CIE 1997).

Unavailability of data prevents us from undertaking a systematic assessment of the employment implications of FDI. According to tentative estimates by the Vietnamese authorities, total employment generated by foreign affiliates during the period 1988–96 amounted to about 250,000. When this figure is related to total realised FDI (as a rough proxy for total cost of investment) of about US$12 billion in 1988–96, investment per worker turns out to be as high as US$48,000 (Nguyen 1998).[2] By contrast, average investment per worker in foreign firms in Malaysian manufacturing is as low as US$18,000.[3]

EXPLAINING DIFFERENCES

How can we explain the startling differences between Malaysia and Vietnam in their experience with promoting FDI? It is usually argued that Malaysia's colonial inheritance – in particular, its well-developed infrastructure and efficient administrative mechanism – has been instrumental in making it an attractive investment location. However, former colonies like Sri Lanka, the Philippines and Ghana have perhaps been better placed for rapid growth than Malaysia without managing to exploit this initial advantage. Malaysia has undoubtedly benefited from its geographical location in a dynamic growth region. This was certainly a factor in the massive direct investment in Malaysia by the NIEs and Japan in the late 1980s and early 1990s, and in the continuous shift by MNEs of relatively labour-intensive production processes from Singapore to Malaysia. But nearby countries such as Indonesia and the Philippines with similar locational advantages have not done nearly as well, suggesting that national development policy has been the key to reaping the benefits of location.

With the second largest population and lowest wage levels in Southeast Asia, Vietnam is perhaps better placed for labour-intensive manufacturing activities than Malaysia ever was. Malaysia, with its low population base, rapid economic expansion through primary export industries and migration of labour to Singapore, has throughout been a relatively high-wage country by developing country standards, and even now its population is no better educated than that of Vietnam. In sum, conditions in Vietnam are not grossly inferior to those that existed in Malaysia when it embarked on its outward-oriented growth strategy through the promotion of export-oriented FDI.

These considerations lead us to consider differences in the investment climate – both policy-induced incentives and the general business environment – in search of an explanation for differences in achievements. The former encompass everything from straightforward incentives such as cash grants and tax holidays to disguised subsidies such as low public utility rates. The latter is a catch-all term for the various factors that influence investment decisions, including political stability and policy continuity: the trade policy regime; administrative procedures for investment approvals and monitoring; the macroeconomic environment; the attitude of the host country to foreign enterprise participation; and the stability and credibility of rules governing foreign investment. Most economists now accept that the general business environment is far more important to investors than specific incentives, and that the latter can work only if appropriately combined with the former (Wells 1986; Guisinger 1985). Tax concessions and other policy-related incentives are relevant only if the country's general business environment is conducive to making a profit. Moreover, as countries compete to attract foreign investment, the incentives offered by one country are often quickly matched by its competitors.

The Investment Climate in Malaysia

The Malaysian policy on FDI has remained highly liberal by developing country standards throughout the post-independence era (since 1958). The emphasis on the promotion of export-oriented FDI, however, dates back to the late 1960s, when specific incentives were offered to export-oriented ventures under the Industrial Incentives Act of 1968 (Lim 1992). The rich assortment of incentives offered to investors under the Act included exemptions from company tax and duty on imported inputs, relief from payroll tax, investment tax credits and accelerated depreciation allowances on investment. This was followed by the introduction in 1970 of the New Economic Policy, which earmarked manufacturing as the growth sector to spearhead economic restructuring and employment generation. The development of free trade zones (FTZs) under an internationally attractive incentive package to entice foreign investor participation in this endeavour was a key element of the New Economic Policy.[4] Special incentives for the electronics industry (including longer tax holidays) were introduced later in 1971. These had been extended to all labour-intensive, export-oriented manufacturing industries by 1973.

While Malaysia is not to be outdone in the sphere of specific incentives, other countries also offer attractive incentive schemes. As we shall see, Vietnam's incentive regime is not markedly different from that of Malaysia. We therefore need to look more closely at the general business environment to assess Malaysia's attractiveness as an FDI destination.

FDI is by no means unrestricted in Malaysia. There are guidelines and regulations governing FDI in conformity with the country's development priorities and overall socio-economic objectives, and these may at times run counter to the profit maximisation objectives of MNEs (Ariff and Chee 1987). Of particular relevance in this connection are attempts under the New Economic Policy to increase the share of *bumiputra* [native Malays] in the corporate sector from 2 per cent in 1970 to 30 per cent in 1990, and to reserve a certain percentage of employment in foreign ventures for *bumiputra*. The

30 per cent equity ownership by *bumiputra* represents a national target and has never been applied on an individual company basis; 100 per cent foreign ownership of export-oriented ventures has always been permitted. Over the years, the government has also adopted a more lenient stance on *bumiputra* employment quotas with a view to ameliorating the adverse impact of the policy on export-oriented FDI (Athukorala 1998, Chapter 8).

Unlike governments in many other countries (including Vietnam), the Malaysian government has taken care to make its policy stance towards FDI unambiguous and transparent. The foreign investment monitoring organisation, the Malaysian Industrial Development Authority (MIDA), has maintained a reputation as a 'one-stop shop' for speedy screening and approval of proposals for new projects. The government has pursued other specific objectives side by side with export promotion, such as location of industry in 'development areas', increasing the use of local inputs and diverting investment into 'priority' industries. But as in other Far Eastern export-oriented economies, these objectives have been pursued largely through prescriptive rather than proscriptive methods.[5] Guarantees against nationalisation are provided by the Constitution,[6] and investment guarantee agreements have been concluded with several capital-exporting countries. A highly liberal foreign exchange rate regime has always assured profit remittances and the repatriation of capital.

These direct government interventions notwithstanding, by and large Malaysia has been able to maintain an outward-oriented policy stance (Sachs and Warner 1995; Riedel 1991a). Despite the early emphasis on import substitution and more recent attempts to promote heavy industries through public sector participation, Malaysia has stayed clear of quantitative import restrictions as a policy tool. By the mid-1990s, only 3 per cent of all import tariff lines (accounting for about 4.5 per cent of annual import value) were subject to licensing requirements. Thus Malaysia differed from many other developing countries in that domestic price signals were not insulated from world market conditions, and direct government involvement through the allocation of import quotas was minimal.

Tariff protection for domestic manufacturing – always low relative to other developing countries – was further reduced over time. By the mid-1990s the weighted average import tariff rate was 8.7 per cent, the lowest in Southeast and South Asia. The average effective rate of manufacturing protection, which increased from about 25 per cent in the early 1960s to 70 per cent in the early 1970s, declined continuously thereafter and was below 30 per cent by the late 1980s (Alavi 1996). In a recent comprehensive study of the patterns and chronology of trade policy reforms in the postwar era, Sachs and Warner (1995, Table 1) identify Malaysia as one of eight developing countries whose trade regimes remained open throughout the period.[7] In this context, Malaysia's FTZ scheme was simply an integral part of an economy-wide liberal investment and trade regime, not an appendage to a highly controlled regime as in many other countries. As such, it provided a conducive setting for export-oriented foreign firms (Riedel 1993). The economy-wide, tariff-based import regime obviously ensured greater flexibility and expediency in procuring imported inputs, for firms located both within and outside FTZs. More importantly, since rent seeking of import entitlements was not a significant influence on private sector behaviour, it was easy to implement and manage the FTZ scheme.

Under the fourth Malaysia Plan (1981–85), the Malaysian leadership experimented with promoting heavy industries through the establishment of public enterprises with foreign capital participation. The Heavy Industries Corporation of Malaysia (HICOM), a public sector holding company, was set up in 1980 to form partnerships with foreign companies in areas such as petrochemicals, iron and steel, cement, paper and paper products, machinery and equipment, general engineering, transport equipment and building materials. Even though the new industrialisation push was often rationalised as an attempt to emulate Japan and Korea – hence the 'Look East Policy', a term coined by Mahathir in 1981 – in practice the selection of projects was based largely on traditional import substitution criteria. These projects were supported with subsidised credit, government procurement provisions and heavy tariff protection, without being subjected to any market-based performance norms. Reforms implemented in response to the severe macroeconomic crisis in the mid-1980s[8] have involved a gradual process of privatisation and restructuring of these enterprises. By the early 1990s state ownership in manufacturing was limited to a few politically sensitive ventures in the automobile manufacturing, petrochemicals, iron and steel, and cement industries.

There is little evidence that either the government's leadership in industrial policy in general or the heavy industrialisation push in particular have affected the export-led industrialisation process. As discussed above, the structure of industry that has evolved over the past two decades is much in line with what one would expect given the nature of Malaysia's comparative advantage and changing factor endowment. Most of the industries set up under HICOM were 'born losers' artificially spawned with subsidies (Chee 1994, p. 249). By the late 1980s HICOM had invested over RM42 billion in projects generating less than 5,000 jobs directly (RM400,000 per job) and almost negligible exports (Chee 1994, Table 10.5). According to a detailed analysis of the productivity of Malaysian manufacturing in 1979–89, most of the three-digit industries dominated by state enterprises recorded negative or zero total factor productivity growth (Alavi 1996, Chapter 5). Apart from the direct economic cost, the inefficient heavy industry projects (which were mostly involved in the production of investment and intermediate goods) added to the burden of downstream industries, which were forced to pay higher prices for protected products (Lim 1992). The firm commitment of the Malaysian government to outward orientation and a flexible investment approval mechanism ensured, however, that state-led industrialisation attempts did not have a backwash effect on the expansion of export-oriented manufacturing through FDI.

In the area of labour market reform, the emphasis of government policy has been on job creation rather than labour legislation to protect workers' rights. The government has attempted to achieve labour market flexibility through industrial relations legislation providing for compulsory arbitration of disputes and prohibition of the right to strike in 'essential services'. Until 1988, all firms with pioneer status and those in FTZs were exempted from mandatory collective bargaining obligations, and unions were not allowed in these firms. Unions have since gained entry to several FTZ industries, but under restrictive conditions.[9] Despite much criticism, this labour market policy has certainly facilitated the process of outward-oriented growth with foreign capital participation. It is probable that the growth of labour-intensive manufactured exports would have been severely constrained had artificially high real wages or regulations driven up labour costs.

The Investment Climate in Vietnam

There has been significant improvement over the past decade in Vietnam's legal framework for the approval and monitoring of foreign investment. Investment incentives and tax laws have also been revised and streamlined. Vietnam's foreign investment code is now more liberal than that of other countries in the region. In 1992 the Foreign Investment Law was amended to permit foreign investors to establish wholly owned enterprises or enter into joint ventures with Vietnamese partners, in the private or public sectors. The law also provided a guarantee against nationalisation of foreign affiliates. The various tax incentives offered by the Vietnamese authorities are also on a par with practices in competing investment locations.

The complex bureaucratic requirements and procedures for getting a project approved and implemented, which often take several years to complete, remain perhaps the biggest obstacle to investors. According to interview-based surveys of investors, this process typically requires the involvement of at least eight central government agencies and numerous local government entities (Riedel and Comer 1997). Although full foreign ownership of domestic ventures is permitted under Vietnamese law, these cumbersome administrative procedures force foreign investors into joint ventures with SOEs.[10] This 'forced' SOE–FDI link not only creates an avenue for inefficient resource use, but also greatly limits the operational flexibility of foreign investors. The experience of Malaysia and many other countries suggests that this latter limitation is a significant deterrent to the entry of export-oriented foreign firms, in particular those in assembly operations in vertically integrated high-tech industries (Athukorala and Menon 1996; Rasiah 1995).

When the Foreign Investment Law was first promulgated in 1987, bureaucratic dominance in economic management was widespread and a market-oriented legal framework did not exist. Over the next four to five years, noteworthy steps were taken to introduce supporting legislation and expand the coverage of the legal framework, with a view to incorporating FDI more effectively into Vietnam's national development strategy. Unfortunately, since the introduction of the Administrative Reform Program in 1995, the development of an institutional framework for the promotion of FDI has been adversely affected by changes in the political and economic environment, propelled largely by an emerging perception that the socio-economic crisis has ended (Truong and Gates 1996). In recent years foreign investment proposals have been subject to strict regulation and more selective screening criteria, including increased emphasis on technological sophistication and technology transfer. Regulatory measures introduced under the 1995 reform program that have had a direct bearing on foreign investment projects include a proposal to establish Communist Party liaison offices in all foreign ventures, the doubling of commercial and residential rents for foreign enterprises and expatriate staff, the imposition of a maximum time limit of three years on work permits issued to foreigners employed in FDI projects, and restrictions on foreign capital participation in labour-intensive industries (Truong and Gates 1996). An amendment to the Foreign Investment Law in 1996 reduced the scope of import duty exemptions for foreign investment projects.

Side by side with the restrictive FDI regime are various obstacles to import trade. In spite of recent reforms and commitments to reform, the Vietnamese trade regime remains complex and highly restrictive. Formal tariffs make up only a limited part of trade restrictions; various kinds of opaque non-tariff barriers, including a stringent licensing mechanism, are equally burdensome. These onerous and arbitrary restrictions pose unnecessary and significant barriers to entry by private firms and are applied in a non-transparent fashion. Tariffs are also subject to frequent fine-tuning and changes. While inputs attract very low or nil rates of duty, outputs often have high rates of duty placed on them. Such a duty structure is bound to provide very high rates of effective protection (CIE 1997, Chapter 1).

To cushion exporters against the constraining effects of the restrictive trade regime, the government introduced a duty rebate scheme in 1993 and an FTZ scheme in 1991. Procedures to support these schemes are complex. Drawback or refund schemes normally require extensive systems for determining production coefficients and cost structures as the basis for calculating the import content of exports. Administrative hurdles have also held back the FTZ scheme, and the government is now reported to be more interested in developing 'industrial concentration zones' (CIE 1997, p. 69). It is evident that, in the context of a highly restrictive trade regime, such piecemeal initiatives are insufficient to ensure a favourable investment climate for export-oriented industrialisation. It has been found time and again that such schemes are not a substitute for broad-based trade liberalisation and that they work effectively only as part of a broad trade liberalisation program (Riedel and Comer 1997, p. 208). Malaysia's experience with its highly successful FTZ scheme is consistent with this view.

The increased emphasis on state of the art technology and the bias against labour-intensive production as part of the investment screening process are clear anomalies in Vietnam's foreign investment policy. As noted, Malaysia's success in generating employment through FDI was a direct outcome of its policy emphasis on the promotion of labour-intensive export industries. In providing incentives, Malaysia placed all export-oriented industries, including labour-intensive consumer goods industries and labour-intensive assembly activities in vertically integrated high-tech industries, on a fairly equal footing.

CONCLUDING REMARKS

Malaysia's success in promoting export-led industrialisation can be attributed to its ability to position itself within a new world order characterised by increased internationalisation of production, spearheaded by MNEs. As a small and open economy, Malaysia's economic policy stance has been, not to isolate itself from these global trends, but rather to respond swiftly to external developments as they arise. Unlike many other developing countries, Malaysia has never imposed stringent quantitative import restrictions. Its longstanding outward-oriented policy stance has seen it well placed to take full advantage of export-oriented FDI to achieve economic development with full employment and equity. The key lesson for Vietnam and other reforming economies is that measures to promote FDI yield handsome development dividends only when implemented as part an overall outward-oriented development strategy.

The Malaysian experience is not that of an unfettered market economy. There have been significant policy interventions, and these have reflected the socio-political challenges posed by a plural society rather than enlightened policy activism of the East Asian type. Under the state-led heavy industrialisation program of the first half of the 1980s, the Malaysian government encouraged MNEs to participate in public sector manufacturing ventures. Despite significant privatisations implemented since the late 1980s, state enterprises still play an important role in key product areas, including automobile manufacturing, petrochemicals, iron and steel, and cement. However, these direct government interventions did not constrain the expansion of export-oriented firms – whether foreign-owned or local – given the virtual free trade status they enjoyed in procuring inputs and Malaysia's flexible investment approval mechanism.

Vietnam has made a promising start in implementing market-oriented reform and promoting FDI as part of it, but it has a long way to go to reap the benefits of this. To be effective, its FDI policy will need to be supported by appropriate trade liberalisation and SOE reforms. Measures to ensure speedy and free access to imported inputs are essential to promote FDI in export-oriented industries. The dominance of SOEs in the economy, which compels foreign investors to form joint ventures with state enterprises as the principal means of gaining market entry, not only nurtures inefficient resource use but also severely constrains the operational flexibility firms need to engage successfully in export-oriented operations.

Vietnam's investment screening criteria are not consistent with national development priorities. As the Malaysian case vividly demonstrates, export-led industrialisation through greater FDI participation is a surer way to generate employment and reduce poverty. With its vast human capital base and strategic location in the world's most dynamic economic region, Vietnam is well placed to follow that path. Under this growth strategy, 'labour intensity' should be treated as a virtue, rather than a drawback, in approving foreign investment projects.

NOTES

1. Manufacturing is defined to include all product sectors belonging to Section 3 of ISIC except petroleum refining.
2. The actual figure may be even higher, because investment contributions to such projects by local joint venture partners are not fully captured in the FDI data.
3. According to the *Survey of Manufacturing Industry 1992* published by the Department of Statistics, average fixed investment per worker in foreign firms was about US$18,000.
4. The first FTZ was established in Bayan Lepas, Penang, in 1992. By the early 1990s Malaysia had ten FTZs. For details, see Rasiah (1995).
5. The terminology is Bhagwati's (1988, pp. 98–100). Under proscriptive regimes, activities that are not specifically permitted tend to be prohibited. The prescriptive approach relies more on incentives to achieve the desired objectives.
6. Transferring a progressively large share of foreign-owned plantation companies to the nationals was a declared government policy. However, the government always adhered strictly to the practice of transferring ownership through formal share market trading rather than arbitrary expropriation (Myint 1967).

7. The other seven were Barbados, Cyprus, Hong Kong, Mauritius, Singapore, Thailand and the Yemen Arab Republic.

8. The blow-out in public expenditure as a result of massive government investment programs under the new industrialisation drive was partly responsible for the macroeconomic crisis (Corden 1996).

9. Only 'in-house' rather than industry-level unions were allowed in plants. Interestingly, workers have been slow to respond to the new opportunity to unionise. One theory is that they have ceased to be militant because of the tremendous improvement in employment prospects and conditions they experienced under the earlier restrictive policy!

10. A foreign investor wanting to set up a fully owned venture or a joint venture with a private sector firm currently has to wait about two years for the necessary permits, compared to less than one year for a joint venture with an SOE (Kokko and Zejan 1996).

10. Experiences in the Region and Private Sector Incentives in Vietnam

Raymond Mallon

BACKGROUND

Introduction

The marked contrast between Vietnam's poor economic performance from the late 1970s through to the early 1990s and the strong economic performance of the Southeast and East Asian market economies during the same period undoubtedly contributed to pressures for economic reform in Vietnam. The recent sharp turnaround in economic conditions in many of these countries has led to some reassessment by Vietnamese policy makers of the implications of the Asian development experience for Vietnam's development strategy. There are also more immediate concerns about the potential impact of the recent turmoil on the competitiveness of Vietnamese business and on regional demand for Vietnamese exports, with considerable debate about appropriate policy responses.

Some domestic analysts have argued that continuing state controls on the Vietnamese economy – and especially controls over capital flows – have insulated Vietnam from the worst impacts of the crisis. They argue that current domestic economic concerns result primarily from external factors and that the appropriate policy response is either to do nothing or, worse still, to tighten controls on capital flows, trade transactions and financial institutions in an attempt to insulate the domestic economy from external factors.

Other analysts argue that weaknesses that have contributed to regional problems – including distorted credit markets, weak financial sector supervision, weaknesses in contract enforcement, close links between bureaucrats, business and banks, protected inefficient industries, lack of transparency and unsustainable external debt financing – also need to be addressed. These weaknesses have previously been masked by the strong growth generated by very high levels of foreign investment inflows relative to GDP. Even before the crisis, doubts had been raised about the sustainability of these high levels of foreign investment in the absence of a greater focus on increasing domestic savings and investment. Moreover, there was evidence of emerging overcapacity in areas that have absorbed a considerable portion of past foreign investment, such as property development (mainly tourist and office facilities) and automobiles. The regional crisis and in particular the fall in approvals of foreign direct investment (FDI) projects since 1996 have increased the urgency of efforts to accelerate institutional and economic reforms in Vietnam.

Recent policy statements indicate that the country's leadership remains committed to sustaining efforts to open up the economy, while also emphasising the need to learn from recent regional problems. Reiterating the need to 'draw lessons from the financial–monetary crisis in some Southeast Asian countries', the new Party Secretary-General, Le Kha Phieu, noted that: 'Modernisation cannot be achieved through a closed door in this era ... no country can close its door to the world. If it tries to do so, the door will one day be opened' (interview published in *Tuan Bao Quoc The* [Weekly International Report], 1 April 1997).

A casual look at recent key indicators of the Vietnamese economy suggests that the measurable impact of the regional turmoil has so far been relatively mild (Table 10.1). Strong economic growth and foreign investment inflows were sustained during 1997. In April 1998, the official growth target for the year remained 9 per cent (but has subsequently been revised downwards), and preliminary first quarter data indicated only a marginal slowing of growth in industrial output, with a more pronounced slowing of growth in exports and imports. The trade and current account deficits fell in 1997, and continued to fall during 1998.

There is, however, cause for considerable concern. The impact of declining competitiveness on exports and output will take time to be reflected in economic aggregates, and it will take time for declines in foreign investment approvals to be reflected in capital inflows. Moreover, signs of an economic downturn were apparent by the first quarter of 1998. Export and import growth rates declined substantially compared with the first quarter of 1997. FDI approvals continued to fall from their peak level in 1996 (when figures were inflated by two massive 'new city' development projects that have yet to start). Tourism growth has slowed, the rental costs of international-standard offices in central urban areas have fallen sharply (from levels that were high relative to those in other Southeast Asian nations), and vacancy rates have increased. Some foreign investors in the property, hospitality, automobile assembly and light manufacturing[1] sectors have reduced their workforces, and declines have been reported in the number of expatriate staff in some offices. The representative offices of a number of South Korean and Thai banks closed in early 1998. The availability of commercial debt financ-

Table 10.1   Key Economic Indicators, 1995–98

	1995	1996	1997	1998*
GDP growth (% growth in 1995 constant prices)	9.5	9.3	8.8	n.a.
Agriculture	4.5	4.4	4.5	n.a
Industry	13.9	14.4	13.2	13.0
Services	10.9	10.0	8.0	n.a.
Inflation (% increase in CPI)	12.7	4.5	4.0	4.5
Exports (% growth in US$ value)	34.4	32.8	20.0	12.2
Imports (% growth in US$ value)	4.0	36.7	0.5	−2.6
Current account deficit (% of GDP)	−10.2	−11.3	−8.0	n.a.
Investment (% of GDP)	27.1	27.9	29.4	n.a.
Foreign investment inflows (US$ million)	2,236.0	1,838.0	2,500.0	n.a.

Note: *The figure for inflation is for the 12 months to March 1998; other data are for the first quarter of 1998 compared with the first quarter of 1997.

Sources: General Statistics Office (1997), *Statistical Yearbook 1996*, Hanoi; unpublished estimates for 1998.

ing from external sources has fallen greatly, and there are increasingly frequent reports of a decline in the financial performance of state enterprises and an accumulation of arrears in the banking system.

There is considerable uncertainty about just how severe an impact the regional crisis will have on the Vietnamese economy but – at least in the medium term – it is unlikely to be as severe as in Thailand, Indonesia or South Korea. Some of the main arguments concerning the potential severity of the impact of the crisis on Vietnam are summarised in the Box (see over).

The usual limitations of economic 'science' in predicting major changes in economic fundamentals are more acute in Vietnam, because of the lack of transparency at all levels, because there is a reluctance to share limited official data and because official statistics are often unreliable. Policy analysts suffer from a dearth of reliable information on key variables affecting the economy, such as capital inflows, foreign reserves, the level of government guaranteed external debt, the financial performance of state enterprises, bad

ALTERNATIVE VIEWS OF THE IMPACT OF REGIONAL TURMOIL ON THE VIETNAMESE ECONOMY

The current account deficit, at 9 per cent of GDP in 1997, is high, and higher than in the major Asian countries now experiencing a financial crisis.	Vietnam is less dependent on short-term flows (short-term debt and portfolio investments) of foreign capital. Most inflows are in the form of FDI, or official development assistance (ODA) provided on a grant or highly concessional basis. The current account deficit has continued to decline since 1996.
Much of Vietnam's trade is with Japan – which has recently experienced very low growth – and other countries with slowing economic growth due to the regional turmoil. Much of the committed foreign investment is also from Asian countries, and this will fall as a result of the region's economic difficulties.	Despite slow growth for some years, economic cooperation with Japan has still grown strongly. Most FDI to Vietnam is from the countries least affected by the crisis (Taiwan, Singapore and Hong Kong). Only Korea (10 per cent of FDI, and less than 5 per cent of 1997 exports) has been severely affected (Table 10.2).
The government still plays a major role in allocating investment. Policy and institutional bias favours larger, more capital-intensive and often less productive investment projects. There is a lack of transparency in the process of public investment decision making.	Possible reductions in FDI inflows will be partially offset by a continuing build-up in inflows of ODA.
Institutional weaknesses limit the entry of new business, the development of private businesses, the exit of loss-making enterprises and the development of competitive markets in Vietnam.	Given the low base of development, there is still considerable opportunity for growth and development within the existing institutional structure.

The Vietnamese currency has appreciated substantially in real terms, with negative implications for the competitiveness of Vietnamese producers. Other Southeast Asian economies are now more attractive destinations for FDI.	Vietnam's financial system is very underdeveloped and not integrated with international markets – partly because of continuing government controls.
The shortage of foreign exchange in official institutions has been particularly acute – transactions in the official interbank market have all but ceased.	Large pools of international funds are still looking for investments. Recent developments have narrowed perceptions of the gap in country risk between Vietnam and other major Southeast Asian countries.
Some enterprises have borrowed relatively large amounts of money in foreign currencies on a short-term basis. Domestic banks have defaulted on letters of credit.	Labour costs are still among the lowest in the region. Other foreign investment costs (land, buildings and some utilities) have declined over the past two years, as have tourism services, while facilities have improved. Markets have overreacted; partial corrections in exchange rates and equity prices are expected in the most badly affected countries.
Lack of transparency is an important problem throughout the economy, not only in financial institutions, but also in the way in which most administrative decisions affecting commercial decisions are taken. Prudential supervision and control in the banking system are particularly weak.	Bad loans from speculative investments (especially in property) appear to be less of a problem in Vietnam. (Banks have not lent because it is difficult to obtain security over property and to foreclose on mortgaged property.) Financial institutions are underdeveloped and are relatively less important in the economy.
The financial performance of Vietnamese enterprises is deteriorating. There is little effective accounting and auditing, and difficulties in initiating bankruptcy action further reduce financial transparency.	The reported declining performance of state enterprises partly results from weak corporate governance and disincentives to report profits. Many of the weakest state enterprises have effectively ceased operations.

Table 10.2   FDI (1988–97) and Exports (1996–97) to Vietnam from Asia (%)

	FDI (1988–97)		Exports	
	Commitments	Disbursements	1996	1997*
Japan	9.8	10.8	12.9	19.2
Singapore	17.7	9.6	25.8	14.0
Hong Kong	7.6	14.8	4.2	1.7
Taiwan	13.0	13.9	7.4	9.1
Korea	10.0	10.8	7.6	4.4
Malaysia	4.2	8.3	1.1	1.7
Thailand	3.3	3.9	1.5	2.7
Indonesia	0.7	0.5	0.6	0.5
Other	33.7	27.4	38.9	46.7
Total	100.0	100.0	100.0	100.0

Notes: *Export data for 1997 are for first ten months of the year.

Source: Preliminary data from the IMF and Vietnam's Ministry of Planning and Investment.

debts in the banking system and levels of domestic private investment. Many of the leading indicators that may indicate future problems – such as trends in the level of non-performing loans in the banking system, the financial performance of state enterprises, the level of inventories in key industrial enterprises and real estate prices – are not available in any systematic form. Improvements in the transparency and reliability of such basic information is needed if analysts are to understand better the implications of the regional economic turmoil and provide more reliable short-term policy advice.

Recent developments have focused attention on the continuing institutional weaknesses and policy disincentives that are restricting private sector development in Vietnam. This is both because business is facing increased competitive pressures, and because the type of institutional weaknesses and policy distortions that constrain private sector development in Vietnam have also contributed to the economic turmoil in neighbouring countries. This chapter briefly reviews some of the institutional and micro-level policy issues that affect incentives to invest in commercial businesses in Vietnam. It argues – in a non-rigorous manner – that there is a need to address these weaknesses for both efficiency and equity reasons, and that recent regional developments increase the urgency of taking action in order to assist in ameliorating emerging macroeconomic imbalances, especially in the domestic savings–investment gap. The chapter does not attempt to cover all the important constraints to private sector investment, and it could be argued that such issues as public investment and trade policies should have received more attention.

The remainder of this section gives a brief overview of the changing role of the private sector in the Vietnamese economy. Some of the institutional weaknesses and policy distortions that continue to affect the investment decisions of Vietnamese enterprises are outlined in the next section.[2] The final section contains recommendations on priorities for reform.

The Changing Role of the Private Sector

The Constitution guarantees that 'enterprises belonging to all components of the economy ... are equal before the law'.[3] In practice, enterprises operating in Vietnam are clearly subject to quite different administrative and regulatory constraints depending on ownership. The country's economic system is still in transition and continues to include elements of both a centrally planned and a market economy regime. Redundant skills, institutions and property relations are being absorbed into a new economic system. In some cases adjustments have been made in a surprisingly flexible manner, but there are also inevitable tensions.[4]

Key indicators of the changing role of the private sector are summarised in Table 10.3. Total state share of GDP declined from almost 45 per cent of GDP in 1986 to less than 33 per cent in 1990. Since 1990 the state share of GDP has increased, reflecting both increased expenditure on state public services and utilities, and the impact of foreign investment in joint ventures with state enterprises. Despite reportedly having a rising share of total output, state enterprise contributions to government revenue declined from 59 per cent in 1990 to 37 per cent in 1996.

Despite the continuing large share of state enterprise in total output, its share of employment has always been relatively small and has fallen consistently over the last decade – from 9.7 per cent of total state employment in 1986 to 5.1 per cent in 1995. The share of civil servants in the workforce fell from 5 to 3.6 per cent over the same period. The private sector has been important in absorbing both workers laid off from the state sector and the large annual increment in new entrants to the workforce.

*Table 10.3   Share of Private and State Sectors in the National Economy,
1986–96 (%)*

	1986	1990	1991	1992	1993	1994	1995	1996
Total state share of GDP	44.7	32.5	33.3	36.2	39.2	40.2	42.3	42.0
Private share of agricultural output	94.9	97.1	97.1	97.2	97.2	97.1	97.2	97.2
Private share of domestic retail trade	41.4	66.9	71.1	74.7	77.3	75.8	76.5	75.7
Non-state share of industrial output*	43.7	32.4	31.5	29.5	28.3	27.6	32.1	32.0
Cooperatives	28.1	9.1	4.8	2.8	2.1	1.1	0.8	0.8
Private enterprises and individuals	15.6	23.2	26.7	26.6	26.1	26.5	31.3	31.2
Share of total workforce employed by the state	14.7	11.3	10.2	9.3	9.1	8.9	8.7	8.9
State administration	5.0	4.4.	4.0	3.7	3.7	3.7	3.6	n.a.
State enterprises	9.7	6.9	6.2	5.6	5.4	5.2	5.1	n.a.
State enterprise share of total budget revenue	n.a.	58.8	60.0	56.3	52.9	49.8	41.0	37.3

Note: *This is an underestimate as it excludes output from foreign joint ventures with state enterprises (shown in Table 10.4).

Source: General Statistics Office (various issues), *Statistical Year Book*, Hanoi.

The private sector accounts for 97 per cent of agricultural output. It also dominates retail trade activity: its share of retail trade nearly doubled from 41 per cent in 1986 to 76 per cent in 1996. The private sector share of all services (including public services such as education and health) has, however, remained largely unchanged at around 55 per cent throughout the 1990s. Excluding such public services, the private sector accounted for about 78 per cent of value added in services in 1996.

Table 10.4   Industrial Output by Ownership, 1994–97 (%)

	1994	1995	1996	1997
All industry	100.0	100.0	100.0	100.0
Domestic enterprises *of which:*	76.2	74.9	73.3	71.5
State enterprises	50.7	50.3	49.2	48.0
Non-state	25.5	24.6	24.0	23.5
Individual	19.0	17.6	16.1	14.5
Private companies	2.2	2.2	2.4	2.5
Cooperatives	0.8	0.6	0.6	0.5
Mixed	3.4	4.2	5.0	6.0
Foreign-invested enterprises *of which:*	23.8	25.1	26.7	28.5
Oil and gas	11.0	10.5	11.0	11.0
Other industries	12.8	14.6	15.8	17.5

Source: Unofficial data supplied by Vietnam's Ministry of Planning and Investment. The data are still subject to revision.

According to the data series reported in Table 10.3 (published on an annual basis), the private sector accounted for only 32 per cent of industrial output in 1996. However, the data may be misleading, for a number of reasons. Output from joint ventures, or business cooperation contracts, between foreign investors and state enterprises is recorded as state output. Non-state enterprises face disincentives to report the full scale of their operations, and their share in the economy is probably understated. On the other hand, output from joint stock and limited liability companies in which state enterprises have equity is reported as non-state output.

The Vietnamese authorities are attempting to provide a data series that records output from foreign-invested enterprises separately. The preliminary summary data for 1994–97 (Table 10.4) show that state enterprises accounted for less than half of total industrial output in 1997. While these unpublished data are consistent with the published data series in terms of trends, there are small differences in absolute values.[5]

Output from foreign-invested enterprises has increased to more than one-quarter of total industrial output since the Foreign Investment Law was approved by the National Assembly in December 1987. While growth in the share of output from foreign investment was initially at the expense of industrial cooperatives, more recently the shares of domestic individual producers and state enterprises have also started to decline. Individuals and households account for some 14.5 per cent of industrial output, but the contribution of registered private companies remains very small at about 2.5 per cent.

One reason for the limited importance of registered private companies in Vietnamese industrial output is that the private sector is only just beginning to develop from a small base. But another, more worrying, factor is the continuing disincentives to private investors to move beyond being small household businesses operating in the informal sector. These disincentives relate to the continuing policy and administrative bias against the private sector, and to poorly developed market institutions.

Emergence of Private Enterprises

The number of private companies has increased consistently since the Company Law was approved in 1990, with an estimated 220 joint stock companies, 9,900 limited liability companies and 23,000 private enterprises registered in 1997 (Table 10.5). Private sector enterprises are mostly small in scale, but a number of medium-sized operations are beginning to emerge. Most of the former industrial and service sector cooperatives have been disbanded or reorganised as private enterprises. The number of household businesses is estimated to have increased from about 0.84 million in 1990 to 2.2 million in 1996.

The small economic contribution of companies is in contrast to the more significant role of private companies in industrialised market economies. Jordan (1997, pp. 90–92) notes that family-controlled corporations (that is, not including public companies) 'in the United States produce more than half of the country's goods and services'. Questions have been raised as to whether there are differences in the business culture of Asian firms that 'require a new and unique form of business vehicle, better suited to their characteristics'. Jordan concludes that: 'Although there are cross cultural differences in terms of degree and intensity ... they are very similar to their Western counterparts on several levels. In terms of size and corporate form, they tend to be small to medium-sized companies with ownership and management concentrated in the hands of a patriarch/matriarch or a small group of family members'.[6]

CIEM (1998) has reported similar characteristics for Vietnamese companies, with the notable difference that the state (and/or state enterprises) holds up to 49 per cent of equity in a number of joint stock companies – and not

Table 10.5   Trends in Numbers of Business Enterprises, 1990–97

	1990	1991	1992	1993	1994	1995	1996	1997 (est.)
State enterprises[a]	12,084	9,832	9,300	5,704	5,835	6,310	5,790	5,960
Centrally managed	1,695	2,331	n.a.	1,675	1,678	1,847	n.a.	1,950
Locally managed	10,389	7,501	n.a.	4,029	4,157	4,463	n.a.	4,010
Domestic non-state enterprises								
Joint stock[b]	–	3	65	106	126	165	190	220
Limited liability[b]	–	43	1,170	3,390	5,258	7,346	8,900	9,900
Cooperatives[c]	n.a.	n.a.	3,231	n.a.	2,275	1,867	n.a.	n.a.
Private enterprises[b]	–	76	3,126	8,684	14,052	18,243	21,000	23,000
Household enterprises (million)[d]	0.84	n.a.	1.50	n.a.	1.53	2.05	2.22	n.a

Notes:
– = not applicable.
n.a. = not available.
[a]Data from 1993 are for state enterprises registered under Decree 388-HDBT. Subsequent figures include registrations of existing unregistered enterprises.
[b]The data are for actual enterprises registered; some may since have ceased operations. Some state enterprises have an equity stake in joint stock and limited liability enterprises.
[c]Excluding agricultural cooperatives.
[d]Data are based on official estimates from survey data.

Source: Based on data provided by the Central Institute for Economic Management and the Enterprise Department, Ministry of Planning and Investment.

just those enterprises that have recently been equitised. The relatively limited contribution of the private corporate sector, and the role of state investments in the 'private' sector, may partly be explained by the fact that the types of institutions needed to protect property rights in a market economy are only just starting to emerge in Vietnam. In the absence of strong market institutions, state involvement may be seen as offering greater protection of property rights. There is a need for further research to compare the role of formal company structures in the industrial development of other East Asian economies, and to contrast that with the current experience in Vietnam. In

particular, there is a need to look more closely at the nature of the relationship between state enterprise management and state enterprise investments in
joint stock companies.

INSTITUTIONAL WEAKNESSES AS A CONSTRAINT TO PRIVATE INVESTMENT[7]

Introduction

Critical to improving incentives for private sector investment and developing
competitive markets is the existence of an effective system of property
rights, including market institutions to facilitate the growth and development
of enterprises, as well as the exit of inefficient enterprises. North (1994,
p. 359) argues that formal and informal institutions 'form the incentive structure of society, and the economic and political institutions, in consequence,
are the underlying determinants of economic performance'.[8] Institutional
development is needed in Vietnam, to provide a framework to facilitate the
formation and growth of enterprises; to develop markets to mobilise and
allocate inputs and final products more efficiently; to improve information
flows; and to provide supporting services and infrastructure. After two general comments, some of the specific institutional weaknesses that restrict
incentives for private sector investment in Vietnam are discussed.

First, it is important to recognise that, compared with most other East
Asian economies, many of the formal institutions required to support investment in a market economy either do not exist or are still at an early stage of
development in Vietnam. The challenges of institutional development are
compounded because formal market institutions need to be developed from
the foundations of institutions that were established to control a centrally
planned economy. The implied change in economic and political power
resulting from institutional change contributes to the tensions noted earlier.
It also means that there are well organised and established interests wanting
to maintain the status quo. The need to address resistance from vested interests to enterprise reform is not unique to Vietnam, but needs to be recognised
by policy advisers if development strategies are to be implemented.

Second, institutional weakness does not affect all enterprises equally.
State enterprises can use close relations with government agencies to protect
property rights, to facilitate contract enforcement and to secure favourable
administrative decisions. At another extreme, small informal enterprises are
less affected because they are mostly involved in spot transactions and can
use social pressure and personal contacts to enforce contracts. Casual observation suggests that the social institutions needed to protect private property

rights and enforce contracts – at least at the local level – exist to a much greater extent in Vietnam than in the transitional economies of Eastern Europe. However, the need for formal institutions is becoming increasingly important as the scale of operations of private business increases. Thus institutional weaknesses are of greater concern to privately owned small and medium-sized business, and partly explain why private companies are still at an embryonic stage of development.

Basic Legal Framework Governing Vietnamese Enterprises

The legislation governing business entities has been promulgated on an ad hoc basis to meet the needs and pressures of an emerging market economy. There is now legislation regulating different categories of ownership and different forms of investment, as well as other legislation applying to different categories of enterprises, as shown in Table 10.6. Other business entities not listed in the table, such as individual and household business, and enterprises owned by social and political organisations and professional associations,[9] are regulated by subordinate legislation.

Incentives for domestic enterprises are also regulated under the Law on the Promotion of Domestic Investment, and those for foreign investors under the Foreign Investment Law. A move towards a more uniform business law addressing the core provisions of business enterprises, regardless of source of investment, would better serve the interests of consistency and transparency. Where the government has clear policy objectives in treating entities differently, these could be stated explicitly and addressed in relevant legislation. This would facilitate both the assessment of the efficiency of policy measures in achieving objectives and the design of more effective policy instruments.

Entry and Development of New Enterprises

Barriers to the entry and development of new enterprises have both economic efficiency and equity implications. Restrictions on new entry will restrict competition and result in higher consumer prices. They will also lead to a growing concentration of wealth by existing owners at the expense of potential new enterprise owners. Such restrictions have contributed to inefficiencies and inequities in income distribution elsewhere in the region. Recently there has been increasing domestic concern about the costs and inequities of the business registration and licensing system in Vietnam.[10]

Current procedures for establishing a business are complex, confusing and overlapping. Registration and licensing responsibilities are spread among different government agencies depending on the ownership and type of the

Table 10.6   Laws Regulating Business Entities*

	Date Approved and Amended	Business Category or Arrangements Addressed under Law
Foreign Investment Law	December 1987 June 1990 December 1992 April 1997	Joint venture entities Foreign-owned entities Business cooperation contracts Build–operate–transfer projects
Company Law	December 1990 June 1994 April 1999 (planned)	Joint stock companies Private limited liability companies
Private Enterprise Law	December 1990 June 1994 April 1999 (planned)	Private unlimited liability enterprises
Bankruptcy of Enterprises Law	November 1993	All business enterprises
Promotion of Domestic Investment Law	June 1994 April 1998 (planned)	All domestically owned business entities
State Enterprise Law	April 1994 1999 (planned)	State corporations State public utility enterprises State business enterprises
Cooperatives Law	March 1996	Cooperatives
Financial Institutions Law	November 1997	All financial institutions

Note: *An amended Promotion of Domestic Investment Law was approved in April 1998. It now seems likely that consideration of a new Company Law will be brought forward to the November session of the National Assembly.

Source: Central Institute for Economic Management; Legal Drafting Agenda of the National Assembly.

business entity. A recent report by researchers from the Central Institute for Economic Management (CIEM) identifies some ten different agencies that must be visited just to register an enterprise (Doanh and Hao 1997), while CIEM (1998, p. 25) notes that applicants must 'have applied for and received 20 different documents with official seals'. Frequently more than one visit to these agencies is needed. Even after registration, additional licences will be required relating to the nature of the activities to be undertaken by the business entity.

There is considerable administrative discretion in the approval process, with bureaucrats having to determine the adequacy of business plans and check the financial background, physical health, mental capacity and curriculum vitae of company founders. Moreover, these bureaucrats are held responsible and liable for checking the accuracy of business registration documents. The approval process contributes to delays, adds to business establishment costs, discourages competition, provides considerable opportunities for corruption[11] and acts as an important disincentive to enterprises that might otherwise move from the informal to the formal sector. Business people complain that they 'have to closely look at the "movement" of their documents, to "investigate" who is in charge of processing their document, in order to "make influence", if necessary' (CIEM 1998, p. 26).

While the information requirements for approval are onerous, the data thus collected are not regularly updated or used following registration of the enterprise. This information is not readily available to policy makers and is not made publicly available. In market economies, information such as the company charter, company address, names of initial shareholders, names and addresses of board members and number of shares issued is considered to provide some protection to minority shareholders and to creditors who may be considering entering into economic contracts with the company (Goddard 1998).

Among other objectives, the government has stated that it is committed to the establishment of small and medium-sized enterprises, an enhanced role for the formal sector, increasing tax revenue and reducing corruption. The realisation of such objectives would be facilitated by the introduction of a simplified business registration and licensing system. Decisions need to be taken on the minimum information that would need to be included in a national business registration database of all enterprises regardless of ownership, and which would be publicly accessible throughout the country. Registration and licensing requirements should be adjusted accordingly. Registration of most enterprises should be automatic, subject to the submission of basic information in a standard format. There may need to be provisions for periodic and ad hoc reporting to maintain an accurate registration database, but to encourage enterprises to register, the process should be simple, fast and inexpensive.

There are related concerns about the specification of rather arbitrary minimum capital requirements for different sectors, and about the need for enterprises to state their business objectives, with transactions outside the specified area being considered illegal (CIEM 1998, p. 61). In practice these regulations are circumvented,[12] and in any case it is not clear what value they would have if enforced.[13] There is also ambiguity about the approvals required and procedures to be followed when an enterprise makes changes to its name, address, shareholding structure or business activities (Goddard 1998, p. 60).

Problems of business registration are compounded by a complicated licensing system. Obtaining business licences can be particularly difficult in areas such as trade and some professional services. The Ministry of Trade must issue import and export licences before a business can engage in foreign trade.[14] Since 1991 such licences have supposedly been available to all enterprises meeting specified criteria, but in practice obtaining them can be time consuming and expensive (Doanh and Hao 1997, pp. 95–105). The criteria used in assessing applications to be registered to engage in foreign trade include minimum capital requirements, past foreign trade experience and the qualifications of personnel. While private manufacturing enterprises have been permitted to trade directly in the products they produce, few foreign trade licences have been issued to private trading companies.

The government also imposes quotas and other controls on the import and export of some major products, including rice, textiles, garments, minerals, petroleum products, fertilisers, motor vehicles, equipment and machinery, and second-hand goods. Mechanisms for securing administrative decisions on quotas remain less than transparent. Most rice and garment export quotas, for example, are allocated to state enterprises. Frequently the actual work is subcontracted to private enterprises, with the state enterprise simply collecting the economic rent associated with the quota, with minimal value added (see, for example, ADB and IFPRI 1996). Trade reforms introduced in early 1998 contain new initiatives to streamline trade administration, including the relaxation of restrictions on foreign investors directly engaged in trade, and the decision to allow more direct private sector participation in rice exports.

Reform of administrative procedures for business registration and licensing over the last two years has reportedly contributed to a reduction in the paperwork and time required to register an enterprise (CIEM 1998, p. 26). However, many of the remaining problems relate to the Company Law, and further substantive progress depends on its being revised. After two years of re-drafting, a revised law was recently submitted to the government, but it is not scheduled to be considered by the National Assembly until April 1999.

The current draft of the new law represents a major improvement in simplifying the procedures and requirements for business registration. Further progress in this area has important implications for private sector incentives and future economic development.

Commercial Transactions, Competition and Expansion

Increasing the certainty that contracts will be enforced and improving mechanisms for resolving disputes related to commercial transactions offer considerable potential to generate short-term improvements in private sector investment incentives and opportunities. Contracting is a central institution in ensuring efficient coordination of economic activity between business entities in a market economy. The ability to conduct intertemporal or interregional commercial transactions depends directly on the cost of making contracts and the probability that contracts will be enforced. Issues of contract enforcement and dispute resolution are not just important in terms of trade transactions, they are also vital in mobilising domestic savings, increasing the availability of commercial financing and reducing the costs involved in financing transactions. Such issues are fundamental to the daily decision making of commercial investors.

Commercial contracts
In many market economies, and especially in Asia, the majority of transactions are conducted with limited reliance on formal contracts and enforcement mechanisms.[15] Instead, parties to a contract rely on relationships to enforce or adjust commitments and/or to address non-performance of commitments. Penalties for non-performance are linked to reputation and opportunities to engage in future business. Such arrangements are very common in Vietnam today among the emerging private sector. Although they can be very effective for a wide range of business activities, as has been demonstrated in East Asia, they also have important limitations.[16]

- As the scale of business grows, the need to deal with 'outsiders', such as foreign bankers and traders, is likely to become inevitable. Either party may doubt that informal mechanisms will result in transparent and equitable outcomes.
- Opportunities to enter contracts depend on established relationships, usually based on past business experience with the entrepreneur or related parties. Thus there is a bias against new entrants, with negative consequences for equity and efficiency.
- As the role of formal and independent financial institutions increases, the costs of assessing and enforcing debt repayment rise. Formal contractual

arrangements reduce the transaction costs of lending and allow financial institutions to provide capital at a lower cost than would otherwise be possible.

• Informal arrangements tend to break down in times of general financial stress. Borrowers continue to operate loss-making businesses longer than they would if legal enforcement mechanisms were in place, compounding their losses. This can lead to the spread of financial difficulties to suppliers and creditors, as has been the case recently in East Asia.

These potential constraints are accentuated in Vietnam because a legacy of the former centrally planned system is that business networks (and their informal 'rules of the game'), which have been important in financing private investment elsewhere in East Asia, remain less developed in Vietnam – except to some extent for small-scale activities at the local level. Moreover, bureaucrats in government agencies and state-owned commercial banks continue to exercise considerable control over a large share of productive assets, but do not face the same profit incentives as owners (or professional managers under performance contracts) to ensure that informal contracts are enforceable and enforced. The scope for collusion could be reduced with greater use of formal and transparent contracts to govern commercial transactions.

Several legal documents dealing with contracts entered into by enterprises have been promulgated since the introduction of *doi moi* [program of economic renovation]. They include the Civil Code (enacted in 1995), the Commercial Code (1997) and the Ordinance on Economic Contracts (1989). There is some confusion about whether the provisions on contracts in the Civil Code apply to economic contracts as a subset of civil contracts, and about the extent to which the restrictive and formal provisions of the Ordinance on Economic Contracts continue to apply to economic contracts. This ongoing uncertainty greatly negates the value of formal contracts in economic transactions. Goddard (1998, p. 21) argues that the Ordinance on Economic Contracts should be repealed because of its restrictive nature, and that attempts to distinguish between civil and economic contracts 'can only produce confusion, inappropriate regulation, and unnecessary costs'. Cumbersome, time-consuming and costly notarisation requirements act as a further disincentive to entering into formal contracts.

Enforcement of commercial contracts and resource mobilisation

Access to capital is frequently cited as a major constraint to the development of both private and state enterprises in Vietnam (Doanh and Hao 1997, pp. 37–51). There are frequent complaints about the particular difficulties faced by the private sector in gaining access to credit (see, for example, Riedel and

Table 10.7   Bank Lending to State and Non-state Enterprises, 1991–97*
              (%)

	1991	1992	1993	1994	1995	1996	1997
State enterprises	90.0	81.8	66.9	61.4	57.0	52.7	50.0
Non-state enterprises	10.0	18.2	33.1	38.6	43.0	46.3	50.0

Note: *End of year.

Sources: IMF (1996), 'Vietnam: Recent Economic Developments', *IMF Staff Paper 96/145*, Washington DC; unofficial data for 1997 was provided by the State Bank of Vietnam.

Tran 1997). Decrees specifying minimum debt to equity ratios, and collateral requirements for bank lending, directly discriminate in favour of state enterprises. Despite continuing difficulties, there have been major increases in the share of bank financing directed to the private sector (Table 10.7).

Strengthening financial institutions to increase access to longer-term credit is also important. In this regard, improved mechanisms for enforcing commitments to repay debt are an urgent priority. A significant constraint to raising capital from 'outsiders' – such as formal banking institutions – is the lack of timely and inexpensive mechanisms to enforce debt repayment. The more effective and credible the commitment the borrower can give to repay, the more likely a financial institution will be to approve a loan, and the lower will be the costs of borrowing. The current system creates considerable uncertainty, giving rise to a need for clear regulations governing the creation, registration and enforcement of security interests in property. Confidence would be increased by the introduction of more automatic judgement procedures for debt recovery where there is no genuine dispute about the debt, and mechanisms for the timely enforcement of judgements against specific enterprise assets. There is a need for easier mortgage foreclosure and bankruptcy declaration procedures, and for improved mechanisms to enforce judgements against general enterprise assets (Goddard 1998).

Some progress has been made towards providing more equitable access to bank credit, with legal clarification that state enterprises are limited liability enterprises, government efforts to commercialise the operations of state-owned commercial banks, and the issuance of regulations restricting government guarantees to state enterprises. Also important are amendments to the implementing regulations[17] of the Land Law to allow companies, cooperatives and private enterprises to mortgage land use rights. However, land use rights can only be mortgaged to Vietnamese banks,[18] and all commercial banks have concerns about the difficulty of foreclosing on mortgages in a cost-efficient manner to recover bad debts.[19] Slow progress with land titling and the insecurity of title to land use rights for commercial and industrial purposes are frequently cited as major constraints to raising capital for private investment.

Interest rate ceilings continue to be imposed, limiting the flexibility of banks to charge higher interest rates for loans with higher transaction costs and/or risks. Banks therefore prefer to lend to enterprises where transaction costs and risks are lower. Because lending to smaller enterprises generally involves both higher unit transaction costs and more risk, interest rate ceilings effectively block small firms' access to credit.

There continues to be a bias against the private sector in accessing foreign investment. Some of this relates to the incentives for foreign investors to have a state enterprise as a partner in order to obtain easier access to decision and policy makers, thereby facilitating administrative approvals. These problems will only be resolved by longer-term administrative reform. There are other areas where substantive short-term improvements could be realised, including the reform of regulations that allow state – but not private – enterprises to contribute land use rights as equity in ventures with foreign investors.[20] Private enterprises are also handicapped by restrictions on the transfer of land use rights.

State preferences for larger foreign investment projects are also a constraint to private sector participation in foreign investment projects. Because private enterprises are only just emerging and have a much lower average capital base than state enterprises, most are in a position to participate only in relatively small projects. Given that small projects have the potential to create greater incremental output and employment for a given level of capital than do larger projects, rather than discouraging such investments, the government should actively encourage them. An important step in this direction would be to provide for automatic approvals of smaller investments in sectors open to foreign investment where privileged treatment is not sought. The recent decision to delegate some foreign investment decisions to selected provincial authorities should also make it easier for smaller enterprises to access foreign investment in those provinces. [21]

Proposed reforms to allow foreign-invested joint venture entities to be incorporated under the Company Law would also facilitate more equitable access to foreign investment, while promoting increased domestic equity participation in foreign-invested projects. Because corporate governance, accounting, auditing and financial reporting systems are generally better developed in foreign-invested joint venture entities than in state enterprises and domestic shareholding companies, domestic investors are likely to be more confident about investing in such entities. The listing of foreign joint venture projects on the proposed stock market – expected to be established in 1999 – could substantially increase incentives for domestic investors to participate in the development of equity markets in Vietnam.

Other institutional constraints on private sector investors
Private business people and professionals continue to face difficulties in accessing the latest business, market, trade and professional information. All technical books and magazines must be imported through a state enterprise with monopoly power, at prices that are higher than elsewhere in the region. Delivery is unreliable. Monopoly pricing means telecommunications costs are much higher than in competing countries. Controls on Internet access were relaxed in late 1997, but because of monopoly pricing, costs remain a constraint. State enterprises are also disadvantaged by these policies to some extent, but are more likely to benefit from a relaxation of restrictions, and from the alternative sources of information available to them through having easier access to foreign investment and technical assistance.

There are many other areas – from obtaining a driver's licence and motor vehicle registration, to securing customs clearance, to inspection by local planning offices, tax authorities and police – where private investors are frequently reported to be at a disadvantage relative to state enterprises. Private sector business people generally face greater difficulty in securing passports to travel abroad on business and in securing visas from foreign embassies than do persons sponsored by state enterprises. An acceleration of state administration reform to clarify and streamline administrative procedures, reduce administrative discretion and increase the professionalism and integrity of the public service must be an integral part of any serious effort to reduce disincentives to private investors.

State Regulatory and Business Activities

Separation of ownership and regulatory functions
Critical to improving private sector incentives is the need to address conflicts of interest arising from government agencies continuing to be both regulator and competitor in key sectors of the economy. Further restructuring of the state enterprise sector will be a crucial part of efforts to level the playing field for private investors. One of the most notable examples of conflict of interest has been the Ministry of Trade having responsibility for allocating export quotas for rice and garments. Most quotas are allocated to state enterprises, including state enterprises 'owned' by the Ministry of Trade.

Although current legislation states that the Ministry of Finance is responsible for exercising state 'financial ownership rights' over state enterprises, line ministries and provincial authorities continue to exercise key ownership rights, such as the right to hire and fire senior management. Because it lacks such powers, and because of personnel resource constraints, the Ministry of Finance has not been able to enforce reforms aimed at improving corporate governance. The removal of the remaining ownership rights over state enterprises of line ministries and provincial authorities is an obvious priority to reduce disincentives to private sector investment. A consolidation of ownership rights is critical to enforcing improved corporate governance and accountability.

The private sector would be in a better position to compete if state enterprises were subject to the same hard budget constraints and incentive structures faced by joint stock companies. Progress has been made towards the commercialisation of state enterprises, including a tightening of budget constraints. This has contributed to the liquidation and/or merger of more than 6,000 state enterprises since the state enterprise re-registration process was announced in late 1991. These were mostly small district-level enterprises. Harder budget constraints for most state enterprises have also contributed to substantive increases in labour productivity in the state enterprise sector, with total employment declining by about one-third as output growth has accelerated. However, progress has stalled over the last few years. A renewed focus on corporatisation and divestiture of small enterprises is now needed to provide more equal opportunities for all economic sectors and to sustain productivity growth.

Corporatisation and equitisation
Full corporatisation implies the incorporation of a state enterprise as a joint stock company under the Company Law. Corporatisation offers a mechanism for restructuring enterprises to improve incentive structures and enterprise accountability. The more dynamic managers of state enterprises could benefit from increased management autonomy and greater flexibility in mobilising capital. Corporatisation would facilitate subsequent equitisation, including the issuance of new share capital. A constraint to corporatisation has been the requirement under the Company Law that a joint stock company have more than one shareholder – thus a state enterprise can only be incorporated if equity in the enterprise is sold to one or more other entities. In Vietnam this is referred to as equitisation.

Full corporatisation is to be encouraged, but it is important that it be done in a way that is enforceable. Under the State Enterprise Law, state enterprises are already required to publish Annual Reports and undergo external audits; key management positions are to be filled on fixed term contracts, with pay related to performance. In practice, however, these provisions have not been implemented. There is a real danger that the same lack of compliance would occur under the Company Law if the government attempted to incorporate all state enterprises in too short a period. Widespread non-compliance could undermine public confidence in the institution, and more generally in the credibility of property rights enforcement. An immediate priority is to get a manageable number of core state business enterprises incorporated under the Company Law and to ensure that they comply with its provisions.

Procedures for equitisation have been clarified in recent years, and some of the decision making has been streamlined and decentralised. There is little doubt that this will lead to some acceleration – from a very low base – of equitisation in 1998. Probably the most important remaining administrative stumbling block relates to valuation. The Ministry of Finance (or its provincial counterpart) has to sign off on the valuation before equitisation proceeds. Frequently the domestic press complains that state officials are selling off state assets too cheaply, while equitisation sponsors complain that overvaluation makes it difficult to get the support of workers and other potential investors. In such a situation there are strong incentives for bureaucrats not to approve the valuation and equitisation of an enterprise. The introduction of transparent mechanisms involving the tender or auction of shares, and the abolition of the requirement for formal valuation of small and medium-sized enterprises, could make an important contribution to accelerating the equitisation process.

Divestiture
There are a large number of state enterprises that are too small for it ever to be economic to establish them as joint stock companies, or for the government to exercise effective corporate governance over them as limited liability companies. Neither corporatisation nor equitisation are viable options for such enterprises. Given rising public concern about the misuse and inefficient use of state assets, the only practical option is for the government to auction, tender or sell them to the higher bidder. Limited government institutional capacity should be redirected to managing more effectively the larger state enterprises that account for the bulk of state assets invested in enterprises.

There appears to be growing pressure to address the inefficiency associated with the government trying to manage large numbers of state enterprises. The government has issued a series of regulations on divestiture since mid-1996;[22] in a speech to the 10th National Assembly in September 1997, Prime Minister Phan Van Khai highlighted the need for action in this area; and the government recently issued specific instructions to accelerate the process.[23] Many loss-making, locally managed state enterprises have effectively ceased operations, so the sale of these assets would impose no additional social costs but would free up resources for more productive investments that could generate increased employment. Accelerated progress in this area will require the introduction of more transparent and streamlined procedures as well as a clearer delegation of responsibilities for implementing divestiture, preferably with clearly monitorable targets.

Competing for state business

Competitive bidding for public contracts and for the provision of public infrastructure and services has considerable potential to increase resource use efficiency and national productivity. Competitive bidding can facilitate the emergence of new and innovative enterprises providing improved services. It can also contribute directly to substantial savings in the government's public expenditure program.

The government has already taken steps in this direction. Recently approved regulations provide a much more transparent basis for procurement and bidding for public projects. Recent regulations have also clarified the right of domestic private investors to invest in build–operate–transfer (BOT) and build–operate–own (BOO) infrastructure projects.[24] The government has introduced ad hoc policy measures allowing private sector provision of education and health services, subject to meeting national standards. Further progress and cost savings might be realised if the government were to introduce broad policies and guidelines requiring all ministries to consider actively the most cost-effective approaches to the provision of public goods and services. Greater use of competitive bidding would facilitate this process. Consideration also needs to be given to establishing consistent mechanisms for providing potential bidders with access to information on business opportunities. Information should be published on contract awards, including price information, to assist in the development of competitive markets.

Exit Procedures

Too many business enterprises continue to operate for too long after they have become insolvent. This problem is particularly pronounced in the state enterprise sector. The result is that resources are tied up in unproductive assets and levels of indebtedness increase unnecessarily. Other entities supplying or otherwise involved in commercial relations with the non-viable enterprise also face unnecessary risks that could have been avoided if it had been declared bankrupt earlier. Difficulties in initiating bankruptcy proceedings increase the risks faced by financial institutions and others in providing credit to enterprises, and make it more difficult and more expensive for all enterprises to secure credit.

Bankruptcy provisions need to be strengthened to facilitate implementation of bankruptcy action.[25] An effective bankruptcy system would ensure that enterprises with the capacity to repay due debts did not have the option to delay payments and force creditors to take court action. The Bankruptcy of Enterprises Law was approved in 1993 but has so far only been used in a limited number of cases. At present it is very time consuming and expensive to take a bankruptcy case to the Economic Court. This is partly because the Economic Courts were established at the same time as the Bankruptcy Law was approved and need time to develop, but it is also due to complexities in initiating bankruptcy proceedings and problems in enforcing action. Insolvency tests are unusually restrictive as well as being vaguely worded, making it possible for insolvent enterprises to delay bankruptcy action for quite some time. It is possible for large creditors holding more than one-third of an insolvent enterprise's debts to frustrate attempts by other creditors to take bankruptcy action. This is a particularly important problem given the substantial cross-borrowings of closely related state enterprises. More automatic bankruptcy procedures and more flexible arrangements for the liquidation of bankrupt enterprises' assets could greatly reduce the constraints mentioned above, while facilitating financial sector development.

In addition there is a need for more effective financial monitoring of state enterprises by the government, and a greater willingness to close state business enterprises that are loss making or that are making an insufficient return on state assets. Failure to take such action acts as a disincentive for potentially more efficient enterprises to enter the market and is a constraint to economic growth. It also reduces the incentive for state enterprise managers to perform well.

CONCLUSIONS AND IMPLICATIONS FOR REFORM

The recent regional economic turmoil will reduce the competitiveness of Vietnamese business enterprises in domestic and international markets, but the direct impact of the crisis is expected to be less severe than in the most badly affected countries in the region. Regardless, it is increasingly clear that 'doing nothing' is not an option if Vietnam is to realise its ambitious targets for socio-economic development.

Prior to the turmoil there was a growing recognition of the need to accelerate efforts to reduce institutional barriers to investment by domestic businesses. Increasing levels of foreign capital inflows and, to a lesser extent, increased public expenditure had been the major source of economic growth during the previous few years. By the mid-1990s the ratio of FDI inflows to GDP in Vietnam was among the highest in the world. This masked some of the underlying constraints to domestic investment. It was doubtful that a growth strategy so heavily dependent on foreign financing was sustainable, or that it would generate equitable growth given the emphasis on larger, capital-intensive projects (Mallon 1997). It was also clear that investment had reached saturation point in some sectors – at least in the short term – with obvious excess capacity in office and hotel development and in the automobile industry.

Recent reductions in approvals for foreign investment projects, and cutbacks in some committed projects, are expected to result in reduced levels of FDI inflows in the short to medium term. Unless domestic sources of investment are increased, growth in economic output and employment can be expected to slow in the medium term. Strong action to reduce continuing disincentives to domestic private sector investment could assist in ameliorating the impacts of reduced foreign capital inflows. Such action could also contribute to more equitable distribution of the benefits of growth, because domestic private investment is more likely to be of much smaller scale, to be relatively labour intensive, and to be more geographically dispersed to include a greater share of investment in rural and isolated areas.

While there are broad principles for economic development that are applicable to and increasingly well understood in Vietnam, there is no simple panacea in addressing the constraints to increased domestic investment. Direct disincentives to private sector investment are still pervasive and are exacerbated by policy distortions and poorly developed market institutions. The market institutions that are sometimes taken for granted when providing policy advice remain substantially underdeveloped in Vietnam relative to other market economies in the region. There is a great need to strengthen the credibility of property rights to provide greater incentives for private sector investment. While reforms require substantive change, investors also need to be assured that the formal rules of business will not be subject to arbitrary change. Reform efforts are further complicated by the resistance to change of vested interest groups that benefit from existing institutional ambiguities and policy distortions. Thus, in establishing a reform agenda that will increase investment incentives, it is important for the government to identify where the expected pay-offs will be greatest. This requires an assessment of both the net benefits of the reform agenda and the probability of success in implementing reform measures.

An immediate priority should be the simplification of administrative procedures and policy interventions to reduce incentives for corruption and lessen resistance to reform. Some specific examples discussed in this chapter include the need for simplified and more automatic business registration and licensing procedures. Removal of ownership rights from line ministries and provincial authorities is also important. Progress in implementing the legislative and administrative changes that are needed to reduce opportunities and incentives for corruption can only increase the probability of success in achieving longer-term institutional development goals.

Elsewhere in the region, the crisis has led to much discussion about the need to take action to establish and enforce stricter supervision of financial institutions. In Vietnam, there remains a more basic need to develop the auditing and accounting standards and professions necessary to make capital adequacy and other prudential controls meaningful. Moreover, key issues constraining the development and viability of financial institutions in Vietnam relate more to the fact that the basic foundations of a market economy – such as contract enforcement, commercial dispute resolution procedures, cost-effective mechanisms for foreclosure of mortgages and more automatic bankruptcy procedures – remain poorly developed. There may be a need for caution and attention to the sequencing of reforms in liberalising the financial sector of an economy where basic market institutions remain substantially underdeveloped. An increased sense of urgency needs to be given to developing the institutions needed to support a market economy.

The fact that the Vietnamese economy has so far managed to continue to perform relatively well despite recent external shocks is encouraging. A slowing of growth below the official forecast level of 9 per cent for 1998 is now anticipated, but there is an expectation that moderate growth will be sustained. Any substantive slowdown can be expected to increase domestic pressures to accelerate reforms. The challenge is to channel these pressures to reduce resistance to change from those with a vested interest in maintaining the status quo. If the recent external shocks contribute to accelerated action to address continuing disincentives to private sector investment, the medium to long-term impact of the regional crisis on the Vietnamese economy, in terms of both growth and equity, may eventually be positive.

NOTES

1. Nike subcontractors from South Korea are one of the most high-profile cases.
2. There are other important constraints, including the role of the state in directing investment resources to particular sectors and the constraints faced by the private sector in accessing international markets, but these are beyond the scope of this study.
3. Article 22, *Socialist Republic of Vietnam Constitution 1992*, Foreign Language Publishing House, Hanoi.
4. Kornai (1992, p. 579) argues that such tensions are inevitable in post-socialist societies.
5. A more detailed breakdown of the state, private domestic and foreign investor share of different industry subgroups is included in Mallon (1998a).
6. The focus of Jordan's study is on family-controlled firms rather than all companies. Given the current lack of confidence in formal market institutions in Vietnam, it is likely that 'family'-controlled firms will be the dominant form of company in Vietnam for some time, even if part of the 'family' connection is close ties with a state investor.
7. Parts of this section have been adapted from Mallon (1998b).

8. North (1994, p. 360) defines institutions as: 'the humanly defined constraints that structure human interaction. They are made up of formal constraints (e.g. rules, laws, constitutions) and informal constraints (e.g. norms of behaviour, conventions, self-imposed codes of conduct) and their enforcement characteristics'.

9. Enterprises belonging to social and political organisations and professional associations are meant to register either as companies or as state enterprises. However, the current status of such organisations is somewhat ambiguous, and they 'operate as a politically specific form of enterprise' (CIEM 1998, p. 16).

10. For a good overview of the problems and inconsistencies of the existing system, see CIEM (1998).

11. Domestic consulting firms (often with close links to government) assist in establishing companies, applying a fee structure that reflects the nature of the approvals required. They will prepare business plans and other documentation needed to obtain approvals.

12. For example 'capital' is borrowed and deposited in a bank account for just long enough to ensure minimum capital requirements are met at the time of business registration. Again, a domestic consulting service may offer to draft a company's business plan in as broad a manner as possible – although this may delay approval and increase its costs.

13. Such requirements have previously been included in company laws in Western companies with the aim of providing some protection to creditors, but were ineffective in achieving this objective (CIEM 1998).

14. Article 4 of Decree No. 89-CP (15 December 1995), 'Revoking the Procedures for Granting Export or Import Permits for Each Consignment', *Government Gazette*, 15 March 1996; Decree 33-CP (19 April 1994), 'State Management of Export–Import Activities'.

15. See Goddard (1998) for a more detailed discussion. This discussion on contract enforcement has benefited greatly from material in Goddard's paper.

16. These points are adapted and expanded from Goddard (1998).

17. Article 13 of Decree No. 85-CP (17 December 1996), 'Guiding Implementation of the Ordinance on the Rights and Obligations of Domestic Organisations with Land Assigned or Leased Land by the State', *Government Gazette*, 28 February 1997.

18. Buildings built on the same land can be mortgaged to both domestic and foreign banks.

19. A mortgage sale generally requires the consent of the government and mortgagor (Circular 217-NHNN, 17 August 1996) and the sale must be conducted by an authorised body (Article 273(2) of the Civil Code).

20. See Article 11(6) of Decree No. 85-CP (17 December 1996), 'Guiding Implementation of the Ordinance on the Rights and Obligations of Domestic Organisations with Land Assigned or Leased Land by the State', *Government Gazette*, 28 February 1997, p. 14.

21. See Decision 386-TTg (7 June 1997), 'Assigning the Licensing of Foreign Direct Investment Projects', *Government Gazette*, 31 July 1997, pp. 25–6. This allows People's Committees in Hanoi and Ho Chi Minh City to approve FDI projects up to US$10 million, and the People's Committees of Hai Phong, Da Nang, Ba Ria-Vun Tau, Dong Nai, Binh Duong and Quang Ninh to approve FDI projects up to US$5 million, subject to certain conditions.

22. Decree No. 50-CP (28 August 1996) 'Establishment, Reorganisation, Dissolution and Bankruptcy of State Enterprises', *Government Gazette*, 15 December 1996; Decree No. 38-CP (28 April 1997), 'Amending and Supplementing a Number of Articles of Decree No. 50-CP of 28 August 1996', *Government Gazette*, 15 June 1997; Decree No. 86-CP (19 December 1996), 'Promulgating the Regulation on Property Auction', *Government Gazette*, 28 February 1997; Circular No. 8-BKH/DN (11 June 1997), 'Guiding Implementation of Decree No. 38-CP and Decree No. 50-CP', *Government Gazette*, 31 August 1997. Circular No. 25-TC/TCDN (15 May 1997), 'Guiding the Order, Procedures and Principles for Financial Settlement when State Enterprises Are Dissolved', *Government Gazette*, 31 August 1997.

23. Government circular issued 21 April 1998 on action by government agencies to reform state enterprises.

24. Decree No. 77-CP (18 June 1997), 'Regulation on Domestic Investment in the Form of BOT Contracts', *Legal Forum*, July 1997.

25. See Goddard (1998, pp. 46–51) for a detailed discussion of the issue.

11. Implications for Vietnam of Rural Industrialisation in China

Yiping Huang*

INTRODUCTION

Development of the township and village enterprise (TVE) sector was one of China's greatest achievements under Deng Xiaoping. In the two decades since rural reform began in 1978, TVEs have grown from being small workshops specialising mainly in maintenance and processing to become a major economic sector accounting for more than half of the country's industrial output.

The development of the TVEs has been unique in at least two respects. First, farmers have been able to stay on the land while earning off-farm income. This seems to offer a solution to the problems of urbanisation faced by many developing countries as they industrialise. Second, TVEs have been exceptionally successful even though most are collectively owned and have a vaguely defined ownership structure. In the literature there has been much speculation as to why China's TVEs have done so well.

From being a large importer of grain in the mid-1980s, Vietnam transformed its agricultural sector to become the world's second largest rice exporter in the early 1990s. At the same time, however, the rural–urban income gap widened, mainly because growth of urban (state) industries outstripped that of agriculture. To accelerate income growth in rural Vietnam, new jobs will need to be created in the non-agricultural sector and rural labour productivity will need to be raised. To many scholars and policy makers, China's TVEs appear to offer an interesting model for Vietnam to learn from as it industrialises.

The purpose of this chapter is therefore to revisit the development of the TVE sector in China and draw some implications for Vietnam. We argue that the two characteristics of TVEs described above did not emerge because they provided the optimal solution to China's industrialisation problems, but were rather the practical response of Chinese farmers to the economic and political constraints of the time. TVEs were successful in China mainly because there was a lack of small enterprises in the early years and because they had a relative institutional advantage over state-owned enterprises (SOEs), not because their property rights were vaguely defined or because they had a cooperative culture.

Recent developments indicate that the enterprises are willing to modify their traditional structure where there is advantage to be gained by doing so. Thus caution must be taken when interpreting the experience of China's rural industrialisation, and especially when drawing implications for other countries.

INDUSTRIALISATION IN RURAL CHINA

While the TVE is mainly a phenomenon of the reform period, its origins lie much further back. In response to calls by the central government for industrial development in the countryside, many commune and brigade enterprises (CBEs), the predecessors of TVEs, were established from 1958 on (Zong, Li and Zhou 1992). By 1960 the total number of CBEs had reached 117,000. In 1962 the government decided that 'communes and production brigades should not run enterprises under normal circumstances',[1] causing numbers to drop sharply to 11,000 by the end of the following year. The CBEs then experienced impressive growth, despite the upheaval of the Cultural Revolution. On the eve of economic reform their gross output had reached 49.3 billion yuan, with a real annual growth rate of 10 per cent between 1960 and 1978, while the number of such enterprises had risen to over 1.5 million. The CBEs were mainly involved in agricultural machinery manufacturing and maintenance, grain processing and the production of building materials.

Since reform began in the late 1970s, the Chinese government has shown increasing interest in the development of the rural industrial sector. In 1978 it stated that 'commune and brigade enterprises should gradually engage in the processing of all farm and sideline products that are suitable for rural processing'[2] as long as this was in conformity with the principle of rational economic development, and that 'urban factories should shift part of their processing of products and parts and components that are suitable for rural processing to commune and brigade enterprises'. In 1981 the government confirmed that the growth of CBEs was in conformity with the comprehensive development of the rural economy, and in 1983 called for further efforts to consolidate and develop such enterprises (Byrd and Lin 1990).

A real breakthrough in policy was not seen until 1984, however. Document No. 1 issued by the central government in that year officially adopted the term 'township and village enterprise' and for the first time strongly encouraged collectives and peasants to pool their funds and jointly set up various kinds of enterprises. Until then policy had been very much preoccupied with agricultural production, especially of grain. This policy change marked the beginning of an important new phase of TVE development.

It was not simply a coincidence that this change in policy approach and the expansion of the TVE sector both occurred in the mid-1980s. In the pre-reform period, the Chinese government had adopted a heavy industry-oriented development strategy (Lin, Cai and Li 1996). Agricultural institutions were organised to facilitate the implementation of this strategy: agricultural production was collectivised; farmers were restricted mainly to producing grain; and agricultural markets were controlled by the state. It was clear that the commune system was damaging to rural development and income, and when the household responsibility system was introduced in the late 1970s it spread rapidly across the country. Reform of the household responsibility system in the early 1980s produced an 'agricultural miracle': total grain output increased by 57 per cent between 1982 and 1984, and rural per capita income almost doubled between 1980 and 1984.[3]

Growth in rural areas in the first half of the 1980s was high by any standard – so high in fact that it has been called 'abnormal growth' by some Chinese economists. Increases in agricultural production, especially grain output, were mainly responsible for the high growth rate. Rapid growth of this type brought new problems. One was that sale of rural products became difficult in some regions because demand did not keep pace with supply. In 1983 and 1984, China was not only able for the first time in its modern history to feed all of its population, it even had a grain surplus. The potential for income growth through further increases in agricultural production had, however, almost been exhausted.

The new policy package announced in 1984 and 1985 included a range of measures to diversify the rural economic structure. Livestock production was strongly encouraged, for instance, as a way of generating a new source of income and of using up surplus grain. TVEs were also recognised as an important vehicle to both reduce surpluses of agricultural products and raise rural incomes.

Until 1984, even though the government had taken a relatively positive approach to CBEs, farmers were ineffective in developing rural industries: resource allocation was controlled by the communes, for whom agricultural production was a priority; the funds to establish factories were available only through bank loans; and there were no free markets on which to sell industrial products (Huang 1998a).

All this changed in the mid-1980s. As households took control of farming, redundant labour became explicit and farmers themselves took charge of the allocation of resources. After a couple of good years, farmers were able to accumulate surplus funds. Even more importantly, most rural markets were open by 1985.

Farmers began to pool their money and labour and start simple factories in their backyards. This style of rural industrialisation has been called *litu bo lixiang* [leaving the land but not the home town] and had the clear advantage of taking pressure off the urban infrastructure. With hindsight it can be seen that it was not the outcome of a calculated decision by farmers, but rather their passive response to changed circumstances. The household registration system introduced in the pre-reform period was still being implemented strictly, and thus farmers could not leave their home towns without official approval. More importantly, the urban economy was still in the early stage of reform and there was nothing to be gained by moving to the city. There were no new jobs or markets in the towns, and without food coupons, farmers would have had great difficulty obtaining food.

The years following 1984 saw dramatic growth in TVEs. The output of industrial TVEs grew at an annual rate of 38 per cent between 1983 and 1986, while employment increased by 16 per cent per annum during the same period. The production structure of TVEs also shifted, from simple agricultural machinery, grain processing and building materials to a wider range of industrial activities including machinery parts, and textiles and clothing.

In 1987–88, the inflation rate soared to around 18 per cent following the introduction of urban reform. This triggered a nation-wide debate on the future of TVEs in the Chinese economy. One popular argument was that TVEs were technologically backward and competed for resources with the SOEs, reducing the efficiency of the national economy. The austerity program subsequently introduced to cool the overheated economy responded to these concerns by placing restrictions on bank loans to TVEs. This situation did not change substantially until early 1992, when Deng Xiaoping toured South China. This heralded a new stage of rapid growth for TVEs.

By this time the location inefficiency of village factories was becoming apparent. Village TVEs were able to operate efficiently if they purchased their inputs and marketed their products locally; those located in remote areas were at a serious disadvantage if transportation and information was an important component of their industry. As a result, many TVEs moved to urban areas or closer to key transportation networks. Those that stayed in the villages remained small and tended to service only the surrounding area. In the long run the TVEs were not able to keep Chinese cities free from the pressure of migrant labour. To date more than 100 million peasants, mainly from the inland regions of China, have migrated to coastal and urban areas to find work.

By the mid-1990s new problems were being felt in the TVE sector. Growth began to slow; financial losses were widespread; and TVEs were said to be performing no better than the SOEs. The enterprises responded with a wave of privatisation, replacing their collective ownership structure with a shareholding system, or 'taking off their red hats' to show that, although previously registered as collective firms, they were in essence privately owned (Sachs and Woo 1997).

CONTRIBUTION TO RURAL EMPLOYMENT AND INCOME

TVEs have contributed significantly to rural welfare by providing employment opportunities and raising incomes. Between 1984 and 1996 the TVE workforce increased from 52 to 135 million, to register an annual growth rate of 8 per cent (SSB 1997). The TVE sector is now the most important in rural China, accounting for nearly one-third of total rural employment and over 60 per cent of total rural output (Table 11.1).

Accordingly, rural income has increased significantly, especially non-agricultural income. The contribution of non-agricultural activities – mainly

Table 11.1   Employment and Output of TVEs in the Rural Economy

	TVE Work-force (million)	Rural Work-force (million)	Share TVE/ Rural (%)	TVE Out-put (billion yuan)	Rural Out-put (billion yuan)	Share TVE/ Rural (%)
1978	28.3	306.4	9.2			
1980	30.0	318.4	9.4			
1984	52.6	365.7	14.4	171.0	502.7	34.0
1988	96.5	400.7	24.1	649.6	1,236.1	52.6
1990	92.7	472.9	19.6	958.1	1,724.3	55.6
1992	105.8	483.1	21.9	1,768.6	2,677.0	66.1
1996	135.1	490.4	27.5	3,667.3	6,010.1	61.0

Source: State Statistics Bureau (various years), *China Statistics Yearbook*, China Statistical Publishing House, Beijing.

TVEs and other off-farm employment – to rural per capita income increased from 35 per cent in 1983 to 44 per cent in 1995 (Table 11.2). Even though income inequality between urban and rural residents worsened as urban reform accelerated in the second half of the 1980s, the urban–rural income gap would be much wider were there no TVEs in rural China.

The success of TVEs has remained largely a coastal phenomenon. According to an annual national survey of 100 villages conducted by the central government, in 1995 villages in the Eastern (coastal), Central and Western regions of China respectively had on average fifteen, eight and nine rural enterprises (Ministry of Agriculture 1996). The contribution to income of non-agricultural activities was above half in the Eastern region but well below 40 per cent in the Central and Western regions. The same survey revealed that the proportion of outward migrant labour in the total labour force was higher in the Western and Central than in the Eastern villages.

The literature offers a number of explanations for this phenomenon, including differences between regions in infrastructure, human capital endowment, capitalist tradition and market environment. In the mid-1990s the government encouraged cross-regional collaboration between TVEs, mainly so that coastal provinces could help inland provinces raise the efficiency of their TVEs.

Along with the positive contribution of rural industrial development to levels of rural income, it has also been argued that TVE growth has contributed to rising inequalities in income distribution in rural China (Rozelle 1994; Huang 1998b). In a study on inequality trends, Rozelle (1994) demonstrated that inequality among counties in an eastern coastal province registered statistically significant increases between 1984 and 1989. His decomposition analysis revealed that the changing patterns of inequality were closely associated with changes in the structure of the rural economy – in particular, policies that stimulated the expansion of rural industry gave rise to greater inequality. While the degree of inequality in rural China is still low compared to other developing countries at a similar stage of development, rising income inequality does cause social and economic problems and needs to be addressed properly.

In a recent study, Huang (1998b) took the analysis a step further by examining the differentiated impact of different types of rural industrialisation on income level and distribution. China has two well-known models of rural industrialisation: the Sunan model, which describes collective TVEs; and the Wenzhou model, which was developed for privately owned TVEs (Chang and Wen 1997). Both types of TVE are represented in Zhejiang, the province chosen by Huang for his empirical inquiry. The data set used in the study was assembled by the author with the assistance of the Statistics Bureau of Zhejiang province. It included indicators for income inequality, income level and

Table 11.2 Rural Income in China, 1983–95

	Rural per Capita Income (yuan)	Rural Agricultural Income (yuan)	Rural Non-agricultural Income (yuan)	Share of Non-agricultural in Total (%)	Urban per Capita Living Expenditure (yuan)	Ratio Rural: Urban
1983	309.8	201.5	108.3	35.0	526.0	0.59
1984	355.3	221.5	133.8	37.7	607.6	0.58
1985	397.6	235.9	161.7	40.7	685.3	0.58
1986	423.8	248.3	175.5	41.4	827.9	0.51
1987	462.6	268.3	194.3	42.0	916.0	0.51
1988	544.9	306.6	238.3	43.7	1,119.4	0.49
1989	601.5	333.4	268.1	44.6	1,260.7	0.48
1990	686.3	416.1	270.2	39.4	1,387.3	0.49
1991	708.6	417.6	291.0	41.1	1,544.3	0.46
1992	784.0	439.5	344.5	43.9	1,826.1	0.43
1993	921.6	522.9	398.7	43.3	2,336.5	0.39
1994	1,223.6	688.3	535.3	43.7	3,179.2	0.38
1995	1,577.7	886.9	690.8	43.8	3,893.0	0.41
Annual growth rate (%)	14.5	13.1	16.7		18.2	

Source: State Statistics Bureau (various years), *China Statistics Yearbook*, China Statistical Publishing House, Beijing.

other relevant variables for each of the province's 67 counties in 1985 and 1995. Huang reached three main conclusions. First, rural industrialisation is favourable for rural income growth. Second, Rozelle was correct in finding that at the current stage of development, rural industrial development contributes to increases in income inequality. And third, industrialisation based on private ownership (the Wenzhou model) leads not only to higher average income but also to greater income inequality, other things being equal, than industrialisation based on collective ownership (Sunan model).

WHY DID COLLECTIVE OWNERSHIP SUCCEED IN RURAL CHINA?

The rise of China's TVEs has been a hot topic since it first caught the attention of the world in the mid-1980s. Some economists were puzzled by the success of TVEs. According to standard economic theory, firms require, at least, clearly defined and properly enforced property rights to be efficient and competitive. However, most Chinese TVEs are controlled by the township or village authorities even though nominally they belong to all the residents of the town or village. There are in fact similarities between rural TVEs and SOEs in their ownership structure, but their performance differed widely throughout most of the 1980s and in the early 1990s.

The literature offers a number of explanations for the TVE phenomenon. One group of economists points to the importance of cooperative culture in China's TVEs. Weitzman and Xu (1994) argued that conventional property rights theory may be missing a critical dimension: the ability of a group to solve potential conflicts internally, without explicit rules, laws, rights and procedures. They speculated that cooperative culture could play an important role in replacing the explicit functions of formal ownership: '[I]f a society can be described by a high λ-value, or people trust each other, then, [even] without formal ownership, parties may still be able to invest in the relationship or to lock together' (Weitzman and Xu 1994, p. 140).

A second group has focused on the role of politics in institutional arrangements for TVEs. Chang and Wang (1994) argued that the ownership structure of TVEs was not the result of free contracting among private agents, as would be the case in a market economy, but rather the product of an environment in which an authoritarian government with monopolistic political power played a dominant role in economic life. The authors state (p. 434) that 'this ownership structure can be viewed as the solution to the central government's problem of improving citizens' welfare subject to the constraints that the current political system be preserved and that local agents be provided with incentives'.

A third group of economists finds the explanation in vaguely defined property rights, including of TVEs, in an imperfect market. Li (1996) theorised that ambiguous property rights could be rationalised by high transaction costs in the market place. He argued that when the government is able to block market transactions, then it may be efficient to invite it to be an ambiguous owner of the firm. In other words (p. 1), '[the] immature market environment in China makes ambiguous property rights often more efficient than unambiguously defined private property'.

This proposition has been supported by some other economists. Naughton (1994), for instance, suggested that local government ownership of TVEs has played a crucial role in financial intermediation because local governments were in a good position to assess the risks of start-up businesses under their control and could serve as guarantors of loans to individual TVEs.

The establishment and development of TVEs in China was the outcome of many factors. Following reform of the household responsibility system, farmers had surplus labour and the funds to pursue new investment opportunities. Theoretically they had two options: move to the city or build factories at home. Most farmers chose to start workshops in their backyards because migration to the cities was not possible at the time. They also had two options for firm ownership: private or collective. Again, collective ownership was chosen as the dominant form for TVEs, first because township and village authorities still had control of a substantial proportion of rural resources (Byrd and Lin 1990), and second because there was discrimination against private ownership in such area as the allocation of bank loans and the granting of tax exemptions (Sachs and Woo 1997).

In the mid-1990s the *China Daily* ('Shareholding System Drives Rural Firms', 14 February 1997) reported that 'although the [township and village] enterprises are nominally owned by townships or villages, no one is actually responsible for the losses or profits of the enterprises. Managers ... [often] take advantage of their power for personal gain, such as hiring their family members or relatives and making extravagant use of public funds'. This sort of behaviour is frequently described in reports on SOEs and would not occur if cooperative culture and the role of local governments were indeed the main driving forces behind the TVEs' achievements.

The initial impetus for the success of TVEs came from the market vacuum that existed in the 1980s. The large urban industries built in the pre-reform period were concentrated mainly in heavy industries, and there was always a shortage of consumer goods. The success of agricultural reform had raised rural incomes and lifted rural demand, but because international trade was controlled by the state and the urban economy was still dormant, there was no readily available supply to meet this demand. Simple consumer goods like footwear, clothing, processed food and toys produced by the TVEs therefore sold as soon as they hit the market. This early stage of TVE development typifies what Sachs (1997) has called the 'small enterprise phenomenon'.

The TVEs also benefited from their relative institutional advantage. While it is true that collective ownership is not necessarily efficient, whether an institution can survive ultimately depends on who it is competing with. In the late 1980s and early 1990s, the TVEs were competing mainly with the SOEs. Although state enterprises are often argued to have more advanced technologies than the TVEs, the latter have an obvious institutional advantage. The TVEs' nominal owners (township or village residents) constitute a smaller and more compact group than those of the SOEs (the people as a whole). Administrative intervention was exercised through a shorter hierarchy for the former (township/village authority to enterprise) than for the latter (central/provincial government to enterprise). More importantly, though both types of enterprises had some soft budget problems, TVEs, unlike SOEs, were forced to stop operating if they continued to make losses.

Today, China's domestic markets are far more competitive. With the rise of private enterprises and joint ventures, it is becoming increasingly apparent that the TVEs now face an institutional *disadvantage*. Even some of the SOEs have improved their performance in the process of reform.

IMPLICATIONS FOR VIETNAM

China's TVEs offer useful lessons for rural development in Vietnam, although these must take into account the different conditions in the two countries.

First, the creation of off-farm job opportunities is necessary if further increases in farm income are to be achieved. During the period 1995–97, average value added per worker in Vietnam was 0.6 million dong for agriculture, 3.5 million dong for industry and 2.5 million dong for the service sector. Transferring labour from the agricultural to the industrial or service sectors implies immediate economic gains.

More importantly, rural Vietnam has the potential to develop a large labour-intensive industry, without factories necessarily having to be located in the villages. Vietnam is a densely populated country with an arable land area of only 0.1 hectares per head. More than 80 per cent of the population resides in the countryside. Per capita income is below US$300, lower than in most other countries. This means that Vietnam is well positioned for economic take-off through a rapid expansion of labour-intensive production.

However, compared to China at a similar stage of development, rural Vietnam does seem to face some additional difficulties. First, the early development of China's TVEs benefited from a market vacuum; they were the only suppliers of consumption goods in the market place. In Vietnam, goods produced by the urban non-state sector, or imported from China or Thailand, already crowd the market. The quality requirements for goods produced by Vietnamese rural enterprises will therefore need to be higher than was the case in China. Furthermore, China has traditionally tended both to save and to invest more, with investment standing at around 30 per cent of GDP even in the pre-reform period. Rapid income growth in the early 1980s meant that Chinese farmers were able to accumulate sizeable surplus funds to establish TVEs. In Vietnam the investment ratio stood at around 10 per cent of GDP before reform, and rose only recently to 29 per cent due to increased domestic saving and FDI. With rural per capita income rising by only 2.7 per cent per year between 1991 and 1995, farmers could accumulate only very limited amounts of investable surplus.

Second, in China collective ownership was the second best choice of farmers, to buy cooperation and protection from local authorities. As rural industries mature in Vietnam, they may be able to avoid this detour if property rights can be defined more clearly from the outset.

The Vietnamese government has a strong motive to promote 'new cooperatives' in rural areas. However, this particular ownership form is unlikely to facilitate healthy development of rural industries or to succeed in building new non-farm enterprises, for several reasons. First, the new cooperative system has in effect been imposed by government from above and does not meet the operational requirements of modern enterprises. Second, cooperatives (even 'new' ones) have a bad reputation among farmers and are unlikely to win their trust. And third, it is of great concern that the members of cooperatives are liable for any losses incurred. In the event of a major natural disaster or a sharp fall in the price of one or more primary commodities, a large number of cooperatives could suffer severe losses, for which their members or the government would be liable. In short, the government should not support one form of establishment in preference to others.

Third, while the ultimate objective of policy should be to create a level playing field for all types of enterprises, rural enterprises can only grow if they are given access to sufficient resources and markets outside central planning. As farmers themselves have very limited surplus funds to invest, the supply of credit will be critical to the development of rural enterprises. TVEs experienced two downturns in growth, in 1989–90 and 1995–97. Both periods coincided with austere macroeconomic policies to bring down inflation, with the TVE sector being the first to suffer when tight monetary policies were implemented.

The creation of a more level playing field requires that the current rice self-sufficiency policy be abandoned and administrative discrimination against the non-state sector reduced. Rice production in Vietnam has reached a very high level, and the returns to additional inputs are likely to decline sharply. The experience of China and other East Asian economies has demonstrated that the self-sufficiency policy has never been successful in achieving food security. Vietnam's SOEs, meanwhile, with their high levels of inefficiency and bias towards urban areas and heavy industry, cannot be depended on to create jobs for the country as a whole or for rural areas in particular. The more resources are allocated to the state sector, the worse unemployment becomes and the more inefficient the economy. In the end, all types of enterprises can contribute equally to the prosperity and income of Vietnam as long as they can survive market competition and grow.

CONCLUDING REMARKS

TVEs in rural China represent one of the greatest achievements of the reform period. China's rural industrialisation has had two important characteristics: off-farm employment has increased without causing an exodus of rural workers to the cities; and collective ownership has dominated as the major institutional form. But the trajectory of rural industrialisation was not painted beforehand by the government; rather, it was carved by farmers in response to political and economic circumstances.

The implications of the TVEs' success should not be overstated. In the early period TVEs were at the forefront of a typical boom of small enterprises to provide commodities China lacked. They continued to succeed because of their relative institutional advantage, especially over SOEs. Locating industries within villages and adopting collective ownership may not have been optimal, but were the best choice farmers could make given the political and economic constraints.

It would be a mistake to assert on the basis of the TVE experience that firms can perform efficiently without clearly defined property rights, even though they can survive and expand under such circumstances. The reality is that a spontaneous drive towards privatisation is sweeping across the country.

The analysis in this study does not give rise to a pessimistic view about the future of TVEs. Their strength lies in their flexibility and their ability to respond quickly to changes in the business environment. They succeeded in the past despite their disadvantage in human capital and despite their public ownership. When human capital became a bottleneck, they made efforts to train their own workers and recruit from outside. When public ownership emerged as a major constraint to development, they opted for privatisation without hesitation. This flexibility and adaptability is sure to make TVEs an increasingly important sector of the Chinese economy well into the next century.

China's experience with TVEs offers important lessons for rural development in Vietnam. In view of its large population, high population–land ratio and very low income level, Vietnam stands a good chance of rapidly developing a large labour-intensive industrial base, This is also the only solution to prevent the rural–urban income gap from widening. To successfully build a rural enterprise sector, however, Vietnam needs to reduce or eliminate existing discrimination against the rural non-state, non-rice sector.

NOTES

*   I am grateful to Fang Cai, Ron Duncan, Ray Trewin, Wing Thye Woo, Wen Hai, Yongzheng Yang and Xiaohe Zhang for earlier discussions of the subject.
1.   'Resolutions on Developing Rural Sideline Production', Central Committee of the Chinese Communist Party and the State Council of the People's Republic of China, 1962.
2.   'Resolution on Several Questions about Speeding Up Agricultural Development (draft)', announced by the Central Committee of the Chinese Communist Party in 1978. This was cited in Byrd and Lin (1990).
3.   Per capita income is measured at current prices. The general price indices for the years 1981–84, however, were all below 3 per cent per annum (SSB 1997).

12. Market Reform and Vietnamese Agriculture

Nhu Che, Tom Kompas and Neil Vousden

INTRODUCTION

Since 1981, Vietnamese agriculture has provided an impressive case study of the benefits of economic reform. As a result of the reforms that have been introduced, Vietnam has made the transition from being a large importer of rice and other foodstuffs in the 1980s to being the world's second largest exporter of rice. The annual growth rate of rice output rose from 0.4 per cent in 1976–80 to 4.2 per cent in the early reform years (1981–87), then to 6.1 per cent in 1988–94. Indeed, output literally doubled between 1981 and 1994 (GSO, various issues). This impressive growth performance coincided with the implementation of widespread reforms in the Vietnamese agricultural sector, involving a move away from the previous collective regime to a system in which farmers were permitted to keep most of the profits from rice production and were increasingly free to trade their product on domestic and international markets.

This chapter gives a concise overview of recent empirical work by the authors on the effects of the different stages of liberalisation on Vietnam's rice output (Che 1997; Che and Vousden 1998; Che, Kompas and Vousden 1998). A distinguishing feature of this work is its attempt to capture the effects of reform on the efficiency of the farmer's labour and management of land resources – the so-called 'incentive' effects of reform. In this respect, our research adds to earlier work on such effects in Chinese agriculture by McMillan, Whalley and Zhu (1989).

Significantly, we find that incentive effects account for a large part of the factor productivity growth associated with liberalisation, ranging from 20 per cent of cumulative growth of total factor productivity (TFP) in the early years of reform to as much as 80 per cent in the later years. We also find that liberalisation can yield large dynamic effects, with the later part of the reform process predicted to produce a significantly higher annual growth rate than the early reforms. As a general conclusion, our work provides strong support for the view that later reforms were more effective than earlier ones in boosting agricultural growth.

In the following section we provide a brief history of the Vietnamese reform experience and the move from a collective regime to a system of relatively open agricultural markets. In the next section we discuss the incentive effects of reform and provide a brief summary of research by the authors on their relative importance. We then consider how the basic framework outlined in the section may be modified to allow for dynamic effects, and present the results of our simulations. In the final section we summarise our main conclusions.

THE STAGES OF REFORM

Although reform of Vietnamese agriculture has been a continual process since 1981, for the purposes of analysis it is helpful to distinguish three main stages: the communal stage (1975–80); the period of output contracts and a tightly controlled domestic market (1981–87); and a third stage involving the gradual freeing up of domestic and international trade in agricultural products (1988 – present). The main features of the respective stages are set out below.

The Communal Stage (1975–80)

During this stage, which commenced shortly after the reunification of Vietnam, all agricultural activities were subject to a compulsory collective regime in which the agricultural cooperative owned 95 per cent of the land of its members and all other assets including farm tools and draft animals. The sole landlord, the state, extracted a lump sum tax (a specified quantity of rice) from the farmers and purchased most of their rice at a 'state price', which was about 20–30 per cent of the black market price. All the usual economic decisions of farmers, including land use and investment decisions, were made by the state. Households could use 5 per cent of their land for the breeding of pigs and chickens and for vegetable production, but trade of produce was not permitted outside the local district. Throughout the collective regime, domestic and international trade of agricultural goods was prohibited.

The Period of Output Contracts (1981–87)

The process of decollectivisation began in 1981 in response to a range of economic crises in 1979–80. Under the newly introduced output contracts system, land was allocated to farmers, who were to organise weeding and harvesting. Other operations continued to be carried out by the cooperative.

A quota for output was set, based on the average yield of the plot of land over the previous three years. Although most commercial decisions remained under the control of the state, these initial reforms were important because they gave farmers some – albeit limited – control over the output and distribution of products and so led to the growth of black markets. A first tentative move had been made towards giving farmers property rights over their land; a system of parallel markets was emerging; and the farmer was given a small measure of responsibility for decision making. Thus were sown the seeds for further liberalisation.

The Gradual Freeing Up of Markets (1988–Present)

Following food shortages in 1987–88, further reforms were initiated in 1988. These gave households conditional use of private land (for a period of 10–15 years) and the right to barter output for inputs. The cooperative retained ultimate control of land and water resources, however, effectively tying the farmer to the cooperative. The farm household now owned its own draft animals, farm tools and other equipment, and after paying a tax had the right to retain income earned from production. Sale of output was still confined to the local district. The significance of these reforms was that they transferred most aspects of the *management* of production to the individual farm household.

The dual price system of one state price and another market price was finally abolished in June 1990, essentially removing all restrictions on domestic trade in agricultural products. From 1989 international trade in these products had gradually been liberalised, an important step being the replacement of quotas by tariffs. These changes were accompanied by a move to a unified exchange rate and the relaxation of exchange controls. Finally, in July 1993, tenure over agricultural land was extended to 20 years and farmers were permitted to sell, lease, exchange, mortgage and bequeath land. Although the ultimate ownership of land still rests with the state, the system of land tenure has shifted considerably in the direction of private property rights, providing farmers with reasonable security of tenure. This has enabled farm households to make investment and land management decisions with less uncertainty about future returns.

The Effects of Reform

In summary, the most recent stage of reforms has encompassed the opening of domestic markets, the gradual freeing up of international trade, increased opportunities and incentives for decision making by individual farmers, and a clear move towards a system of private property rights. Although we have found it convenient to divide the reform process into two stages, it should be clear from the above summary that the reforms were in fact continual and occasionally overlapping.[1] Nevertheless, for the purposes of the broad analysis, there is much to be gained from considering reform as if it had proceeded in two clearly defined stages, the first tentative and relatively limited, the second more ambitious and pervasive. The data for rice output neatly reflect this dichotomy, with the growth rate of rice output being significantly higher in the second stage of reform than in the first, and growth performance in both stages being well above that under the collective regime.

This is evident in Figure 12.1 and Table 12.1, which track rice output and average annual growth in output for the period 1976–94. Rice output grew by 0.4 per cent in 1976–80, 4.2 per cent in 1981–87 and 6.1 per cent in 1988–94. Table 12.2 allows us to compare this impressive performance with the growth rate of factor inputs. While output growth rose steadily as reform proceeded, labour increased only slowly and the sown area of land declined slightly. Material inputs grew more slowly than output in each period.

Of interest is the case of capital, which grew slowly during the first stage of reform but increased dramatically (by 10.6 per cent per annum) in the second stage. This suggests that the later reforms induced substantial new investment, which appears to have been an important contributing factor in the high output growth of those years. (We shall have more to say about this later when we consider the dynamic effects of the reforms.) Induced capital accumulation is not the whole story, however, as the last column of Table

Figure 12.1   Rice Output in Vietnam, 1976–94 (million tons)

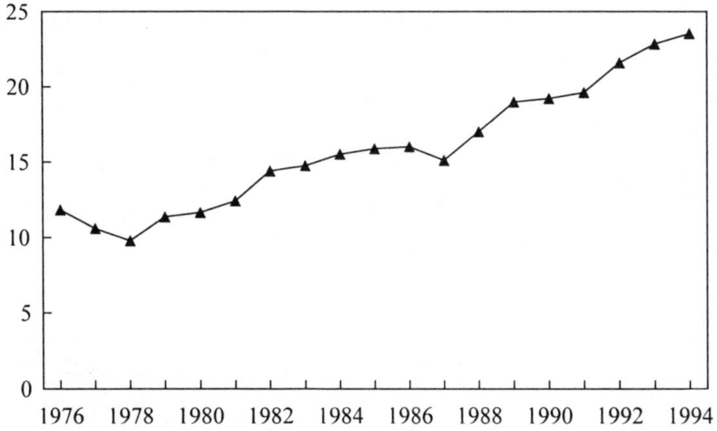

Source: Che (1997), Table 7.1.

Table 12.1   Rice Output in Vietnam, 1976–94

	Output (thousand tons)	Annual Growth Rate (%)
1976	11,827.2	
1977	10,597.1	−10.40
1978	9,789.9	−7.62
1979	11,362.9	16.07
1980	11,647.4	2.50
1981	12,415.2	6.59
1982	14,390.2	15.91
1983	14,743.3	2.45
1984	15,505.6	5.17
1985	15,874.8	2.38
1986	16,002.9	0.81
1987	15,102.6	−5.63
1988	17,000.0	12.56
1989	18,996.3	11.74
1990	19,225.2	1.20
1991	19,621.9	2.06
1992	21,590.3	10.03
1993	22,836.6	5.77
1994	23,528.3	3.03
1976–80		0.4
1981–87		4.2
1988–94		6.1

Source: Che (1997), Table 7.1.

Table 12.2 Annual Growth Rates (%)

	Output	Labour	Land	Materials	Capital	TFP
1976–80	0.4	0.4	–0.8	–1.1	2.2	0.6
1981–87	4.2	0.3	–1.2	3.3	1.7	3.3
1988–94	6.1	1.3	–0.5	5.6	10.6	3.1

Source: Che (1997), Table 7.1.

12.2 shows. This column provides annual growth rates for TFP, calculated as Solow residuals (Solow 1956). In all three stages TFP exhibits positive growth, although the growth rate is slightly less in 1988–94 than in 1981–87, probably because of the high rate of capital growth in the later years.

THE INCENTIVE EFFECTS OF REFORM

An aspect of reform that has received relatively little attention in the empirical literature is the effect of liberalisation on the incentive to work harder and to manage existing resources more efficiently. In particular, there has been little attempt to estimate the likely size of such incentive effects. A notable exception is McMillan, Whalley and Zhu (1989), who used the device of an 'institutional production function' to estimate the effects of reforms in Chinese agriculture on farmer effort, represented as an efficiency coefficient of the labour input in the production function.

McMillan, Whalley and Zhu assume that agricultural output is produced via a Cobb–Douglas production function using the inputs of labour, land, capital and intermediate goods (such as fertiliser). The effective labour input into production is the number of efficiency units of labour given by the product εN, where N is a physical unit of labour (the number of workers or the number of hours worked) and ε is individual worker 'effort'. In general this approach may be hard to implement because effort is difficult to observe. The problem is solved by assuming that each farmer chooses a level of effort to maximise a utility function containing a separable disutility of effort. The farmer's consumption is assumed to be equal to profit, which is the value of production at prevailing prices minus input costs. It is thus possible to solve for the farmer's optimal effort level as a function of the other inputs. This effort level can then be substituted for ε in the production function, to give the production function in its 'institutional' form as a function of a technology parameter (which depends on the optimal value of ε among other things) and the four observable inputs of labour, land, intermediate goods and capital. This institutional production function can then be estimated using observed output and input data, without requiring data on unobservable effort. It is also of the Cobb–Douglas form and so is readily estimated in the log-linear form. Moreover, the output elasticities of the respective factors can easily be used to generate estimates for the factor shares in the original production function. It is then possible to estimate the effects of liberalisation on farmer effort and so ascertain the relative importance of the incentive effects of reform. In this work, reform is represented by its effect on product price.

In Che (1997) and Che and Vousden (1998), a generalised version of the McMillan, Whalley and Zhu model is used to estimate the incentive effects of the respective stages of reform in Vietnamese agriculture. The authors assume that the farmer's effort choice has two dimensions, ε_1, effort that directly increases the productivity of the labour input, and ε_2, effort directed towards better management of the farmer's land. The latter includes such things as the planning of crop rotation and timing, and decisions on the number of crops per year on a particular plot of land and on the application of fertilisers. This second category of effort may therefore reasonably be assumed to affect the productivity of the land directly. Although both types of effort may enter the farmer's utility function in the same way, they have rather different effects on production. The technical production function used in Che and Vousden (1998) is

$$Q = \alpha_0 (\varepsilon_1 N)^{\alpha_1} (\varepsilon_2 L)^{\alpha_2} (K_1)^{\alpha_3} (K_2)^{\alpha_4} \qquad (12.1)$$

where Q is output of rice and N, L, K_1 and K_2 are the inputs of labour, land, materials and physical capital respectively. The α's are all positive constants.

The Che and Vousden model also allows for estimation of the effects of different stages of the reform process. It uses the classification outlined in the previous section, of an initial communal (pre-reform) stage (1976–80), an 'output contracts' stage (1981–87) and a 'market opening' stage (1988–94). Each stage is represented by its effect on an 'average' price of rice defined as

$$\beta p \ldots \beta_0 p_S + \beta_1 p_M + \beta_2 p_W \qquad (12.2)$$

where β_0, β_1 and β_2 are respectively the proportions of rice output allocated to the state, the domestic market and the international market (the β_i's sum to unity); and p_S, p_M and p_W are respectively the prices received by the farmer from the state, the domestic market and the world market. Changes in both the proportion of output sent to different markets (the β's) and prices in the respective markets will occur as the sector moves from one stage of reform to the next. Clearly, in the initial communal stage $\beta_0 = 1$, so that $\beta_P = \beta_0 p_S$ (that is, all output is sold to the state at the state price, p_S, which is well below any market price). As the reform process continues, more will be sold to the domestic market and subsequently to the world market. Thus β_1 and later β_2 will increase over time. With increased competition from the private market, p_S will also increase. Finally, as restrictions on rice exports are lifted, the effective price faced by the farmer for sales to the world market (p_W) will rise.

Using the annual data from Che (1997), it is possible to graph the time path of β_P (Figure 12.2). As shown in the figure, the average price of rice output has increased in nearly every year since 1981. However, reform can also affect the prices of inputs, which may have been kept at artificially low levels under the communal regime. It is thus possible that any increases in β_P may overstate the actual effect of reform on profits because of induced increases in input costs. To capture this, Che and Vousden derive estimates of the average cost of production for each year from 1981 to 1994 and use this information to estimate average farm profits. As Figure 12.3 shows, average profits rose steadily during most of 1981–94, suggesting that increases in input costs have been smaller than, or lagged behind, increases in the product price.

From Figures 12.2 and 12.3, it is clear that the reform process has led to an almost uninterrupted upward movement in average price and profits. To analyse the effects of these price changes on farmer productivity and effort, it is necessary to estimate the underlying rice production function. To do this, the farmer's optimal effort levels are solved for[2] and substituted in (12.1) to generate a Cobb–Douglas institutional production function, which is then estimated using cross-sectional data for 53 provinces for 1993. This estimated production function – which is found not to deviate significantly from constant returns to scale[3] – can then be used to estimate the time path of the Solow residual using time series data for rice output and inputs. The Solow residual is the sum of many factors, and it is clearly not possible to account for all of them. However, it is possible to calculate the part of the residual attributable to changes in the effort variables ε_1 and ε_2, the 'incentive effects' of reform. The results of this calculation, explained in full in Che and Vousden (1998), are illustrated in Figure 12.4, which shows the cumulative growth paths of output, TFP and the component of TFP reflecting incentive effects.

It is clear from Figure 12.4 that incentive effects constitute an important component of TFP growth. The calculations in Che and Vousden (1998)

Figure 12.2 Index of Average Rice Price, 1981–94

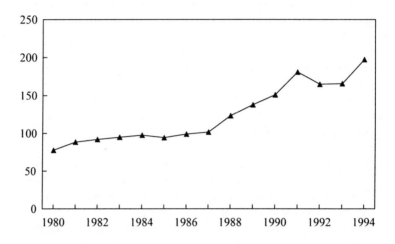

Source: Che (1997), Table DA.10.

Figure 12.3 Average Variable Profit in Rice Production

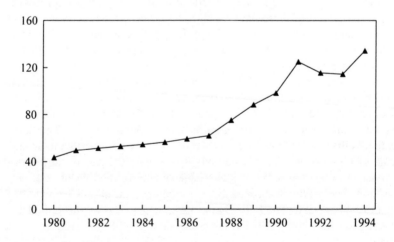

Source: Che (1997), Tables DA.10 and DA.12.

*Figure 12.4   Cumulative Growth of Rice Output, TFP and 'Incentive'
             Component of TFP (%)*

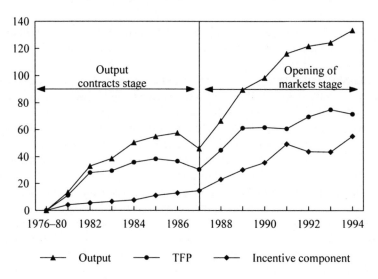

Source: Che and Vousden (1998).

indicate that in cumulative growth terms, such effects accounted for at least
20 per cent of TFP growth in the early 1980s and up to about 80 per cent in
the 1990s.

DYNAMIC CONSIDERATIONS

The research discussed in the previous sections is essentially static in nature.
Although it does consider rates of output and productivity growth, these are
based on comparison of static equilibria from one year to the next, taking
capital inputs as exogenously given. No allowance is made for the effect of
reform on the capital accumulation process itself. However, it seems likely
that liberalisation would encourage further investment in physical capital by
increasing the farmer's marginal product of capital. To incorporate such considerations, Che, Kompas and Vousden (1998) develop a dynamic version of
the model in Che and Vousden (1998), by allowing farmers to maximise an
intertemporal version of the objective function used in the static model (see
endnote 2) subject to a neoclassical capital accumulation equation of the
form:

$$\frac{dK_2(t)}{dt} = I(t) - \mu K_2 \tag{12.3}$$

where $I(t)$ is the farmer's investment in new machinery at time t (obtained by forgoing current consumption) and μ is the exogenous rate of depreciation of capital.[4]

This system tends to a steady-state level of capital stock and rice output. Moreover, later stages of liberalisation converge to higher steady-state values of capital and output than do earlier stages because, as shown in Figure 12.2, the average price of rice is higher during the later stages of liberalisation. This means that, *ceteris paribus*, the marginal product of capital is also higher at later stages of liberalisation, implying an increased return from the forgoing of current consumption to accumulate capital. Thus capital accumulation proceeds to a higher steady-state level in the later stages of reform. A byproduct of this increased capital accumulation is a rise in the marginal product of both types of effort, so that the induced increase in effort is also greater in the later stages of liberalisation. In other words, induced capital accumulation by farmers amplifies the incentive effects of reform.

To quantify the long-run effects of each stage of reform, Che, Kompas and Vousden solve for the steady state that would be reached if a given stage of reform, as reflected in given values of βp and farm average cost, continued indefinitely without further changes in parameters. The approximate convergence time can then be computed and an implied annual rate of output growth derived.[5] To compute this rate of growth requires some assumption about the rate of TFP growth. TFP is observable up to the last year of a particular stage of liberalisation (1987 for the output contracts stage, 1994 for the market opening stage), but there is no information on how or whether it would continue to grow if that stage continued indefinitely. It may continue to grow at the same annual rate as for the years observed (the optimistic case); it may not grow at all after the last year observed (the pessimistic case); or it may grow at a rate somewhere between these extremes. Table 12.3 summarises the estimated annual rates of growth for each stage under both optimistic and pessimistic assumptions about TFP growth. In both cases a clear result emerges: the predicted annual growth rate is significantly lower in the earlier than in the later stage of reform, suggesting that the emergence of free markets and strengthening of private property rights that has occurred since 1987 is crucial to economic growth and investment.

The effects of reform on annual growth rates identified in Table 12.3 give us some idea of the likely dynamic effects of liberalisation, but offer no normative conclusions. For these, it is necessary to use the approach of Baldwin (1992) to estimate dynamic gains from trade. In Baldwin's model, static gains

Table 12.3   Implied Growth Rates of Rice Output during Stages of Liberalisation

	Approximate Convergence Time (years) (%)	Predicted Annual Growth Rate	
		Optimistic Case (%)	Pessimistic Case
Output contracts stage	22	3.7	1.2
Market opening stage	33	5.1	2.0

Source: Che, Kompas and Vousden (1998).

from trade are those that occur at the original capital stock, while dynamic gains (or losses) are those associated with the induced movement of the capital stock to a new steady state. Although this may sound straightforward, there is a measurement problem. With no capital market distortions, we would expect that the usual 'Harberger triangles', which are intended to measure the static gains from trade, would include dynamic gains if estimated using long-run elasticities. Dynamic gains would already have been captured in the standard measure and there would be no additional gains to estimate. The interesting case is where capital market distortions are present – specifically, if the private and social costs of capital differ. Separate measurable dynamic gains could then be estimated. Baldwin attempted to estimate these gains using European data. He found gains to be relatively small, suggesting that the pursuit of dynamic gains may be inappropriate. However, capital market distortions for European countries are, for the most part, small. The procedure outlined in this section offers the basis for estimating dynamic gains from liberalisation for an economy with much larger capital market distortions and perhaps correspondingly larger dynamic gains. Estimation of these gains would be a worthwhile focus for future work.

CONCLUSIONS

This chapter has provided a brief overview of the effects of the post-1980 reforms of Vietnamese agriculture on rice output, TFP in rice production, and the implied rates of growth for each of the main stages of reform. It has also focused attention on the effects of the reform process on economic incentives. Reform-induced increases in farmer 'effort' are estimated to account for at least 20 per cent of TFP growth in the early years of reform and as much as 80 per cent in the later years. Capital stock data and the underlying theory both suggest that reform has brought about a large increase in farm investment in new capital equipment, particularly in the second, more ambitious, stage. The predicted average annual growth rate associated with transition to a steady state is also significantly higher in the second stage of reform than in the first. These results suggest that the second wave of reform, which opened markets and provided greater security of land tenure, has been the real engine for growth in the Vietnamese rice sector.

NOTES

1. In our empirical work we have been able to capture some of these subtleties by analysing the data on an annual basis.
2. These are chosen to maximise the utility function

$$U = \Pi - \frac{\varepsilon_1^z}{z\delta} - \frac{\varepsilon_2^z}{z\delta}$$

where Π is the farmer's profits and z and δ are positive constants. Che and Vousden estimate the value of z to be about 3. There is no need to estimate δ separately as it is subsumed in other estimated constants.
3. The estimated values for the share parameters of (12.1) are approximately $\alpha_1 = 0.4$, $\alpha_2 = 0.3$, $\alpha_3 = 0.2$ and $\alpha_4 = 0.1$.
4. The model is an extension of the basic neoclassical optimal growth model (Cass 1965). A neoclassical framework is used in preference to an increasing returns endogenous growth framework (Grossman and Helpman 1991, for example) because agriculture is a constant returns to scale industry.
5. These estimated rates of growth are derived by working out the (constant) annual growth rate which would take the sector from the observed initial level of output to the steady state in the estimated convergence time (22 years for the first stage and 33 years for the second). This is very much an approximation because the actual growth rate converges to zero as the steady state is approached.

References

Abiad, V.G., C.E. Cuevas and D.H. Graham (1988), 'Borrower Transaction Costs and Credit Rationing in Rural Financial Markets: The Philippines Case', *Working Paper No. 88-09*, Presented during the workshop 'Financial Intermediation in the Rural Sector: Research Results and Policy Issues', Central Bank of the Philippines, Manila.

ADB (Asian Development Bank) and IFPRI (International Food Policy Research Institute) (1996), Rice Market Monitoring and Policy Options Study, ADB, Hanoi.

Ahmed, Z.U. (1982), Transaction Costs in Rural Financial Markets in Bangladesh: A Study of a Rural Credit Market, Unpublished PhD Dissertation, University of Virginia, Virginia.

Alavi, Rokiah (1996), *Industrialisation in Malaysia: Import Substitution and Infant Industry Performance*, Routledge, London.

Amsden, A. (1989), *Asia's Next Giant: South Korea and Late Industrialization*, Oxford University Press, New York.

Anderson, D. (1982), 'Small Industry in Developing Countries: A Discussion of Issues', *World Development*, 10 (11), pp. 913–48.

Anon. (1971), 'Survey of Recent Developments', *Bulletin of Indonesian Economic Studies*, 7 (3), pp. 1–29.

Anwar, M. Arsjad and Iwan Jaya Aziz (1987), 'Perkembangan Ekonomi Indonesia 1987 dan Proyeksi 1988', in M. Arsjad Anwar et al. (eds), *Ekonomi Indonesia: Masalah dan Prospek 1988/1989*, University of Indonesia Press, Jakarta.

Ariff, M. (1991), *The Malaysian Economy: Pacific Connections*, Oxford University Press, Singapore.

Ariff, M. and H. Hill (1985), *Export-oriented Industrialization: The ASEAN Experience*, Allen & Unwin, Sydney.

Ariff, M. and Chee Peng Lim (1987), 'Foreign Investment in Malaysia', in V. Cable and B. Persaud (eds), *Developing with Foreign Investment*, Croom Helm, London, pp. 9–22.

Arndt, H.W. (1974), 'Survey of Recent Developments', *Bulletin of Indonesian Economic Studies*, 10 (2), pp. 1–34.

Aswicahyono, H.H., K. Bird and H. Hill (1996), 'What Happens to Industrial Structure When Countries Liberalize? Indonesia Since the Mid 1980s', *Journal of Development Studies*, 32 (3), pp. 340–63.

Athukorala, Prema-chandra (1998), *Trade Policy Issues in Asian Development*, Routledge, London.

Athukorala, Prema-chandra and Jayant Menon (1996), 'Foreign Direct Investment and Industrialisation in Malaysia: Exports, Employment and Spillovers', *Asian Economic Journal*, 10 (1), pp. 29–44.

—— (1997), 'Export-led Industrialisation, Employment and Equity: The Malaysian Case', *Agenda*, 4 (1), pp. 63–76.

Baldwin, Richard E. (1992), 'Measurable Dynamic Gains from Trade', *Journal of Political Economy*, 100, pp. 162–71.

Bank Indonesia (1968), *Report for the Years 1960–1965*, Jakarta.
—— (1984), *Report for the Financial Year 1983/1984*, Jakarta.
Bautista, R.M. and C.M. Gonzales (1992), 'Domestic Stabilization of Export Crop Prices: Philippine Copra and Malaysian Rubber', *The World Economy*, 15 (6).
Bernanke, Ben and Mark Gertler (1995), 'Inside the Black Box: The Credit Channel of Monetary Policy Transmission', *Journal of Economic Perspectives*, 9 (4), pp. 27–48.
Berry, A. and D. Mazumdar (1991), 'Small-scale Industry in the Asia–Pacific Region', *Asian-Pacific Economic Literature*, 5 (2), pp. 35–67.
Bhagwati, Jagdish (1988), *Protectionism*, MIT Press, Cambridge MA.
Bhattacharya, Amar and Mari Pangestu (1996), 'Indonesia: Development Transformation and the Role of Public Policy', in Danny M. Leipziger (ed.), *Lessons from East Asia*, University of Michigan Press, Ann Arbor.
Binhadi and Paul Meek (1992), 'Implementing Monetary Policy', in Anne Booth (ed.), *The Oil Boom and After: Indonesian Economic Policy and Performance in the Soeharto Era*, Oxford University Press, Singapore, pp. 102–31.
Binhluc District Statistical Office (1996), *Binhluc Statistics: 1995*, Binhluc, Namha.
Binhluc District VBA Branch (1996), *Annual Report: 1994*, Binhluc, Namha.
Bird, Kelly (1996), 'Survey of Recent Developments', *Bulletin of Indonesian Economic Studies*, 32 (1), pp. 3–32.
—— (1998), An Analysis of Market Structure and Competition in Indonesian Manufacturing Industry, Unpublished PhD dissertation, Australian National University.
Bosworth, B., S.M. Collins and Y.-C. Chen (1995), Accounting for Differences in Economic Growth, Paper presented to a conference on 'Structural Adjustment Policies in the 1990s: Experience and Prospects', Institute of Developing Economies, Tokyo.
Brash, Donald (1997), 'Prudential Supervision and Globalization of the Banking Sector: A National Supervisor's View', in Charles Enoch and John Green (eds), *Banking Soundness and Monetary Policy: Issues and Experiences in the Global Economy*, IMF, Washington DC.
Bruch, M. and U. Hiemenz (1984), *Small- and Medium-scale Industries in the ASEAN Countries: Agents or Victims of Economic Development?*, Westview Press, Boulder.
Byrd, W.A. and Q. Lin (1990), 'China's Rural Industry: An Introduction', in W.A. Byrd and Q. Lin (eds), *China's Rural Industry: Structure, Development and Reform*, Oxford University Press, Oxford.
Calvo, Guillermo, Leonardo Leiderman and Carmen Reinhart (1996), 'The Capital Inflows Problem: Concepts and Issues', *Contemporary Economic Policy*, 12 (3), pp. 54–66.
Calvo, Guillermo and Enrique Mendoza (1996), 'Mexico's Balance of Payments Crises: A Chronicle of a Death Foretold', *Journal of International Economics*, 41 (3–4), pp. 235–64.
Caprio, Gerard and Daniela Klingebiel (1997), 'Bank Insolvency: Bad Luck, Bad Policy, or Bad Banking?', in Michael Bruno and Boris Pleskovic (eds), *Annual World Bank Conference on Development Economics, 1996*, World Bank, Washington DC.
Cass, David (1965), 'Optimum Growth in an Aggregative Model of Capital Accumulation', *Review of Economics Studies*, 32, pp. 233–40.
Chanda, Nayan (1998), 'Rebuilding Asia', *Far Eastern Economic Review*, 12 February, pp. 46–50.
Chang, C. and Y. Wang (1994), 'The Nature of the Township–Village Enterprise', *Journal of Comparative Economics*, 19 (3), pp. 434–52.
Chang, G.H. and J.G.Z. Wen (1997), 'Wenzhou Model versus Sunan Model: Two

Forms of Non-state Enterprise in China', in W. Hai (ed.), *Zhongguo Xiangzhen Qiye Yanjiu* [Chinese Township and Village Enterprises: Nature, Experience and Reforms], China Industry and Commerce Publishing House, Beijing.

Chang, Roberto and Andres Velasco (1997), 'Financial Fragility and the Exchange Rate Regime', *Working Paper No. 97-16*, Federal Reserve Bank of Atlanta, Atlanta, November.

Chant, John and Mari Pangestu (1994), 'An Assessment of Financial Reform in Indonesia, 1983–90', in Gerard Caprio Jr, Izak Atiyas and James A. Hanson, *Financial Reform: Theory and Experience*, Cambridge University Press, Cambridge UK, pp. 223–75.

Che, Nhu (1997), The Effects of Internal and External Trade Liberalisation on Agricultural Growth: A Case Study of Vietnam, PhD dissertation, Australian National University, Canberra.

Che, Nhu, Tom Kompas and Neil Vousden (1998), Liberalisation, Incentives and Vietnamese Agricultural Growth, Paper presented to the 'Conference on Vietnam and the Region: Asia–Pacific Experiences and Vietnam's Policy Directions', Australian National University, Canberra, 20–21 April.

Che, Nhu and Neil Vousden (1998), Liberalisation and Agricultural Productivity: The Role of Incentives in Vietnamese Agriculture, Unpublished working paper, Australian National University, Canberra.

Chee Peng Lim (1994), 'Heavy Industrialisation: A Second Round of Import Substitution', in K.S. Jomo (ed.), *Japan and Malaysian Development in the Shadow of the Rising Sun*, Routledge, London, pp. 244–62.

Chen, E.K.Y. (1997), 'The Total Factor Productivity Debate: Determinants of Economic Growth in East Asia', *Asian-Pacific Economic Literature*, 11 (1), pp. 18–38.

Chia S.Y. (1996), 'The Deepening and Widening of ASEAN', *Journal of the Asia Pacific Economy*, 1 (1), pp. 59–78.

CIE (Centre for International Economics) (1997), *Vietnam's Trade Policies 1997*, CIE, Canberra.

CIEM (Central Institute for Economic Management) (1998), Review of the Current Company Law and Key Recommendations for Its Revision, Draft paper financed by the United Nations Development Program (Project VIE/97/016), Hanoi.

Cole, W. (1998), 'Bali's Garment Export Industry', in Hal Hill and Thee Kian Wie (eds), *Indonesia's Technological Challenge*, Institute of Southeast Asian Studies, Singapore, pp. 255–78.

Corden, W.M. (1996), 'Pragmatic Orthodoxy: Macroeconomic Policies in Seven East Asian Economies', *Occasional Papers No. 61*, International Center for Economic Growth, San Francisco.

Cuevas, C.E. (1984), Intermediation Costs and Scale Economies of Banking under Financial Regulation in Honduras, Unpublished PhD Dissertation, Ohio State University, Columbus.

Cuevas, C.E. and D.H. Graham (1984), 'Agricultural Lending Costs in Honduras', in D.W. Adams, D.H. Graham and J.D. Von Pischke (eds), *Undermining Rural Development with Cheap Credit*, Westview Press, Boulder.

—— (1985), 'Transactions Costs of Borrowing and Credit Rationing in Agriculture: A Simultaneous-Equations Approach', *Economics and Sociology Occasional Paper No. 1180*, Agricultural Finance Program, Ohio State University, Columbus.

Dean, Judith M., Seema Desai and James Riedel (1994), *Trade Policy Reform in Developing Countries since 1985: A Review of the Evidence*, World Bank, Washington DC.

Djiwandono, Soedradjad (1995), Sambutan Gubernor Bank Indonesia pada Rapat

Pleno I Perbanas [Speech of the Governor of Bank Indonesia at the First Plenary Meeting of Perbanas], Batam, 10 June (mimeo).

Doanh, Le Dang and Tran Kim Hao (1997), 'Evaluation of Macroeconomic Policies and Administrative Formalities on Promotion of Small and Medium Scale Enterprises in Vietnam', Draft report to CIEM and UNIDO, Hanoi.

Dobson, W. (1997), 'East Asian Integration: Synergies between Firm Strategies and Government Policies', in W. Dobson and Chia S.Y. (eds), *Multinationals in East Asian Integration*, International Development Research Centre, Ottawa, and Institute of Southeast Asian Studies, Singapore, pp. 3–27.

Dollar, David (1996), 'Economic Reform, Openness and Vietnam's Entry into ASEAN', *ASEAN Economic Bulletin*, 13 (2), pp. 169–84.

Dooley, Michael (1994), 'Globalization, Speculative Bubbles, and Central Banking', in Shakil Faruqi (ed.), *Financial Sector Reforms, Economic Growth and Stability: Experiences in Selected Asian and Latin American Countries*, World Bank, Washington DC.

Edwards, C. and Jomo K.S. (1993), 'Policy Options for Malaysian Industrialisation', in Jomo K.S. (ed.) *Industrialising Malaysia: Policy, Performance, Prospects*, Routledge, London, pp. 316–34.

Edwards, S. (1983), 'The Short-run Relation between Growth and Inflation in Latin America: Comment', *American Economic Review*, 35, pp. 85–103.

El-Erian, M. (1988), 'Currency Substitution in Egypt and the Yemen Arab Republic', *IMF Staff Papers*, 35, pp. 85–103.

Feder, G. et al. (1988), *Land Policies and Farm Productivity in Thailand*, Johns Hopkins Press, Baltimore, for the World Bank.

Feder, G., L.J. Lau, J.Y. Lin and X. Luo (1989), 'Agricultural Credit and Farm Performance in China', *Journal of Comparative Economics*, 13, pp. 508–26.

Fernald, John, Hali Edison and Prakash Loungani (1998), 'Was China the First Domino? Assessing Links between China and the Rest of Emerging Asia', *International Finance Discussion Paper No. 604*, Board of Governors of the Federal Reserve System, Washington DC, March.

Glick, Reuven and Ramon Moreno (1999), 'Is Pegging the Exchange Rate a Cure for Inflation? East Asian Experiences', in Richard Sweeney, Clas Wihlborg and Thomas Willett (eds), *Exchange Rate Policies for Emerging Market Economies*, Westview Press, Boulder, Chapter 8.

Go Iwaki (1992), 'SMI Development and the Subcontracting System in Japan', in Kim S.J. and Suh J.-W. (eds), *Cooperation in Small and Medium Scale Industries in ASEAN*, Asian-Pacific Development Centre, Kuala Lumpur, pp. 309–51.

Goddard, David (1998), 'Enterprise Reform: Legal and Regulatory Issues', Draft report of legal consultant to Asian Development Bank/Ministry of Planning and Investment, Enterprise Reform Technical Assistance Project.

Goldfajn, Ilan and Rodrigo O. Valdes (1997), 'Capital Flows and the Twin Crises: The Role of Liquidity', *IMF Working Paper No. 97–87*, IMF, Washington DC, July.

Goldstein, Morris and Phillip Turner (1996), *Banking Crises in Emerging Economies: Origins and Policy Options*, Bank for International Settlements, Basle.

Golin, Jonathan (1998), 'Should You Bank on It? Assessing Vietnam's Bank Credit Risk', *Vietnam Business Journal*, February, pp. 37–9.

Government of Indonesia (1989), Himpunan Ketentuan Lanjutan (Penyempurnaan) Pakto 27 1988 [Compilation of Stipulations (Refinements) Further to the Package of 27 October 1998], Jakarta.

—— (1994), *Rencana Pembangunan Lima Tahun Keenam 1994/95–1998/99* [Sixth Five-year Development Plan 1994/95–1998/99], Jakarta.

Graham, D.H., M. Schreider and J. Leon (1996), 'Transactions Cost Issues in Rural Finance: A Review of the Arguments and Recent Evidence in Asia', in Asian Productivity Organisation (ed.), *Transaction Costs of Farm Credit in Asia*, Asian Productivity Organisation, Tokyo, pp. 82–98.

Greenaway, D. (1993), 'Liberalising Foreign Trade through Rose Tinted Glasses', *Economic Journal*, 103, pp. 208–22.

Grenville, Stephen (1977), 'Survey of Recent Developments', *Bulletin of Indonesian Economic Studies*, 13 (1), pp. 1–32.

Grossman, Gene M. and Elhanan Helpman (1991), *Innovation and Growth in the Global Economy*, MIT Press, Cambridge MA.

GSO (General Statistics Office) (various issues), *Statistical Yearbook*, Statistical Publishing House, Hanoi.

Guisinger, Stephen (1985), *Investment Incentives and Performance*, Praeger, New York.

Habir, Manggi (1994), 'Bank Soundness Requirements: A Commercial Bank Perspective', in Ross H. McLeod (ed.), *Indonesia Assessment 1994: Finance as a Key Sector in Indonesia's Economic Development*, Research School of Pacific and Asian Studies, Canberra, and Institute of Southeast Asian Studies, Singapore, pp. 171–85.

Hai Bang (1998), 'Con Bao Tein te Dang ye Dan' [The Financial Storm Is Weakening], *Thoi Bao Kinh te Vietnam*, 12, 11 February, p. 4.

Harberger, A.C. (1997), 'Reflections on Economic Growth in Asia and the Pacific', *Journal of Asian Economics*, 7 (3), pp. 365–92.

Hausmann, Ricardo and Liliana Rojas-Suarez (eds) (1996), *Banking Crises in Latin America*, Interamerican Development Bank, Washington DC.

Hill, Hal (1996), 'Indonesia's Industrial Policy and Performance: "Orthodoxy" Vindicated', *Economic Development and Cultural Change*, 5 (1), pp. 147–74.

—— (1997a), *Indonesia's Industrial Transformation*, Institute of Southeast Asian Studies, Singapore, and Allen & Unwin, Sydney.

—— (1997b), 'Towards a Political Economy Explanation of Rapid Growth in Southeast Asia', in Hadi Soesastro (ed.), *One Southeast Asia in a New Regional and International Setting*, Centre for Strategic and International Studies, Jakarta, pp. 93–149.

—— (1997c), 'Myths about Tigers: Indonesian Development Policy Debates', *Pacific Review*, 10 (2), pp. 256–73.

Hill, Hal and Thee Kian Wie (eds) (1998), *Indonesia's Technological Challenge*, Institute of Southeast Asian Studies, Singapore.

Hobday, M. (1995), *Innovation in East Asia: The Challenge to Japan*, Edward Elgar, Cheltenham.

Huang, Y. (1998a), *China's Agricultural Reform: Getting Institutions Right*, Cambridge University Press, Cambridge UK.

—— (1998b), Rural Industrialization and Income Inequality in China, National Centre for Development Studies, Australian National University, Canberra, mimeo.

Hughes, Helen (ed.) (1988), *Achieving Industrialization in East Asia*, Cambridge University Press, Cambridge UK.

—— (1993), 'An External View', in L. Low, Toh Mun Heng, Soon Teck Wong, Tan Kong Yam and Helen Hughes (eds), *Challenge and Response: Thirty Years of the Economic Development Board*, Times Academic Press, Singapore, pp. 1–25.

Iqbal, Farukh (1995), Deregulation and Development in Indonesia, Paper presented at the conference 'Building on Success: Maximizing the Gains from Deregulation', Indonesian Economists Association, World Bank and University of Indonesia, Jakarta, 26–28 April.

Johnson, C. (1982), *MITI and the Japanese Economic Miracle*, Stanford University Press, Stanford.

Jomo K.S. (ed.) (1993), *Industrialising Malaysia: Policy, Performance, Prospects*, Routledge, London.

Jordan, Cally (1997), 'Family Resemblances: The Family Controlled Company in Asia and Its Implications for Law Reform', *Australian Journal of Company Law*, 8 (1), pp. 89–104.

Jorgenson, D.W. and Z. Griliches (1967), 'The Explanation of Productivity Change', *Review of Economic Studies*, 34 (3), pp. 249–83.

Jun, Kwang W., Minh Pham Duc, V. Kwakwa, Kevin Peters Jr. and Long Tong Thang (1997), Foreign Capital Flows in Vietnam: Trends, Impact and Policy Implications, Background Paper for the World Bank's Economic Report 'Vietnam: Deepening Reforms for Growth', World Bank, Washington DC (mimeo).

Kaminsky, Graciela, Saul Lizondo and Carmen Reinhart (1997), 'Leading Indicators of Currency Crises', *IMF Working Paper No. 97–79*, IMF, Washington DC, July.

Kaminsky, Graciela and Carmen Reinhart (1996), 'The Twin Crises: The Causes of Banking and Balance-of-Payments Problems', *International Finance Discussion Paper No. 544*, Board of Governors of the Federal Reserve System, Washington DC, March.

Keenan, Faith (1997), 'Lesson One: Vietnam's Banks Have a Lot to Learn about Commercial Lending', *Far Eastern Economic Review*, 17, July, pp.·80–81.

Kim Linsu (1997), *Imitation to Innovation: The Dynamics of Korea's Technological Learning*, Harvard Business School Press, Boston.

Kirkpatrick, C.H., N. Lee and F.I. Nixson (1984), *Industrial Structure and Policy in Less Developed Countries*, Allen & Unwin, London.

Kokko, Ari (1997), Managing the Transition to Free Trade: Vietnamese Trade Policy for the 21st Century, Stockholm School of Economics, Stockholm (mimeo).

Kokko, Ari and Mario Zejan (1996), 'Planned and Failed Foreign Direct Investment in Viet Nam', *Asian Pacific Development Journal*, 3 (1), pp. 37–54.

Kornai, Jonas (1992), *The Socialist System: The Political Economy of Communism*, Norton, New York.

Krugman, Paul (1994), 'The Myth of Asia's Miracle', *Foreign Affairs*, 73 (6), pp. 62–78.

—— (1995), 'Growing World Trade: Causes and Consequences', *Brooking Papers on Economic Activity*, 25th Anniversary Issue, Brookings Institution, pp. 327–77.

Krugman, Paul (1998a), 'What Happened to Asia?', Downloaded from http://web.mit.edu/krugman/www/.

—— (1998b), 'Fire Sale FDI', Downloaded from http://web.mit.edu/krugman/www/.

Ladman, J.R. (1984), 'Loan Transaction Costs, Credit Rationing, and Market Structure: The Case of Bolivia,' in D.W. Adams, D.H. Graham and J.D. Von Pischke (eds), *Undermining Rural Development with Cheap Credit*, Westview Press, Boulder.

Lall, S. (1992), 'Technological Capabilities and Industrialization', *World Development*, 20 (2), pp. 165–86.

—— (1996), 'Paradigms of Development: The East Asian Debate', *Oxford Development Studies*, 24 (2), pp. 111–32.

Leung, Suiwah (1997), 'Financial Deregulation and Trade Expansion', in David Robertson (ed.), *East Asian Trade after the Uruguay Round*, Cambridge University Press, Cambridge UK, pp. 78–100.

Leung, Suiwah and Le Dang Doanh (1998), 'Vietnam', in Ross H. McLeod and Ross Garnaut (eds), *East Asia in Crisis*, Routledge, London and New York, pp. 120–30.

Li, David D. (1996), 'A Theory of Ambiguous Property Rights in Transition Economies: The Case of the Chinese Non-state Sector', *Journal of Comparative Economics*, 23 (1), pp. 1–19.

Lim C.Y. and Associates (1988), *Policy Options for the Singapore Economy*, McGraw-Hill, Singapore.

Lim, David (1992), 'The Dynamics of Economic Policy-making: A Study of Malaysian Trade Policies and Performance', in A.J. MacIntyre and K. Jayasuriya (eds), *The Dynamics of Economic Policy Reforms in South-east Asia and the South-west Pacific*, Oxford University Press, Singapore, pp. 94–114.

Lim, L.Y.C. (1996), 'The Evolution of Southeast Asian Business Systems', *Journal of Asian Business*, 12 (1), pp. 51–74.

Lin, J.Y., F. Cai and Z. Li (1996), *Zhongguo De Qiji: Fazhan Zhanlu Yu Jinji Gaige* [China's Miracle: Development Strategy and Economic Reform], Chinese University Press, Hong Kong.

Lin, O.C.C. (1998), 'Science and Technology Policy and Its Influence on Economic Development in Taiwan', in H.S. Rowen (ed.), *Behind East Asian Growth: The Political and Social Foundations of Prosperity*, Routledge, London, pp. 185–208.

Lindsay, H. (1989), 'The Indonesian Log Export Ban: An Estimation of Foregone Export Earnings', *Bulletin of Indonesian Economic Studies*, 25 (2), pp. 111–23.

Little, I.M.D., R.N. Cooper, W.M. Corden and S. Rajapatirana (1993), *Boom, Crisis, and Adjustment: The Macroeconomic Experience of Developing Countries*, Oxford University Press, New York, for the World Bank.

Low, L., Toh Mun Heng, Soon Teck Wong, Tan Kong Yam and Helen Hughes (1993), *Challenge and Response: Thirty Years of the Economic Development Board*, Times Academic Press, Singapore.

Mallon, Raymond (1997), '*Doi Moi and Economic Development in Vietnam*', in Adam Fforde (ed.), *Doi Moi: Ten Years after the 1986 Party Congress*, Conference proceedings, Australian National University, Canberra.

—— (1998a), Enterprise Restructuring to Create More Equitable Opportunities for Private and State Enterprises in the Industry Sector, Consultant Report to the Asian Development Bank, Hanoi.

—— (1998b), Mapping the Playing Field: Options for Reducing Private Sector Disincentives in Vietnam, Report prepared for the Swedish Embassy, Hanoi.

Manzano, George and Ramon Moreno (1998), 'Supporting Regional Consultations: Research, Policy Analysis and Surveillance', in *Asia: Responding to Crisis*, Asian Development Bank Institute, Tokyo, pp. 29–44.

McCallum, Bennett T. (1992), 'A Specification of Policy Rules and Performance Measures in Multicountry Simulation Studies', *IMF Working Paper 92-41*, IMF, Washington DC, June.

McKinnon, Ronald I. (1973), *Money and Capital in Economic Development*, Brookings Institution, Washington.

McKinnon, Ronald and Huw Pill (1997), Overborrowing: A Decomposition of Credit and Currency Risks, Unpublished manuscript, November.

McLeod, Ross H. (1984), 'Financial Institutions and Markets in Indonesia', in M.T. Skully (ed.), *Financial Markets and Institutions in Southeast Asia*, Macmillan, London, pp. 49–109.

—— (1996), 'Control and Competition: Banking Deregulation and Reregulation in Indonesia', *Working Paper No. 96/7*, Department of Economics, Research School of Pacific and Asian Studies, Australian National University, September.

—— (1997a), 'Policy Conflicts in Indonesia: The Impact of the Current Account

Deficit Target on Growth, Equity and Stability', *ASEAN Economic Bulletin*, 14 (1), pp. 32–45.

—— (1997b), 'Explaining Chronic Inflation in Indonesia', *Journal of Development Studies*, 33 (3), pp. 392–410.

—— (1998), 'From Crisis to Cataclysm? The Mismanagement of Indonesia's Economic Ailments', *The World Economy*, 21 (7), pp. 913–30.

McMillan, J., J. Whalley and L. Zhu (1989), 'The Impact of China's Economic Reforms on Agricultural Productivity Growth', *Journal of Political Economy*, 97 (4), pp. 781–807.

Medalla, E.M., G.R. Tecson, R.M. Bautista and J.H. Power (1995), *Catching up with Asia's Tigers: Philippine Trade and Industrial Policies*, Philippine Institute for Development Studies, Manila.

Medhi Krongkaew (ed.) (1995), *Thailand's Industrialization and its Consequences*, Macmillan, London.

Meyanathan, S.D. (ed.) (1994), 'Industrial Structure and the Development of Small and Medium Enterprise Linkages: Examples from East Asia', *EDI Seminar Series*, World Bank, Washington DC.

Mingsarn Santikarn Kaosa-ard (1992), 'Manufacturing Growth: A Blessing for All?', in Thailand Development Research Institute, *Thailand's Economic Structure: Towards Balanced Economic Growth?*, Thailand Development Research Institute, Bangkok, pp. 2–1/63.

Ministry of Agriculture (1996), *China Agricultural Development Report '96*, China Agricultural Publishing House, Beijing.

Mishkin, Friedrich (1997), The Causes and Propagation of Financial Instability: Lessons for Policy Makers, Unpublished manuscript, Columbia University, New York, September.

Moreno, Ramon and Mark Spiegel (1997), 'Are Asian Economies Exempt from the Impossible Trinity? Evidence from Singapore', in Monetary Authority of Singapore (ed.), *12th Pacific Basin Central Bank Conference: The Impact of Financial Market Development on the Real Economy*, Monetary Authority of Singapore, Singapore, pp. 9–26.

Muir, Ross (1991), 'Survey of Recent Developments', *Bulletin of Indonesian Economic Studies*, 27 (3), pp. 3–27.

Myint, Hla (1967), 'The Inward and Outward Looking Countries of Southeast Asia', *Malaysian Economic Review*, 12 (1), pp. 1–13.

Naughton, B. (1994), 'Chinese Institutional Innovation and Privatization from Below', *American Economic Review*, 84 (2), pp. 266–70.

Nehru, V. and A. Dhareshwar (1994), 'New Estimates of Total Factor Productivity Growth for Developing and Industrial Countries', *Policy Research Working Paper*, 1313, World Bank, Washington DC.

Nguyen, Xuan Tu (1998), 'Foreign Direct Investment in Vietnam', Paper presented at the conference, 'Vietnam and the Region: Asia–Pacific Experiences and Vietnam's Economic Policy Directions', 20–21 April, Australian National University, Canberra.

North, Douglas C. (1994), 'Economic Performance through Time', *American Economic Review*, 84 (3), pp. 359–68.

Pangestu, Mari (1990), Trade Policy Reforms in Indonesia: Towards an Explanation, Paper presented to the 'International Conference on Economic Policy Making Process in Indonesia', Yayasan Padi dan Kapas, ISEI-Jaya, and Asia Foundation, Bali, September.

—— (1991), 'Managing Economic Policy Reforms in Indonesia', in Sylvia Ostry (ed.), *Authority and Academic Scribblers: The Role of Research in East Asian Policy Reform*, International Center for Economic Growth, San Francisco.

—— (1996), *Economic Reform, Deregulation and Privatization: The Indonesian Experience*, Centre for Strategic and International Studies, Jakarta.

Panglaykim, J. and D.H. Penny (1968), 'The New Banking Laws', *Bulletin of Indonesian Economic Studies*, No. 9, February, pp. 75–7.

Papageorgiou, D., M. Michaely and A. Choksi (eds) (1991), *Liberalizing Foreign Trade*, Basil Blackwell, Cambridge MA, for the World Bank.

Patten, R.H. and J.K. Rosengard (1991), *Progress with Profits: the Development of Rural Banking in Indonesia*, International Center for Economic Growth, San Francisco.

Pomfret, R. (1996), 'ASEAN: Always at the Crossroads?', *Journal of the Asia Pacific Economy*, 1 (3), pp. 365–90.

Puhazhendhi, V. (1995), *Transaction Costs of Lending to the Rural Poor: Nongovernmental Organisations and Self-help Groups of the Poor as Intermediaries for Banks in India*, Foundation for Development Cooperation, Brisbane.

Rasiah, R. (1995), *Foreign Capital and Industrialisation in Malaysia*, Macmillan, Houndmills.

Remolona, Eli (1990), 'How Safety Nets Work: Dealing with Financial Institutions in Distress: The Experience of Four Countries', *Central Banking*, No. 2, pp. 61–72.

Riedel, James (1991a), 'Intra-Asian Trade and Foreign Direct Investment', *Asian Development Review*, 9 (1), pp. 111–46.

—— (1991b), 'Strategy Wars: The State of Debate on Trade and Industrialization in Developing Countries', in A. Koekkoek and L.B.M. Mennes (eds), *International Trade and Global Development: Essays in Honour of Jagdish Bhagwati*, Routledge, London.

—— (1993), 'Vietnam: On the Trails of the Tigers', *World Economy*, 16 (4), pp. 401–22.

—— (1997), 'The Vietnamese Economy in the 1990s', *Asian-Pacific Economic Literature*, 11 (2), pp. 58–65.

Riedel, James and Bruce Comer (1997), 'Transition to a Market Economy in Vietnam', in Wing Thye Woo, Stephen Parker and Jeffrey D. Sachs (eds), *Economies in Transition: Comparing Asia and Eastern Europe*, MIT Press, Cambridge MA, pp. 189–213.

Riedel, James and Chuong S. Tran (1997), *The Emerging Private Sector and the Industrialization of Vietnam*, Washington DC.

Riedel, James and William S. Turley (1998), *The Politics and Economics of Transition to an Open Market Economy in Vietnam*, OECD, Paris.

Rojas-Suarez, L. (1992), 'Currency Substitution and Inflation in Peru', *IMF Working Paper, WP/92/33*, IMF, Washington DC.

Rozelle, S. (1994), 'Rural Industrialization and Increasing Inequality: Emerging Patterns in China's Reforming Economy', *Journal of Comparative Economics*, 19 (3), pp. 362–91.

Sachs, J. (1997), 'Ownership Reform in TVEs', in W. Hai (ed.), *Zhongguo Xiangzhen Qiye Yanjiu* [Chinese Township and Village Enterprises: Nature, Experience and Reforms], China Industry and Commerce Publishing House, Beijing.

Sachs, J. and A. Warner (1995), 'Economic Reforms and the Process of Global Integration', *Brookings Papers on Economic Activity*, 25th anniversary issue, pp. 1–95.

Sachs, J. and W.T. Woo (1997), 'Understanding China's Economic Performance', *NBER Working Paper 5935*, Cambridge MA.

Schiller, J. and B. Martin-Schiller (1997), 'Market, Culture and State in the Emergence of an Indonesian Export Furniture Industry', *Journal of Asian Business*, 13 (1), pp. 1–23.

Sheng, Andrew (ed.) (1995), *Bank Restructuring: Lessons from the 80's*, World Bank, Washington DC.

Smith, H. (1995), 'Industry Policy in East Asia', *Asian-Pacific Economic Literature*, 9 (1), pp. 17–39.

Soesastro, Hadi (1989), 'The Political Economy of Deregulation in Indonesia', *Asian Survey*, 24 (9), pp. 853–69.

—— (1998), 'Domestic Adjustment in Four ASEAN Economies', in Charles E. Morrison and Hadi Soesastro (eds), *Domestic Adjustments to Globalization*, Japan Center for International Exchange, Tokyo.

Soesastro, Hadi and M. Chatib Basri (1998), 'Survey of Recent Developments', *Bulletin of Indonesian Economic Studies*, 34 (1), pp. 3–54.

Solow, Robert M. (1956), 'A Contribution to the Theory of Economic Growth', *Quarterly Journal of Economics*, 70 (1), pp. 65–94.

SSB (State Statistics Bureau) (1997), *China Statistics Yearbook*, China Statistical Publishing House, Beijing.

Syahrir and Colin Brown (1992), 'Indonesian Financial and Trade Policy Deregulation: Reform and Response', in Andrew J. MacIntyre and Kanishka Jayasuriya (eds), *The Dynamics of Economic Policy Reform in South-east Asia and the South-west Pacific*, Oxford University Press, Singapore.

Tran Mai Huong (1998), 'Vietnam Alert to Impact of Financial Crisis', *Vietnam News*, 11 February, p. 2.

Tran, T.D. (1996), Segmented Rural Credit Markets and Borrower Transactions Costs: A Study of Rural Credit Market in Vietnam, Paper presented to the AusAID/NCDS Vietnam Economic Research Project, Canberra, December.

Tran, T.Q. and T.H.P. Nguyen (1998), 'Rural Finance Mini-market,' *Economic Studies*, 238, Institute of Economics, National Centre for Social Sciences and Humanities, Hanoi, pp. 35–43.

Tran, T.V.A., V.T. Ngo, C.N. Nguyen, V.H. Dao, H.T. Nguyen, T.H. Tran, T.H. Pham and B.Q. Lam (1992), *Survey on Rural Credit, Vietnam*, Study commissioned by the Swedish International Development Authority, Development Cooperation Office, Hanoi.

Tripathi, S. and John McBeth (1998), 'Tale of Two Banks: Indonesia's Push for Big Banks May Sideline the Fittest', *Far Eastern Economic Review*, 26 March, pp. 68–9.

Truong, David H.D. and Carolyn L. Gates (1996), 'Vietnam in ASEAN – Economic Reform, Openness and Transformation: An Overview', *ASEAN Economic Bulletin*, 13 (2), pp. 159–68.

UNDP (United Nations Development Program) (1996), *Catching Up: Capacity Development for Poverty Elimination in Vietnam*, UNDP and UNICEF, Hanoi.

Wade, R. (1990), *Governing the Market: Economic Theory and the Role of Government in East Asian Industrialization*, Princeton University Press, Princeton.

Wardhana, Ali (1989), Structural Adjustment in Indonesia: Export and the 'High-cost' Economy, Keynote address, '24th Conference of South-east Asian Central Bank Governors', Bangkok, 25 January.

Warr, P.G. (1989), 'Export Processing Zones: The Economics of Enclave Manufacturing', *World Bank Research Observer*, 4 (1), pp. 65–88.

—— (1995), 'Myths about Dragons', *Agenda*, 1 (2), pp. 215–28.

—— (1997), 'General Equilibrium Welfare and Distributional Effects of Thailand's

Rice Export Tax', *Working Papers in Trade and Development*, No. 97/1, Australian National University.

Weitzman, M.L. and C. Xu (1994), 'Chinese Township–Village Enterprises as Vaguely Defined Cooperatives', *Journal of Comparative Economics*, 18 (2), pp. 121–45.

Wells, Luis T (Jr) (1986), 'Investment Incentives: An Uneasy Debate', *TNC Reporter*, 22, Autumn, pp. 17–19.

Wisarn Pupphavesa (1996), Competition Regulation and Policy in Thailand, Paper presented to the 23rd Pacific Trade and Development (PAFTAD) Conference, Taipei.

Wolf, Holger (1998), 'Exchange Rate Regimes', in *Asia: Responding to Crisis*, Asian Development Bank Institute, Tokyo, April, pp. 45–57.

World Bank (1993), *The East Asian Miracle: Economic Growth and Public Policy*, Washington DC.

—— (1995), *Vietnam: Financial Sector Review, An Agenda for Financial Sector Development*, Report No. 13135-VN, Washington DC.

—— (1997), *Vietnam: Refining Reform for Growth*, World Bank, Washington DC.

—— (1998), Vietnam: Rising to the Challenge, Economic Report for the World Bank Consultative Group Meeting for Vietnam, World Bank, Washington DC, 7–8 December.

Young, A. (1994), 'Lessons from the East Asian NICs: A Contrarian View', *European Economic Review*, 38 (3/4), pp. 964–73.

Zong, J., Z. Li and F. Zhou (1992), 'Development of Non-agricultural Industries: The Current Situation, Problems and Prospects of the Township and Village Enterprises', in S. Guo (ed.), *The Changing Countryside and Agriculture: A Positive Study of Rural Economic Reform in China*, China Finance and Economy Press, Beijing.

Index

ADB *see* Asian Development Bank
Administrative Reform Program, 161
AFTA *see* ASEAN Free Trade Area
agricultural sector, 7, 12–13, 31, 121,
    129, 172, 195, 206–28
    reform, 207–11
Albania, 87
APEC *see* Asia–Pacific Economic
    Cooperation
arm's-length lending, 46, 47
ASEAN *see* Association of South East
    Asian Nations
ASEAN Free Trade Area (AFTA), 19,
    56, 63, 132
Asia–Pacific Economic Cooperation
    (APEC), 56, 63
Asian Development Bank (ADB), xiii,
    xv, 54(fn)
Asian Development Bank Institute,
    52(fn)
Asian Tigers, 10, 11
assignment problem, 45, 54(fn)
Association of South East Asian Nations
    (ASEAN), 3, 19, 42, 49, 121–45
    ASEAN-3, 6, 42, 49
Augmented Dicky–Fuller (ADF) test, 92
AusAID/NCDS Vietnam Economic
    Research Project, xiii, xv
Australian Agency for International
    Development (AusAID), xv

baht, 19–20, 33, 39, 42, 69
balance of payments, 5, 6, 35, 70, 71,
    75, 92
Bali Summit, 132
Bangkok Bank of Commerce, 20, 39, 47
Bangkok International Banking Facility,
    53(fn)
Bangkok Metropolitan Bank, 39
Bangladesh, 101–3, 112, 115(fn), 148,
    149, 154
Bank Bumi Daya, 82(fn)

Bank Danamon, 38
Bank Duta, 38
Bank of England, 47, 54(fn)
Bank Indonesia, 39, 53–4(fn), 69, 71,
    72, 74, 75, 78, 80, 81(fn), 82(fn)
Bank Negara Indonesia, 82(fn)
Bank One, 39
Bank Pembangunan Indonesia
    (Bapindo), 38, 82(fn)
Bank of Thailand, 19, 39
Bank Umum Majapajit, 38
bankruptcy, 80, 188–9
    see also banks, insolvencies
Bankruptcy of Enterprises Law (1993),
    178, 189
banks, 20, 62
    closures, 39, 47, 77, 78, 79, 166
    controls on borrowing, 75–6
    foreign, 22
    guarantees, 53(fn)
    insolvencies, 38–9, 47, 62, 77
    lending, 70–3, 183
    licensing, 72, 76–7
    regulation, 7, 22, 32, 46–8, 62, 77,
        82(fn), 191
    reserves, 73–5, 81(fn)
    restructuring, 78–9
    weaknesses, 22, 23, 237
    see also central banks; financial
        sector; runs on currencies/
        financial institutions
Bapindo *see* Bank Pembangunan
    Indonesia
Barings Bank, 47, 54(fn)
Basle Accord, 46
Binhluc, 4, 96–117
Bolivia, 101
BOO *see* build–operate–own
BOT *see* build–operate–transfer
Brazil, 12
Bretton Woods system, 49
build–operate–own (BOO), 188

build–operate–transfer (BOT), 188
Bulgaria, 87
bumiputra, 157, 158
bureaucracy, 19, 58, 71, 127, 130, 131,
    141–2, 143(fn), 145(fn), 161, 179,
    180, 182, 185
business enterprises
    law, 177, 178
    new, 177–81
    registration procedures, 177–81
    trends, 175
    see also small and medium-sized
        enterprises

capital
    account liberalisation, 59–60
    inflows, 4, 5, 21, 32, 37, 48–50,
        54(fn), 62, 72, 82(fn), 140, 190
    mobility, 23, 83, 165, 186
    outflows, 70
causes of financial crisis, 3–4, 32, 37,
    42, 47, 78
CBEs *see* commune and brigade
    enterprises
central banks, 40, 44, 50, 62, 69, 71, 73,
    74, 76, 77, 78, 81(fn)
Central Committee, 26
Central Provident Fund (Singapore), 127
certificates of deposit (SBIs), 69, 70, 74,
    75, 81(fn)
chaebol, 26, 44, 62
Chile, 54(fn)
China, 7, 12, 13, 14, 21, 33, 54(fn), 62,
    87, 104, 121, 126, 193–205
China Daily, 201
Civil Code (1995), 182
Commercial Code (1997), 182
commune and brigade enterprises
    (CBEs), 194
Company Law (1990), 174, 178, 180,
    184, 186, 187
competition/competitiveness, 24, 56, 61,
    67, 76, 77, 139–42, 166, 170, 188,
    202
Constitution, 18
    Indonesia, 57
    Malaysia, 158
    Vietnam, 18
consumer price index (CPI), 31
contagion effect, 4
contracts, 181–2

Cooperatives Law, 178
corporatisation, 186–7
corruption, 20, 127, 131, 133, 179, 191
    see also cronyism
CPI *see* consumer price index
credit
    availability, 16–17, 62, 183–4, 203
    government directed, 3, 22, 32, 47
    guarantees, 17
    informal, 17, 98, 104
    letters of, 17, 22, 38, 43, 54(fn), 78
    policies, 96–117
    risk, 4
    subsidised, 4, 6
cronyism, 61, 64, 141
    see also corruption
Cultural Revolution, 194
current account deficits, 22, 23, 168

debt ratios, 40, 44, 53(fn), 183
Deng Xiaoping, 193, 196
Department of Finance (Indonesia),
    82(fn)
derivatives, 47
devaluation, 20, 24, 42, 68, 69, 78, 85,
    94
dirigisme, 55
divestiture, 186, 187–8
doi moi, 8, 27, 31, 87, 182
    see also liberalisation
dollarisation, 5, 51, 82–95
    definition, 83
domestic investment, 190
domestic savings, 8, 14, 35
Do Muoi, 16
dong, 24, 25, 85, 86, 91, 94, 99–104,
    113
duty rebate scheme, 161

Ecuador, 103
Economic Court, 189
Economic Development Board
    (Singapore), 127, 144
economic renovation *see doi moi*
education, 128
emerging markets, 4, 20, 37, 53(fn)
employment, 6, 12, 121, 136, 151–2,
    157, 162, 163, 166, 171, 186, 195,
    196, 197–200, 202, 204
equitisation, 186–7
Euro-bond, 20

exchange rates, 45, 57, 68–82, 85
  Bretton Woods system, 49
  fixed, 49, 67, 68
  floating, 32, 48, 54(fn), 68, 69, 70
  pegged, 3, 4, 8, 32, 35, 42, 48,
    53(fn), 54(fn)
  real, 5, 53(fn), 58
  risk management, 3–4, 6
export-oriented industrialisation, 5–7,
  10, 11–14, 25, 27, 121–8, 137,
  150–1, 157, 162
  Korea model v. Taiwan model, 26
export pessimism, 11–12
exports, 5, 12, 24, 26, 60, 129–34, 142,
  145(fn), 148–51, 153, 154, 155, 170,
  193, 206
  direct, 26
  quotas, 185
  restrictions, 180
external debt *see* foreign borrowing
external financing *see* foreign
  borrowing; foreign direct investment

FDI *see* foreign direct investment
financial assistance, 21
financial crisis
  causes, 3–4, 32, 37, 42, 47, 78
  nature, 19–20
  possible impact on Vietnam, 3–5,
    22–5, 50–2, 168–9
Financial Institutions Law (1997), 178
financial sector
  deregulation, 8, 66–7, 72
  prudential supervision, 7, 22, 78, 79,
    82(fn), 191
  structural weaknesses, 3, 4, 16–17,
    18, 20, 22, 32, 36, 37, 50–1, 168,
    169
  vulnerability to shocks, 32, 36, 40,
    42, 46, 49, 53(fn)
  see also banks; central banks
First Bangkok City, 39
fiscal incentives, 127, 138
fiscal policy, 14, 45, 63, 133
Five-year Development Plan, 72
foreign borrowing, 20, 40, 41, 43, 49,
  51, 62, 69, 75–6, 169
foreign currency debt *see* foreign
  borrowing
foreign currency deposits, 84–8
foreign direct investment (FDI), 5, 6, 9,

  21, 23, 51, 52, 58, 125–7, 129, 133,
  146–64, 166, 168, 170, 189, 192(fn)
  declining, 24–5, 166, 190
foreign exchange controls, 4, 14, 23, 86
foreign investment code, 160
Foreign Investment Law, 58, 161, 174,
  177, 178
foreign reserves, 22, 40, 42, 43, 53(fn),
  84
free trade, 11, 14, 19, 130–32, 157
  zones (FTZs), 130–31, 157, 159,
    161–2, 163(fn)
  see also tariffs
FTZs *see* free trade, zones

G-7 governments, 53(fn)
G-10 standards, 46
GDP, 4, 5, 14, 19, 20, 26, 27, 31, 35, 40,
  44, 45, 48, 51, 53(fn), 122, 135, 137,
  144(fn), 165, 168, 171, 189, 203
  private/state sector split, 172
General System of Preferences, 147
Ghana, 156
globalisation, 56, 64
government-directed credit, 3, 22, 32, 47
government guarantees, 17, 36, 43, 46,
  77–8
gradualism, 59
growth, 3, 27, 31, 32, 33, 35, 51, 58, 67,
  73, 121, 122–3, 135, 191, 166,
  195–6, 206, 211
  sources, 134–6

Habibie, President, 125
Hanil Bank, 39
Heavy Industries Investment Corporation of Malaysia (HICOM), 159
hedging, 4, 32, 36, 42, 48, 69
HICOM *see* Heavy Industries Investment Corporation of Malaysia
Honduras, 112, 115(fn)
Hong Kong, 6, 11, 14, 34, 40, 76, 127,
  135, 148, 149, 151, 170
household businesses, 15, 16, 174
Hungary, 87
hyperinflation, 5, 57, 81(fn), 86, 134

IMF *see* International Monetary Fund
import substitution, 11, 12, 14, 146, 149
imports, 5, 14, 24, 60, 206
  duties, 19

import licensing, 57, 61
  reform, 60
  restrictions, 17, 24, 57, 61, 128, 132, 161, 162, 180
incentives, 157, 165–91
India, 12, 111–12, 148, 149
Indonesia, 4, 6, 8, 12, 20, 21, 22, 34, 35, 37, 38, 40, 41, 43, 53(fn), 54(fn), 55–65, 87, 96, 121, 122, 123–5, 127, 128, 130, 131, 133, 135, 137, 140, 141, 148, 149, 156, 167, 170
Indonesian Bank Restructuring Agency, 39, 82(fn)
Industrial Bank of Korea, 39
Industrial Incentives Act (1968), 157
industrialisation, 194–7
  see also export-oriented industrialisation
industrial policy, 123–5, 142–3
industry
  competition policy, 139–42
  distribution, 154
  output by ownership, 173, 191(fn)
  size distribution 136–9
inflation, 5, 9, 14, 24, 27, 31, 35, 46, 48, 51, 58, 62, 67, 68, 69, 70–1, 72–3, 74, 76, 81(fn), 83, 84, 85, 86, 91–4, 133–4, 196
institutional weaknesses, 176–7
  see also financial sector, structural weaknesses
interest rates, 20, 24, 35, 58, 70, 72, 104–5, 114(fn)
International Monetary Fund (IMF), xiii, xv, 53(fn), 54(fn), 64, 77, 89
intervention, 123–5, 143(fn)
investment climate
  Malaysia, 157–60
  Vietnam, 160–2
investment, private, 17
IPTN, 128

Japan, xiii, 33, 34, 121, 123, 126, 156, 170
Johnson Matthey, 54(fn)

Khai, Prime Minister, 25
Kia Group, 39
Korea, 4, 6, 21, 22, 33, 34, 35, 39, 41, 87, 123, 126, 168, 170
  see also South Korea

Korea Exchange Bank, 39
Korea First Bank, 39
Korea Long Term Credit Bank, 39

Land Law, 184
land prices *see* real estate
land use, 7, 17–18, 31, 184
Latin America, 86, 94
Law on the Promotion of Domestic Investment, 177
lending policies, 4, 36, 62–3, 70–3, 183
letters of credit, 17, 43, 54(fn), 78
  deferred, 22
  unsecured, 38
liberalisation, 55–65, 84–8, 125, 133, 155, 206–18
  effects, 211–15, 216–17
  see also doi moi
Lippo Bank, 38
liquidity, 36, 40, 61, 73, 81(fn)
litu bo lixiang, 196
'Look East Policy', 151, 159

M1, 72, 73, 89, 91, 92
  see also M2; money supply
M2, 4, 51, 53(fn), 72, 73, 87, 89, 91, 92
  see also M1; money supply
macroeconomic policy, 14, 32, 43, 44–6, 48, 55, 56, 58, 59, 66–70, 125, 133–4, 144(fn), 203
Mahathir, Prime Minister, 21, 151, 159
Malaysia, 6, 12, 20, 21, 33, 34, 38, 40, 41, 121, 122, 123–5, 126, 128, 129, 132, 135, 137, 140, 143, 144(fn), 146–64, 170
Malaysian Industrial Development Authority (MIDA), 158
Malaysia Plan, 159
manufacturing, 7, 15, 18, 121–2, 148–53
market reform *see* liberalisation
Mexico, 43–4, 48, 53(fn)
microeconomic policy, 70–80, 125, 133
MIDA *see* Malaysian Industrial Development Authority
Ministry of Finance (Indonesia), 38
Ministry of Finance (Vietnam), 186, 187
Ministry of Trade, 180, 185
MNEs *see* multinational enterprises
monetary policy, 45, 70, 133
  see also exchange rates

money supply, 68, 83
   see also M1; M2
Mongolia, 87
Moody's, 39
moral hazard, 47, 53(fn)
multinational enterprises (MNEs), 126,
   130, 140, 148, 150–4, 157, 162, 163

National Banking Rehabilitation Agency
   (NBRA), 80
NBRA *see* National Banking Rehab-
   ilitation Agency
net open position (NOP), 78, 82(fn)
New Economic Policy, 157
New Zealand, 48, 49, 54(fn)
newly industrialising economies (NIEs),
   6, 121, 128, 156
NIEs *see* newly industrialising
   economies
Nigeria, 54(fn)
non-performing loans, 38, 170
NOP *see* net open position

ODA *see* official development assistance
OECD *see* Organisation for Economic
   Cooperation and Development
official development assistance (ODA),
   146, 153, 168
oil, 8, 12, 56, 58, 59, 60, 61, 67, 68, 71,
   81(fn), 133, 135
OPEC *see* Organisation of Petroleum
   Exporting Countries
open economy, 11, 35–6, 49, 55, 126,
   127, 129, 130, 133, 136, 158, 166
   see also free trade; liberalisation
Ordinance on Economic Contracts
   (1989), 182
Organisation for Economic Cooperation
   and Development (OECD), 129,
   144(fn)
Organisation of Petroleum Exporting
   Countries (OPEC), 67, 81(fn)

Pakistan, 148
Panama, 103
Peru, 103
peso, 43–4, 53(fn)
Phan Van Khai, Prime Minister, 187
Philippines, 10, 33, 34, 38, 40, 41, 47,
   87, 101, 111, 121, 122, 130, 135,
   137, 144(fn), 148, 149, 156

Plaza Accord, 61, 147
Poland, 87
political systems/leadership, 20, 21, 27,
   123, 133, 142
poverty, 58, 152, 163
Private Enterprise Law, 178
private sector, 7, 26
   changing role, 171–4
   constraints, 185
   development, 10, 11–16
   emergence, 174–6
   incentives, 165–91
   reform priorities, 16–19
   small and medium-sized enterprises,
     10, 15–16, 17, 18, 27, 136–9,
     144(fn)
Promotion of Domestic Investment Law,
   178
property and land use rights, 7, 17–18,
   175, 176, 184, 190, 200, 201, 203
   see also real estate
prudential supervision, 7, 8, 22, 78, 79,
   82(fn), 191

R&D *see* research and development
real estate, 20, 22, 33, 47, 78
   see also property and land use rights
reform
   priorities, 9–28
renminbi, 42, 53(fn)
research and development, 128–9
resources
   labour, 13, 156
   mineral, 12
   natural, 12
rice, 12, 131, 185, 193, 203–4, 206,
   output, 209–10
   price, 214
risk management, 3, 4, 31, 32, 46, 52
Romania, 87
rouble, 84
runs on currencies/financial institutions,
   3, 35, 36, 38, 39, 53(fn), 78
   definition, 52(fn)
rupiah, 68, 69, 75, 76, 77, 78
rural income in China, 199
rural sector, 97–117, 193–205

SBIs *see* Certificates of Deposit
semiconductors, 42, 148
sequencing, 8, 59–60

Shinhan Bank, 39
Siam City Bank, 39
Singapore, 6, 11, 14, 33, 34, 49, 53(fn),
    121, 123, 126–7, 129, 130, 132,
    135–6, 137, 143(fn), 148, 149, 151
small and medium-sized enterprises
    (SMEs), 6, 10, 15–16, 17, 18, 27,
    136–9, 144(fn)
SMEs *see* small and medium-sized
    enterprises
smuggling, 86
Socialist bloc, 61
Soeharto, President, 55, 74, 81(fn),
    82(fn), 125, 133, 141
SOEs *see* state-owned enterprises
South Korea, 11, 20, 40, 42, 43, 44, 45,
    47, 53(fn), 148, 149, 151, 167
    see also Korea
Soviet bloc, 8, 135–6
Sri Lanka, 148, 149, 154, 156
Standard and Poor's, 39
State Bank of Vietnam, 17, 50, 89, 94,
    98
State Enterprise Law, 178, 186
state enterprise sector, 185–6
state-owned enterprises (SOEs), 4, 14,
    15, 16, 17, 27, 28, 51, 146, 154, 160,
    163, 164(fn), 194, 196, 197, 200,
    201, 202, 204
sterilisation, 68–9, 75
stock market, 17, 140, 185
stock prices, 33
subsidies, 4, 6, 28, 139, 156, 159
Sukarno, President, 66, 73, 81(fn)
Sunan model, 198, 200
surveys
    rural credit market, 96–117
    villages in China, 198

Taiwan, 6, 11, 13, 14, 15, 17, 26, 34, 40,
    41, 123, 128, 151, 170
Tanaka, Prime Minister, 58
tariffs, 57, 60, 61, 63, 158, 161
    see also free trade
taxation, 18, 58, 91, 127, 160
technology policy, 128–9
TFP *see* total factor productivity
Thailand, xiii, 4, 6, 13, 19, 20, 22, 33,
    34, 35, 38, 40, 43, 44, 45, 53(fn),
    54(fn), 121, 123, 125, 128, 129, 130,

131, 132, 135, 141, 143, 148, 149,
    167, 170, 203
total factor productivity (TFP), 125,
    134–6, 206, 213, 215, 216, 217, 218
township and village enterprises (TVEs),
    7, 193–205
trade barriers *see* free trade
trade deficit, 17
    see also balance of payments
trade reforms, 180
transaction costs, borrower, 96–117
    determinants, 105–12
    quantification, 98–104
Turkey, 12
TVEs *see* township and village
    enterprises

UNCTAD *see* United Nations Con-
    ference on Trade and Development
unemployment *see* employment
United Nations Conference on Trade and
    Development (UNCTAD), 86
United States, 20, 21, 24, 48
US dollars, 5, 15, 19, 34, 51, 68, 83–95
    propensity to hold, 88–91

VBA *see* Vietnam Bank for Agriculture
Vietnam Bank for Agriculture (VBA), 4,
    98, 113, 114(fn)
Vietnam War, 84

Wenzhou model, 198
won, 39
World Bank, xiii, xv, 87
World Trade Organisation, 19, 56, 63

yen, 33, 42, 53(fn)
yuan, 194

Zhejiang, 198